THE MOBILE MIND SHIFT

THE MOBILE MIND SHIFT

Engineer Your Business to Win in the Mobile Moment

Ted Schadler

Josh Bernoff

Julie Ask

FORRESTER RESEARCH

GROUNDSWELLPRESS
Cambridge, Massachusetts

Published by Groundswell Press
Cambridge, MA
www.mobilemindshift.com

Distributed by Greenleaf Book Group LLC

For bookstore ordering information or discounts, please contact
Greenleaf Book Group LLC at PO Box 91869, Austin, TX 78709, 512.891.6100

For corporate or event bulk purchases, please contact Forrester Research,
www.mobilemindshift.com, 617.613.6000

Design and composition by Greenleaf Book Group LLC
Cover design by Forrester Research, Inc.
Cover photo by AP Photo/Michael Sohn, copyright 2013, used by permission.

Cataloging-in-Publication data
Schadler, Ted.
   The mobile mind shift : engineer your business to win in the mobile moment /
Ted Schadler, Josh Bernoff, Julie Ask, Forrester Research.—First edition.
     pages : illustrations ; cm
   Issued also as an ebook.
   Includes bibliographical references and index.
   ISBN: 978-0-9913610-0-7
   1. Internet marketing. 2. Mobile commerce. 3. Mobile communication systems.
4. Smartphones. I. Bernoff, Josh. II. Ask, Julie. III. Title.

HF5415.1265 .S334 2014
658.872/02854678   2014935730

Part of the Tree Neutral® program, which offsets the number of trees
consumed in the production and printing of this book by taking proactive
steps, such as planting trees in direct proportion to the number of trees
used: www.treeneutral.com

TreeNeutral®

Printed in the United States of America on acid-free paper

14 15 16 17 18 19 10 9 8 7 6 5 4 3 2

First Edition

CONTENTS

INTRODUCTION

· · · · · · · · ·

The age of the customer is upon us.

Some surprising things happened in 2013. Netflix, streaming entertainment to PCs, TVs, and mobile devices, amassed twice as many subscribers as Comcast, the largest US cable company. Weight Watchers blamed poor financial results on competition from apps like MyFitnessPal. The Home Depot announced that it would spend $300 million to serve customers whose "shift to mobile technology" took the company by surprise. And globally, one in four information workers brought mobile apps to work to help get the job done.

Not so long ago, companies dominated their markets with strength in manufacturing or distribution. With complete control of prices, buying locations, and information about products and customers, the balance was tipped in the company's favor. But now, the same forces that once favored companies instead create advantage for customers. With a mobile device, you can compare prices, get product reviews, and buy from anywhere. Customers rule.

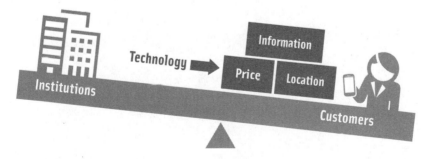

Here's what this means.

Your sales efforts must acknowledge a powerful customer who can choose from a virtually infinite set of suppliers. Your marketing must be focused on utility. And your decisions must acknowledge the shift in power. In short, you must become customer-obsessed.

The same shift transforms what happens within companies, especially in corporate technology departments. They're experiencing a budget squeeze just as mobile technologies ramp up the demands on corporate systems. It's a hard time for technology executives: 32% of business decision-makers believe that their IT department actually hinders business success.

The answer for technology managers is to focus on *BT*—business technology—the technology, systems, and processes that win, serve, and retain customers. The new BT agenda focuses on technology that provides superior *customer experiences* over maintaining corporate systems with shrinking resources. This includes leveraging the huge stream of customer data that new digital touchpoints are generating to learn about and better serve customers.

This is the context in which we wrote *The Mobile Mind Shift*. Mobile is the biggest, most pervasive, most powerful, and most global trend driving us toward the age of the customer. It creates demands not only on customer-facing parts of the business, but also on the systems that technology managers own, systems that must be re-engineered for the demands of mobile.

If you want your company to succeed, you must retool it for the age of the customer. The best way to connect with and satisfy customers is on a mobile device. And to do that properly, you must refocus your strategy, your systems, and your people to deliver mobile engagement.

We'll show you how.

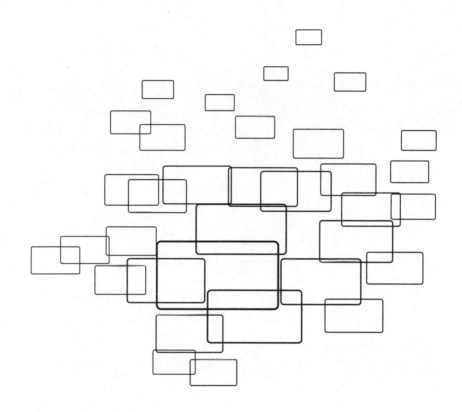

PART I
Master the Mobile
Mind Shift

1

. . . .

The Mobile Mind Shift

A World Transformed by Mobile Moments

Michael Sohn was on his second day of waiting, in the rain, in St. Peter's Square in the Vatican. Michael is a German living in Berlin and a Catholic, but he was not in the Vatican as a tourist. He was there with his 16-megapixel digital camera to do his job, which was to get a photograph of the next pope for his employer, the Associated Press (AP).

Michael huddled in the rain with dozens of other photographers and thousands of people, staring out at the chimney above the Sistine Chapel, hoping to see the white smoke that would signal the election of a new pontiff. In the wake of the retirement of Pope Benedict XVI the College of Cardinals had convened, and twice each day black smoke had risen from the chimney, once in the morning and once in the afternoon. For 48 hours, nobody had seen anything but black smoke—which meant the cardinals had not yet made a decision.

But now, late on the second day, white smoke rose from the chimney. Michael and the other photographers and pilgrims buzzed excitedly. Their long, damp wait was about to pay off. People began to jostle for position. Minutes ticked by. As if by divine command, the rain ceased. But as day darkened into evening, Michael, 200 meters from the balcony, began to wonder if he would be able to capture the shot he'd been waiting so long to get.

A man came out on the balcony. His amplified voice floated above the crowd with a single Italian word: "*Buonasera.*" The pilgrims prepared to experience this moment in a way that would etch it into their memories.

Nearly as one, they raised their smartphones and tablets.

The man looking from the balcony saw the entire crowd brightly lit with the flashes of the smartphones. And at that moment, the photographer Michael Sohn realized that the most profound transformation taking place was not on the balcony, but in the eyes and hands of the crowd. He got the shot.

His photo of the crowd brandishing their mobile devices to capture the world's first view of Pope Francis I has become an iconic image, spreading across the planet in the blink of an eye. (You can see part of it on the dust jacket for this book.) With a photographer's unique perspective, Michael had noticed how visitors to Rome experienced every sight through smartphone cameras. "They leave, they never knew what they saw," he told us. And now they were doing the same in St. Peter's Square. At this transcendent moment, their photos and videos of the scene in the square began spreading across Facebook, Twitter, Instagram, Vine, YouTube, Flickr, Tumblr, and WhatsApp . . . and ricocheting from person to person in endlessly forwarded emails and text messages. Their mobile devices had become such a central part of their experience that raising them at that moment was second nature—they and their phones experienced the moment together.

They had made the mobile mind shift. And now the rest of the planet is shifting as well. Are you ready to meet their demands?

What Is the Mobile Mind Shift?

What's happening here?

The iPhone launched in 2007. By 2013, the convenience and control afforded by the iPhone and its competitors has caused our expectations to rise. Like those pilgrims in Rome, we have learned that anything we need will be available anywhere, at any time, on our smartphones. You have a smartphone; you know this. Your ability to control your personal sphere, the things you care about both in your life and your work, has dramatically improved. Your mind has shifted to expect all that and more. And you've made the shift without even thinking about it. Your control over the things you care about is so ubiquitous and natural as to be invisible. You expect to have apps (and mobile sites) that empower you with information and service as a fundamental privilege of living.

Almost without realizing it, you and a billion other people worldwide have made smartphones your constant companion. Whenever we have a free moment, we pull out our smartphone and check our email or our Facebook, play a game, watch a film clip, or search the Internet. In China, we might use WeChat instead of Facebook, but the dynamic remains the same. Mobile devices have become our go-to tool for the basic things of life. But they are also much more than that. With 1 million apps in Apple's and Google's app stores, mobile devices have become high-value tools *for getting things done.*[1] No longer do we wait to sit down to go online. We just tap the app and refill a prescription, pay a bill, check in for a flight, buy a movie ticket, browse job listings, or set the thermostat so the house is warm when we get home. Or snap a photo of a car accident and file an insurance claim. Or any of a thousand other things.

Mobile devices are not just improving our personal lives. They are also accelerating the way we work. All our files are available in Dropbox. And we can pull up a customer record on our tablet before walking into a meeting and see the latest status of an order. We can tap into the sales data right in a budget meeting. We expect to be able to get work done anywhere, on any device, at any time. And we act on our own to get things done regardless of whether our company helps us or tries to stop us.

The shift is accelerating. We can get more things done every day because entrepreneurs and innovators seize on the new opportunities created by a billion mobile devices. Using a car service website to book a ride to the airport is nice. Uber is nicer. You tap the app and see what limos are available and how far away they are right in the moment you need one. A few more taps and you set up a place to connect with your driver.

eBay is nice. You can order things when you're in front of your computer and have them shipped to your home. eBay Now is nicer. You can order just about anything and have it delivered in an hour to the park bench at the southwest corner of Union Square where you are will be eating lunch.

Our lives have become a collection of *mobile moments* in which we pull out a mobile device to get something done immediately wherever we are.

The result of this accumulated experience with mobile apps is that our minds have shifted. Not only can we *do new things.* We now also *expect new things.* We expect to be able to get whatever we want whenever we want it wherever we are. We're disappointed when it's not there.

When we don't immediately find what we want, we turn to the app store on our phone or tablet and look for a service that can help us directly: Twitter for news, ESPN for sports updates, Google Maps for finding the best train to Firenza, Instagram for photo bragging, LoseIt! for calorie counts before ordering lunch, Yelp for dinner recommendations, and OpenTable for booking a table at that restaurant.

Mobile moments are global. In Beijing we use Didi Dache to order a taxi or Anjuke to find an apartment or Touch China to get a recommendation for a late night bar with live music. In Paris we use Solocal to find the nearest family-owned bakery. TootPay facilitates our payments in Indonesia, Thailand, Cambodia, and Myanmar. Sky Go in the UK broadcasts the live sports matches we crave. In Korea, we play games published by Anipang on the KakaoTalk platform.[2]

The mind shift and rise of mobile moments in our day are just getting started. By 2017, 2.4 billion people will own smartphones and 651 million people will use tablets at home and work—nearly three times as many as in 2013.[3] That's a lot more customers perpetually connected to the information and services they need. And the services they can receive on a smartphone or tablet are also still in their infancy. A million apps is a lot, but the world has over 900 million public websites and at least that many internal company sites.[4] So we're betting that those million apps will become 10 million by 2020.

All this convenience and control is creating a Pavlovian response: We feel a need, no matter how fleeting, so we pull out an app to satisfy it. We call this Pavlovian response *the mobile mind shift*.

The mobile mind shift is the expectation that I can get what I want in my immediate context and moments of need.

What, exactly, has shifted? Our behavior, of course. There's no waiting to go online. We are always online. We can pull out a smartphone or tablet and immediately get the information and service we need to act. We're never lost or without resources. But it's not just our behavior. Our minds have shifted, too.

Our minds have shifted in two fundamental ways. There is a *shift in expectations:* We expect that we can get what we want on any device at any time. Already, 52% of highly mobile people are frustrated when something they want isn't available on their smartphone.[5] And there is a *shift in control over the things we care about*: our files and photos, our financial information, even our glucose meter and the smoke detector in our house. We also expect to control things at work, such as information we need in meetings or to serve our customers.

Redefining Relationships One Mobile Moment at a Time

The mobile mind shift has rewritten the rules for relationships between companies and their customers. Customers and employees who have made the mobile mind shift take out their phones or tablets and expect service in a mobile moment. What do we mean by a mobile moment? Simply:

A mobile moment is a point in time and space when someone pulls out a mobile device to get what he or she wants immediately, in context.

Mobile moments redefine every customer relationship. If a customer wants information or service in a mobile moment, that is your moment to shine. Be there, and your customers will come to depend on you, deepening their loyalty and providing valuable information that your company can use to further improve the relationship.

This truly is the age of the customer—winning, serving, and retaining customers has become the one and only way a company can profit and differentiate itself.[6] But serving customers now means serving them in their mobile moments. If you are absent in those moments, that customer will turn to someone else who is providing a better mobile service. Who is ready to serve them in a mobile moment? Increasingly, it's an entrepreneur.

How Entrepreneurial Minds Exploit *and Create* the Mobile Mind Shift

A handful of innovative companies and a horde of entrepreneurs have figured out how to apply technology to solve problems in a customer's mobile moment. These digital disruptors swarm around your customers and attack your markets.[7] They relentlessly experiment with new business models that serve people in their immediate context and moments of need. They *think differently* and they *execute differently* to serve customers and employees primed by the mobile mind shift. They don't just build apps; they design a complete *mobile engagement* from the experience on the glass through to execution and fulfillment.

These entrepreneurs and innovators, unencumbered by legacy business and operating models optimized for the PC or Web era, have mastered a key concept: When someone gives you permission to be in their pocket, this creates the potential for a profitable mobile moment.

When entrepreneurs from every walk of life and business spot a mobile moment, they attack. Cody Rose, who as the son of a family of restaurateurs calls himself a "restaurantrepreneur," says: "We look for annoying things in everyday life that can be fixed with a mobile app. Then we jump on it." His first app, at NoshList, helped greeters in restaurants send texts to people when their tables were ready. He now leads enterprise products at mobile payment startup Square, the app that many companies use to process payments anywhere.

Entrepreneurial companies and services like Deezer, Flipboard, Hailo, HotSchedules, Intuit, MyFitnessPal, Line, M-Pesa, Nest Labs, Parrot, Proteus, Roambi, Sound World Solutions, Square, Tencent, Twitter, Uber, WhatsApp, WTSO, and many others are building substantial new businesses sometimes by disrupting an existing market. There are tens of thousands of them. Every one of these apps exploits a mobile moment to plug the gap between what people want to do and what a mobile device helps them to do. And each new app *advances the mobile mind shift* as people become aware of their new power. When people see that they can do a new thing—or an old thing more conveniently and immediately—they incorporate it into the way they live and work (see Table 1-1).

Intel's former chairman Andy Grove famously wrote "Only The Paranoid Survive."[8] But you're not paranoid if they're really out to get you. And these entrepreneurs really are out to get you. Every mobile entrepreneur and every competitor is attacking your customer's mobile moments.

Every industry and every market and every economy will shift under this onslaught of entrepreneurial energy. We'll revisit this theme of entrepreneurial energy throughout the book because it reveals lessons on how to identify and win the mobile moments in your customers' and employees' days. Two examples demonstrate the impact of entrepreneurs on the mobile mind shift: Uber for car services and Roambi for business data.

Table 1-1: Mobile Moments Change Every Part of Life and Work

What part of life?	How does a mobile moment change the expectation?
Shopping	As a shopper, you can walk into a store confident that you have all the information you need to make the best decision. When choosing between two grills, the experiences of other buyers and the pricing at the Walmart down the street are available to you right from the aisle.
Parenting	As a parent, the phone is a blessing and a curse. It's a blessing because you can get things done from anywhere, or you can hand it to a fussy child so they can play a game. It's a curse because your teenager keeps sneaking a look at WhatsApp at the dinner table and sometimes does something colossally stupid like posting a picture of a body part.
Healthcare	As a patient, you can use your smartphone, wearable devices, and apps like LoseIt! to care for yourself better than ever before. You can track vital signs and demonstrate medication compliance through connected medical devices. A doctor can interpret the combined data to create a holistic picture of your health.
Work	As an employee, you bring a smartphone to work to get things done. And if your company issues you a smartphone, but locks it down to just company email, you carry two phones. Employees are too busy to sit at their desks. That's why they take Evernote or Google Docs with them wherever they go.
Managing	As an executive, you are empowered with a smartphone or tablet and ready access to critical data. You can move forward with a decision right in a meeting because you have the data you need to act rather than waiting until later when someone can run the right report for you.
Citizenship	As a citizen, you can check the polls, read position statements, and compare candidates from outside the voting place. You can control the things you care about: pay your water bill, register your car, and check the vacation garbage pickup day while waiting to sign the paperwork on your new car.
Sports	As a sports fan, you have more options to watch and follow the game. You stay directly in touch with the game, the players, the fans, the stats, and the rumors. Whether you're watching the game from Fenway Park or in your own living room, your phone and tablet connect you to your community and the entire experience.
Athletics	As an athlete, your phone alone or in combination with a wearable device crammed with sensors (worn on your wrist, feet, or ankle) provides real-time feedback not only on your pace and distance, but also on your stride. Sensor-laden basketballs from 94Fifty measure the backspin on the ball or arc of your shot.

continued . . .

Table 1-1: Mobile Moments Change Every Part of Life and Work (*continued . . .*)

What part of life?	How does a mobile moment change the expectation?
Traveling	As a traveler, you are no longer in an information vacuum, wandering on the edge of the time horizon and wondering if you'll get to your meeting on time. The TripIt app on your phone has everything you need to check status, make connections, order cars, check into your hotel, alert your team of a delay, and even help you rebook a flight.
Driving	As a driver, the combination of Google Maps and Waze gives you confidence to know where you're going and the fastest way to get there. If you are using Google Now, a bad traffic situation will reset your day including setting your alarm for an earlier time and devising a new route for you.

Uber Exploits the Mobile Mind Shift to Redefine the Market for Car Services

Travis Kalanick is the founder and CEO of car service Uber. Travis was early to recognize the size of the mobile mind shift. He saw how passengers and drivers carrying mobile phones could share their location and connect. A passenger wanting a ride could use a mobile device to find a driver. A driver waiting for a fare could be alerted in that same moment that someone needed a ride.

Uber has been so successful that it has raised the hackles of power players in the industry it disrupts. The mark of a successful digital disruption is when customers are joyous even as existing companies and players are angry and striking back.

Travis saw that people—drivers and passengers—were ready to exploit the mobile mind shift even if the existing limousine and taxi services weren't. The gap between what people wanted and what the market could provide was big enough for a new business model. It was a great place for an entrepreneur to be, so he launched Uber. Now car services customers can act with confidence that they'll get a ride when needed.

But it doesn't stop there. Uber also changes the fundamental economics of supply and demand in the car service industry. Passengers seeking rides are the demand. Drivers seeking fares are the supply. Supply and demand meet up through their Uber app. The entire market becomes more transparent and more efficient. Ultimately, passengers will wait less and drivers will drive more. Everybody wins. Except, of course, the taxi authorities and limo services that have built their livelihoods on controlling supply and demand. They will be forced to adapt, as taxi services in cities like London and Boston already have.

Travis set out to meet the car service needs of customers and wound up shifting the dynamics and economics of an entire market.

Roambi Exploits the Mobile Mind Shift to Inject Business Data into Decision Moments

When Apple introduced the iPhone in 2007, Quinton Alsbury, a graphic artist turned software entrepreneur, saw the potential to bring business data to life through its touchscreen interface. He saw that the same mobile mind shift happening in consumers could also happen in business, and he cofounded a company now called Roambi.

As Quinton describes it, "We believed we could bring consumer experiences to business applications. So we hacked the iPhone in 2007 to see if it could work. Our vision was to use multitouch gestures to interact with business data, to use motion to tell the stories buried in the data."

Roambi's customers can pull out their iPhone or iPad and click on a chart, such as a pie chart, formatted with the big picture data. A sales manager or CEO can tap the chart to drill down into the important details, swipe over to find the specific transactions, and zoom back out and see the big picture again. If a new question comes up—and it always does in business meetings—then the data to help answer it is readily available on a tablet or smartphone. People quickly grow addicted to the insight that data in a Roambi app can provide in every moment.

It turns out that ready access to business data for executives changes things for everybody. In a company in the packaged food industry, once executives had access to real-time data through Roambi, senior managers needed that access, too. The need for real-time data quickly spread to every manager and key employee in the firm. Data became a single source of truth that all managers could use to act in concert. To accommodate the demand, the company's technology department had to beef up the technology platforms for data. A simple mobile app caused a Fortune 500 company to rethink entirely how it operates.

The Mobile Mind Shift Transforms Your Customer Strategy

If you don't engage your customers on the mobile device of their choice with the information and services they want, then some entrepreneur or competitor will. If you're Bank of America or Barclays, can you satisfy customers who've been spoiled with a complete view of their finances from their Mint.com app? If you're Blue Cross Blue Shield, how do you meet the expectations set by patients wedded to Fitbit's bracelet and app to track their fitness? If you're American Airlines, what happens if your most loyal customers trust the FlightCaster and Hipmunk apps for flight data more than they trust you? And the same applies to your employees. How can your company empower employees with business solutions when they already have what they need on their mobile devices with Google Apps and Skype and a hundred other personal apps?

Unless your company is very unusual, your strategy for engaging with customers probably hasn't shifted. You are connecting with those customers using technology and processes first developed in the 1990s. You may have mobile apps, but they probably deliver the same static experience you did on the Web: self-service, complex, and unaware of someone's *physical context*.

There are three things terribly broken with applying old Web thinking to serve customers whose minds have shifted. First, people are no longer sitting in one place; they are innately and incessantly mobile and connected at every waking moment regardless of where they are. Second, they are not happy to slog through the complex linear processes you've developed for your business. Third, they are not willing to serve themselves if they think you should anticipate their needs and serve them immediately.

Entrepreneurial apps have created this mind shift in your customers. They know they can deposit a check in the Bank of America account in 20 seconds by taking a picture of it, rebook their Delta flight while standing at the gate, and place their order at the McDonald's in Paris while walking to the restaurant. They expect the same from you.

Your company is stuck in a static Web and physical world while your customers and employees live in a mobile world. They expect service *at their convenience* in every tiny moment of their day, whether to solve a problem, get information, entertain themselves, or get something done. Yesterday's physical or Web-only interaction models fail in the mobile world. So why not engage your customers on their phones and tablets?

It's time to embrace the mobile mind shift.

You have the opportunity to live up to your customer's expectations and delight her. You can save her time and provide her with valuable services. And you can do it at her convenience, when she's looking for help.[9] Isn't this what any good company wants—to be more engaged with its customers' needs, to become more essential?

Your customers are ready. You can be, too.

Your Mobile Mind Shift Strategy

Entrepreneurs have an advantage: They start with a blank slate. They can go straight at the mobile moments in the hands of a billion people. They can envision new mobile experiences, design for mobile first, and deliver immediately. You will have to do the same. To engage your customers and employees in their mobile moments, everybody in your company will have to *think differently* and *execute differently*. You need a *mobile mind shift strategy*—a strategy to serve customers in their mobile moments of need.

Serving customers with mobile is easy to imagine, but very difficult to achieve. Why? Because your company and its processes and information systems were never designed with mobile moments in mind. Your technology is too rigid, your processes too linear, and your organization too siloed. The expectation of customers in their mobile moments massively disrupts these well-intentioned but calcified ways of doing business.

Winning in the mobile moment will mean changing how you organize, operate, and deliver products and services. You can win in a mobile moment, but only if your entire corporation gets behind it. You may not have a blank slate to work from, but you must have the courage to pretend that you do.

Start with the mind of your customer. Then think backwards from there, proceeding to her device, to the application running on that device, and to the systems—platforms, processes, and people—that power that mobile moment (see Figure 1-1). This is where courage kicks in. Re-engineering your company's technology platforms, business processes, and the way people work is like moving a mountain—it's where the big costs lie. But you have no choice.

Figure 1-1: Deconstructing the Mobile Mind Shift

Operating Principles of the Mobile Mind Shift

To keep your company focused on winning in the mobile moment, we have created a set of operating principles in the form of customer promises. Your customers should be able to agree with these statements:

- **Wherever I am, your company is available.** That means on a smartphone and tablet, but it might also mean on a wearable, gadget, computer, or television. If one out of 10 of your customers has a new device, you'd better be on it because you can be sure that those early adopters are the most influential and often the most valuable to you.

- **Whenever I choose, your business service is at my fingertips.** We pay our monthly mobile data bill so we can immediately get what we want where we want when we want. If your service is sluggish or offline or missing, you will disappoint your customer.

- **Whatever my next step, you have anticipated my needs.** On a mobile device, you know someone's immediate context—where they are, what they did last, how they present themselves, and maybe even their emotional state. All of this information gives you the opportunity to serve a customer before they even ask for it. If you really don't know what your customer needs next, go find out. Walk around your retail store; ride around with your sales reps; instrument your apps and touchpoints to collect the data that will help you. This level of customer knowledge is now a basic business competency.

- **Whatever my action, you are ready to respond.** The mobile app hands someone a tremendously powerful lever to take action, share an experience, capture a moment, or ask for help. If your mobile app doesn't help someone complete an action, you have failed. If the result of a click is a dead end on a customer journey or a roadblock on an internal process, then customers will complain and maybe defect.

How This Book Gets You Ready for Mobile Moments

We wrote this book based on our analysis and work with hundreds of companies that have succeeded—and sometimes failed—to engage customers in their mobile moments over the past seven years. The book is in four parts.

In part one, "Master The Mobile Mind Shift," we focus on the tools you need to design great mobile engagements, the "how" of your mobile strategy. This starts in chapter 2, where we introduce the business discipline for mastering mobile moments, the IDEA cycle. In chapter 3, we show you how to create a plan to execute on the IDEA cycle, including how to conduct a mobile moment audit to identify mobile moments, prioritize them, and determine the impact on your operations. And in chapter 4, we describe the Mobile Mind Shift Index, a way to understand the mobile intensity, expectations, and behaviors of your Shifted customers.

Chapters 5 through 8 make up part two, "The Mobile Business Shift," in which we focus on *what to do* by analyzing the impact of the mobile mind shift on your business—your sales, marketing, product development, and business models. We reconstruct these functions through the lens of mobile moments. Our goal in these chapters is to share the stories of large companies and entrepreneurs to help you envision how to make mobile experiences the beating heart of your customer strategy.

Chapters 9 through 12 are part three, "The Mobile Systems Shift," where we describe how to re-engineer your systems, including platforms, processes, and people, to deliver a great mobile experience. We show how mobile will affect your workforce. We analyze technology platforms, business processes, and the teams and organizations that deliver great mobile moments. Armed with these examples and analysis, you and your teams will know what to do to serve customers and employees in their immediate context and moments of need.

We close with part four, "The Future Shift," a single chapter on what happens to the mobile mind shift as mobile devices are deconstructed and disappear into wearable devices, as connected products increase the number of mobile moments in which you can serve a customer, and as society digests the impact of the mobile mind shift.

It's a long journey, but you're ready to take the first step. In the next chapter, we unravel the mystery of mobile moments and explain how the best companies take advantage of it.

2

· · · · · · · · ·

Master the IDEA Cycle

A Business Discipline for Winning in Mobile Moments

The retailer Alex and Ani was on a tear. The Rhode Island-based company was opening a new retail store every month to sell its unique bangles, earrings, and necklaces. Alex and Ani's jewelry was popular because of its unique message: All of its pieces incorporate symbolism and designs that enable the wearer to express her individuality in an organic, spiritual way. Alex and Ani stores showcase the products and are also a venue for customers to explore different fashion scenarios, often with the help of store associates. The 10 employees working a store at any one time are an essential component of the Alex and Ani shopping experience, advising customers on ways to customize their purchases to express themselves through the positive symbols and charm meanings.

But in the run-up to Mother's Day in 2012, success had overwhelmed the capacity of the stores to serve customers. Customers at some stores had to wait over an hour just to check out at one of three registers. That was a disaster. For Joe Lezon, the company's newly hired chief technology officer, and Susan Soares, its head of retail operations, it was clear that something had to change.

As an experienced technology executive from Fidelity, Joe thought he knew how to solve this customer experience challenge using mobile technology. By putting Wi-Fi in the stores and giving employees an iPod Touch and a credit card reader/printer (known as a "sled"), he could build a mobile point-of-sale system, thereby tripling the number of checkout points. This would give his fashion-advisor employees the tools they needed to help customers choose pieces as well as to process their transactions. Joe knew what to do, but he needed help figuring out how to do it.

Joe turned to Ty Rollin, chief technology officer, at Boston-based Mobiquity for help in implementing his idea. Susan's operations people, Joe's technology people, and Mobiquity's developers formed a team that worked on the problem for six months. Then they deployed the solution.

There's a lot to learn from their approach.

Alex and Ani has a retail store right downstairs from its Rhode Island headquarters, so the extended team started by watching how employees in that store engaged with customers at various points while shopping and checking out. They then designed an iPod Touch application to assist employees in the context of each interaction. They tied the application directly into their point-of-sale system, added analytics to know how it worked, and tested it in the store downstairs. Then the team made it better. They streamlined the app, simplifying interactions to help employees remain focused on customers. After that, they rolled the platform out to all 32 of their stores in time for the holiday season.

The results were astounding. Joe now tracks the checkout in seconds, not minutes or hours, even in the busy holiday season. Susan has data to help her further optimize inventory processes. Operations are streamlined and customers are happy.

It took way more than a mobile app to do this. It took a *disciplined approach to designing for mobile moments*. This holistic approach included an end-to-end technology solution, employee training, new learning based on staff experience, and a revised process for store operations. All this led to an ideal tool for serving customers. The team from Alex and Ani and Mobiquity did more than just build a mobile point-of-sale system. They designed and implemented a new and evolving platform for succeeding in mobile selling moments.

A New Business Discipline: the IDEA Cycle

Making a mobile app or site is relatively easy. Making it an ongoing business success isn't.

Alex and Ani succeeded because instead of the quick and easy solution ("let's build an app"), they took a disciplined approach to understanding what problems to solve, how to design the best solution, what systems would be affected, and what analytics were needed to keep improving the solution.

Learn from what Alex and Ani—and other companies with mobile success—have done. They didn't just build an app. In our work with dozens of entrepreneurs and more than 100 companies, we have seen that success comes from a new, *disciplined* way to tackle mobile moments. Even though mobile moments in sales or marketing are different from mobile moments for products or services, and even though customer mobile scenarios are completely different from employee mobile scenarios, your need to serve individuals on mobile devices is a *universal* business activity. You need a structured business discipline to deliver great mobile moments in every facet of your business. We call this business discipline the *IDEA cycle* (see Figure 2-1).

Master the IDEA cycle and your company will master the discipline of mobile mind shift strategy and execution. Your company will learn how to identify mobile moments in your customers' and employees' days. Your sales and marketing people will understand the goals of engaging in a mobile moment and what it will take to achieve them. Your product teams will see how to enhance products through mobile moments. Your operations people will see what processes need to change, and your technology management staff will understand the requirements of the new technology platform. The IDEA cycle aligns all parts of your business to win in mobile moments.

The IDEA cycle includes four steps:

1. **Identify** the mobile moments and context. In this step, you map out all the situations and scenarios in which you can serve someone on a mobile device.

2. **Design** the mobile engagement. This is the step where you bring business people, designers, and developers together to decide how you will engage a customer in his mobile moments.

3. **Engineer** your platforms, processes, and people for mobile. Mobile engagement requires much more than an app. What changes will you need to make to your core operations and systems?

4. **Analyze** results to monitor performance and optimize outcomes. Your mobile application is not complete if you're flying blind. Capture, track, analyze, and act on the data to improve the engagement.

Figure 2-1: The IDEA Cycle

These four steps form a *cycle* because you can't do them just once. Your best chance of getting a mobile moment done while getting it right is to start small. But you'll inevitably want to extend the mobile moments as you learn, which means going through the cycle again. To do this effectively, you will need to invest in a team and execution platform that you can extend over time

These four steps spell IDEA (**I**dentify, **D**esign, **E**ngineer, **A**nalyze), which makes the cycle easy to remember. It is also a simple way to make sure you do things in the right order without leaving out the hard parts. Trust us; as we've seen in many companies, skipping any of the IDEA steps will lead to problems, either right away or in the long term, and those problems will be expensive, difficult, and embarrassing to fix.

The IDEA cycle is *how* you plan and execute your mobile moments. *What* you apply it to—what problem you are trying to solve—depends on your specific situation and goals. For example, Walgreens' retail stores focused on the mobile moments surrounding photos. By contrast, at Alex and Ani, Joe and Susan focused on improving customer checkout. If you take a peek at the different chapters coming up, you'll see that many of them show how to use the same IDEA cycle to solve different problems— marketing problems, sales problems, product problems, field service problems, and so on.

Now let's get a close look at each of the four steps.

Step 1: Identify the Mobile Moments and Context

The first step in the IDEA cycle is identifying the mobile moments and the context of each one. What matters most in a mobile moment is giving someone *exactly* what they want in the simplest way possible— sometimes before they even know they need it. And that means you need to know what they want and what they're doing when they want it. You must walk in their shoes, observe their actions, and be able to describe what you have observed to the rest of the team. Regardless of whether you are serving employees or customers, you must *identify* their mobile moments and context.

At Alex and Ani, Joe and Susan worked with Mobiquity to map out the moments in which employees interact with customers on the floor, at the register, and at the door. By observing and cataloguing the *context*— the situation, preferences, and attitudes—of employees and customers in these key moments, they were able to identify and define the important details of the engagement: where in the store the moment happens, for how long, at what stage in the shopping or checkout process, with what information available, with what customer expectations, and so on.[1] For example, they could see the sequence of operations that takes place the moment a sales associate completes a transaction for the customer and what information (such as customer details and previous purchases) would be useful at that moment. Context makes mobile moments very different from web experiences, because you know more about where and who someone is in a mobile moment.

Understanding the mobile moment and context helps you create something "simple, delightful, and beautiful," as Charles Teague, CEO of the company that makes the popular weight control app LoseIt!, puts it. "Our goal isn't just to make you use our app. It's to make you keep at your health management. And that means *you have to want to come back*." When people reach for their phone in front of that deli counter to decide if they should have a meatball sub or a vegetarian sandwich based on their calorie goals, what's their frame of mind? What have they told you about their breakfast? Have they worked out already today? What's *the most important thing* they need to do—in this case, it's understanding their calorie budget for lunch. If LoseIt! gets the mobile moment wrong because it lacks the appropriate context, then the app will fail to engage a customer in that mobile moment.

Observing and recording people's activities as they go about their lives is called ethnographic research. Advanced companies like Procter & Gamble use this technique to figure out how people use or might use its products. As Dave Wolf, VP of research and development from digital experience developer Cynergy (now part of KPMG) says, "Relying on our insights alone would lead to failure." In the mobile mind shift, every company must master ethnographic research so they are smart about people in their mobile moments of engagement.

Step 2: Design the Mobile Engagement

Once you have identified the mobile moments and context, the next step in the IDEA cycle is to design your mobile engagement. This is where you match your customer's motivations in his mobile moment to your business goals. And of course that engagement is severely constrained by a tiny screen and the huge expectations set by five-star consumer apps. As digital agency EffectiveUI's Brett Johnson explains, "Mobile requires more attention to detail than the Web. On mobile, consumers can't and won't hop about. You have to plan much more intensely for what the customer is going through." If an individual doesn't use your app or site in the mobile moment, then the moment will pass, and you'll have missed the opportunity to solve his problem.

In a process of relentless refinement using only a whiteboard, the eight-person team assembled by Alex and Ani and Mobiquity drew pictures to design the mobile engagement, mapping out how an employee would use the iPod Touch to engage a customer more effectively. They included the screen layouts, the sequence of events and information or transaction needed at each step, and the contingencies to cover the common scenarios. For example, if a promised item turned out not to be in inventory, what information would an employee need to help the customer over that hurdle?

Step 3: Engineer Your Processes, Platforms, and People for Mobile

Mobile engagement is much more than an app. If the app has a pretty face, but doesn't help a customer accomplish a goal, then the engagement is weak. And if a customer is ready to take another step and the app instead launches him off to the website or call center, he'll think twice before coming back.

To make a mobile moment successful, you must engineer your business and its platforms, process, and people to deliver the experience. Engineering your systems and operations is also where you will face the true cost of mobile success. It's what turns a $250,000 mobile marketing app into a $2 million mobile transaction app. Based on many interviews with companies that have built successful mobile apps, here is our rule of thumb: Expect to spend 20% of your budget on designing and developing a great app and 80% of the budget on the technology and process redesign required to support it.

For most companies, this requires a substantial investment. Home Depot learned this lesson in 2013. As the chief caretaker of the business model, Home Depot CEO Frank Blake recently reported to shareholders, "Our customers' shift to mobile technology has been much faster than we anticipated. We're having to play catch up in this area and it will be a major focus of our investment in 2014."[2] The company plans to spend $300 million on "supply chain, technology, and online improvements."[3] That's a Fortune 500 company spending to re-engineer its business for mobile moments.

Let's look more closely at three elements of the Engineer step: platforms, processes, and people.

Build a technology *platform* for mobile moments. The technology platforms to support mobile moments look very different from those you use for the website or for internal PC applications, because they must support touchscreen apps and sites on any mobile device and deliver an

intuitive, task-oriented, contextual experience. We call the technology platforms that support mobile and other digital initiatives "systems of engagement" to reflect their focus—delivering engaging human experiences.[4]

Most eCommerce teams struggle to mobilize their service for just this
reason: mobile engagement is *not* just an extension of your self-service website. For example, when the online apparel retailer Zappos first attempted
a mobile commerce app, it had to replicate the product catalogue, but the
implementation ended up showing different inventory in the mobile app
than on the website.[5] This revealed a deep flaw in the retailer's back-end
systems and operations that it has since rectified with a hybrid mobile app
that uses the online catalogue and capabilities.

Intuit's journey to mobile moments has led it to redesign and redeploy
its entire technology platform, using the cloud and advanced techniques
from the software industry. The company has been re-engineering its core
platforms for four years now. (We dive deeper into the new technology
platform in chapter 10.)

Transform business *processes* through mobile moments. If you
deliver a new capability on a mobile device without fundamentally
rethinking your processes, you will fail to reap the benefits. For example, giving a salesperson an iPad or a customer a hotel-booking app
won't drive a business outcome unless you are also prepared to change
the way you handle transactions. When McDonald's in France launched
a mobile app for ordering and pre-paying for food, it couldn't stop with
an app. It had to design new restaurant processes for staff to make and
serve orders so they were ready when customers walked in. In chapter
11, we will tell you how to engineer your processes so employees can
serve customers directly in a mobile moment.

**Organize your *people* for continuous improvement in your mobile
experience.** The mobile mind shift is relentless. What delighted your customers a few months ago is table stakes today and will be humdrum next
year. You have to deliver something quickly just to get your service in
play. But you will also have to improve it continuously with new capabilities based on new insight. That takes an agile development process. You
must build, test, learn, and extend your entire engagement—not just your
mobile app—on a constant upgrade cycle. If you try to get it all right and
all done the first time around the IDEA cycle, you will almost certainly
miss the mark.

Here's an example. The bank ING Direct in Australia wanted to deliver an exceptional "outside in" mobile experience that started with the customer. The company's ethnographic research showed that bank customers wanted three things on a mobile app: to check their balances, view their check history, and move money. As ING Direct's Janelle McGuinness said, "If we could get these things right, we knew we would satisfy the needs of most people." Janelle's team knew they didn't need to have every piece of functionality at launch. But importantly, since they knew that the app would need frequent updates, they used an agile development process to deliver improved releases frequently.

In chapter 12, we will introduce you to the process and organizational model for building mobile applications. A mobile steering committee makes the decisions. The workers are organized into IDEA teams, dedicated teams of designers, developers, and business people that work together to build, not just the app, but also the complete mobile engagement. At Nordstrom, the IDEA team started with a simple commerce app and a mobile point-of-sale system like Alex and Ani's. That was in 2011. Now, Nordstrom has many agile business and development teams in full flight focused on a variety of digital initiatives. At mobile startups, this is just the way of doing business. At large companies, this is a new way of working.

Step 4: Analyze Results to Monitor Performance and Optimize Outcomes

Analytics is the critical last step of the IDEA cycle. Why? Because without instrumenting the app and the technology platforms to know what's going on, you are flying blind; you cannot possibly improve your service or develop insight into what your customer wants from you. Don't treat data collection and analytics as an afterthought. Build it into the original mobile moment and continue to refine it as you enhance the offering. At Alex and Ani, Joe Lezon knows that analytics are a critical business tool for measuring store operations, including the effectiveness of the iPod checkout application. That's how he knows that checkout times are now in seconds instead of minutes or hours.

Collecting and analyzing data to help you improve the mobile experience is a basic building block of successful mobile experiences. Start with basic data like downloads, logins, and clicks on features to know who's using the app and when. Think of that as "little data." It's a good start. But the real business benefit of mobile moments lies in optimizing a business outcome such as room nights booked, referral fee collected, or premium products sold. To optimize these, you must collect and analyze the big data generated by mobile applications to find patterns and insights across a large number of customers and transactions.

Gregory Wright, vice president of product management at Intuit, is responsible for the Mint.com mobile app. He has this to say about the importance of analytics at Intuit: "We use the agile process so we are rapidly building and shipping features. But at Intuit, we have this notion of 'doneness:' You're not done unless you've instrumented it for data collection and analytics. So we build that into each release cycle."

We hear this same commitment to data collection and data analytics from entrepreneurs and innovators like Adam Pisoni at Microsoft's Yammer, Tony Fadell at Nest Labs, and Bill Ruh at General Electric. They have hired data scientists to help identify what data to collect, software developers and toolkits to instrument the app and the back end, and data operations staff to build and operate the data platform. The scientists also build new models of execution into the analytics engine. Data analysis is a new competency, an essential business skill in the mobile mind shift.

· · · · · · · · ·

What we've described here is a framework—IDEA—for thinking about how to engage your customers in their mobile moments. But how can you move forward—what do you actually have to *do*? You need a plan. In the next chapter, we show you how to build that plan.

3

· · · · · · · ·

Plan Your Mobile Engagement
Conduct a Mobile Moment Audit

Phil Easter knew he could soothe a world of pain in travelers' lives. And that's a lot of lives. Phil's company, American Airlines, flies 350,000 passengers to their desired destinations every day. Phil is American's director of mobile apps. In 2009, shortly after Apple announced the app store and a way for developers to build apps, he realized that the iPhone gave him a great way to help customers when they needed it most—in the anxious scurry of a travel day.

Supported by American Airlines' CIO Maya Leibman, Phil and his mobile team started with two questions: What do travelers do in the days and hours leading up to and following a flight? And how can we help them on a mobile device? Guided by these simple questions, Phil's team catalogued a traveler's moments in time—days before, hours before, minutes before the flight—and mapped them against the mobile services they could provide: checking in, viewing boarding passes, seeing departure gates, and so on. This technique is called *plotting the mobile moments in a customer journey* (see Figure 3-1).

Armed with a description of the mobile moments in which a traveler might look for help, the team next figured out how best to engage a traveler in each moment. They started with the service to be delivered: book reservations, check in, and so on. They then enlisted the aid of designers with experience in mobile screen layout and touchscreen interactivity to see if they could deliver that service well on a mobile device.

Figure 3-1: Plotting the Mobile Moments in a Customer's Journey

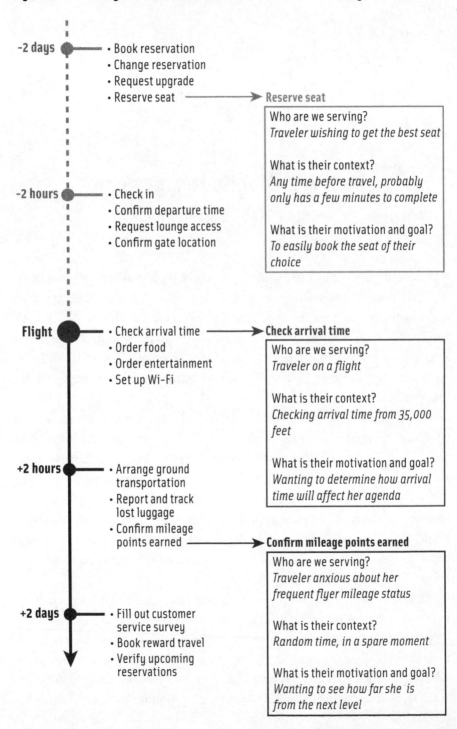

Phil and his team then built the app and linked it to the back-end transaction systems. As a result, when a traveler loaded the app, it pulled up her most current information, and when she clicked the "check in" button, it updated the right record. While this sounds simple, it required Phil's team to work with 10 different groups who were responsible for the technology systems involved. American Airlines' mobile app is very complicated behind the scenes, but travelers never experience that complexity—they can check in or change seats with a single tap.

The last step in Phil's team's process was to "instrument" the app so they would know how many times someone opened the app, how frequently they logged in, how long it took them to complete a task like checking in, and so on. These metrics are American Airlines' eyes and ears into what's really going on in a traveler's mobile moments.

American Airlines' mobile app has been very successful. The app has been downloaded more than 10 million times. Phil works hard to make the app experience great. For example, when Apple introduced its iOS 7 mobile operating system with its completely different look and feel, Phil helped make sure that American Airlines' app was one of the first available in the new format. In the 48 hours leading up to a flight, people use the mobile app 10 times as often as they do the AA.com website. And today, 10% of American's customers use a mobile boarding pass, up from zero just a few years ago. Phil expects that percentage to rise much higher as more travelers integrate American Airlines' mobile moments into their travel day. The app is so successful that American now plans to double the size of its mobile team.

Great Mobile Experiences Start with a Mobile Moment Audit

Mobile apps can do just about anything.

And that's the problem.

According to Maya, who chairs American Airlines' mobile steering committee, "the list of new feature requests is longer than Phil's arm." Doing all that would not only have sucked up resources—it would have created an incoherent traveler experience.

Because apps are a magnet for feature suggestions, you need a *disciplined* way to deliver an enjoyable, effective mobile experience.

Figure 3-2: Mobile Moment Worksheet

Identify the mobile moments and context.

Assess audience
- Who are we serving?
- What devices do they use?
- What is their motivation and goal?

Determine context
- What is their situation and location?
- What is their emotional state or attitude?
- What are their preferences and history?

Design the mobile engagement.

Engage your customer
- What service will you provide?
- What will it accomplish?
- How will they find it?

Calculate customer benefit
- Does it improve a customer's experience?
- Does it accomplish a customer's goal in seconds?
- Is it convenient and enjoyable to use?

Determine the value to you
- Does it accomplish your goal?
- Is it cost effective? Does it drive revenue?
- Are you committed to it for the long haul?

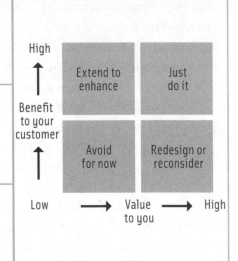

Engineer your platforms, processes, and people for mobile.

Build platforms
- What systems will the engagement use?
- Do you have access to those systems?
- Are they ready for mobile?

Transform processes
- What processes will the engagement touch?
- Where will your current processes break down?
- What changes will you have to make?

Align people
- What skills will you need?
- Will your organization support the engagement?
- Do you have resources to make these changes?

Analyze results to monitor performance and optimize outcomes.

Identify the data you need
- What are the business metrics?
- What are the engagement metrics?
- What are the technical metrics?

Determine if you're ready to use it
- Can you collect the data?
- Do you have the analysis tools?
- Do you have analytics expertise?

Maya and Phil at American Airlines started with who needed what and why. They then created a complete design for engagement—not just an app. They moved methodically through all four steps in the IDEA cycle and have continued to add functionality and capability with each new release of the app.

This is a systematic process, and you can do it, too. But to light the path, you need a plan, a way to figure out what to do, how to do it, and what changes you'll need to make to your technology and operations to deliver it. Based on the successes and failures of the companies we have worked with, we created a planning guide we call a *mobile moment audit* to help you consider the universe of possible mobile moments, then sketch out your path through the IDEA cycle.

In chapter 2, we described the steps in the IDEA cycle. The mobile moment audit helps you determine how to execute each step. Our worksheet for the mobile moment audit includes a comprehensive overview of the steps you'll need to take and the questions you'll need to answer (see Figure 3-2). In the rest of this chapter, we'll go through those steps in detail, so you can do your own mobile moment audit and create your own plan. As in Chapter 2, what we say here about customers applies equally well to employee mobile applications.

Identify the Mobile Moments and Context

Start with customers. That's nearly always the right way to begin a new project, and it certainly applies to mobile projects.

Maya and Phil knew a lot about their customers. The American Advantage loyalty program, the first ever frequent flier program for a major airline, gave the company deep insight into the travel habits and preferences of their best customers. But entries in a database didn't provide enough knowledge to understand a customer's travel context and moments of need. To figure that out, Maya and Phil's team spent time observing and cataloguing where customers were and what they were trying to accomplish in the airport.

You must do the same. Or you could go further, as Delta Air Lines did. It created emotional maps of its customers' in-airport experience at check-in, security, boarding, and even looking out the window at the baggage coming up the conveyer belt. The company looked for the moments when anxiety wrinkled travelers' brows. Where anxiety lurks, there's often a good opportunity for a mobile moment.

In the first step of the mobile moment audit, you will analyze customers, catalogue the mobile moments, identify the context, and determine their motivations. You can use the same process for employee mobile engagement—just substitute the word "employee" for "customer" in what follows. Here's how to do it.

Analyze Customers' Mobile Mind Shift

Are your customers ready for mobile?

Start your mobile moment audit by analyzing the level of mobile intensity, expectations, and behaviors of your audience. (We show how to do this in detail in our description of the Mobile Mind Shift Index in chapter 4.) For example, it won't help you to assume that someone wants to buy your product on their mobile device if they only buy in a store. Instead, they may just want to find out if you have it in stock before stopping at the store on their way home.

Then spend some effort to determine what their motivations are. Ethnographic and other research techniques like the ones Delta used can help here. Once you understand what your customers want, you can look at the moments in which you can help them.

Catalogue the Mobile Moments

Have you really thought through all the moments in which your customers could benefit from a mobile app or mobile site? Take another look at Figure 3-1, the map of some of the moments in the journey of an American Airlines traveler. Could you create a map like this? You should.

Customer experience experts use a discipline called journey mapping to determine the path customers follow. Now that mobile is so central to solving problems in many customer journeys (and not just for air travelers!), your task is to find the moments in which you can help customers anywhere on that journey.

We have catalogued some common types of mobile moments and their associated customer or employee motivations (see Table 3-1).

Table 3-1: Envisioning Mobile Moments in Different Scenarios

Scenario	Customer or employee motivations	Mobile moments
Consumer sales	Find a product, learn about it, check a price or review, make a purchase.	• A customer sees a display while in a store and needs comparison information to make a decision. • A consumer sees a movie ad while on a bus and wants to purchase two tickets for tonight. • A customer sees a print ad for a car in a magazine and wants to know the cost and features.
Business sales	Prepare for a meeting, deliver value during the meeting, or follow up after the meeting.	• A salesperson working for a global consumer packaged goods (CPG) company monitors shelf and promotion placement at a store using the Trax mobile app. • A rep for medical device maker Medtronic uses a tablet to show a doctor how the new stent works. • A Trane air-conditioning installer taps her app to send follow-up information to a potential customer by email.
Marketing	Discover, explore, engage, or act.	• A Krispy Kreme customer gets an alert on her iPhone any time the Hot Light goes on at her local doughnut shop. • A teenager in China virtually "grabs" coupons during a TV commercial for the new Neo Adidas products. • Amazon Local pushes out daily deals to registered users for everything from cupcakes to massages to glass blowing classes.
Product development	Interact with the product to install, upgrade, control, or maintain it.	• A consumer with a Nest thermostat asks for an alert whenever the power goes out. • A MyFitnessPal customer with a Withings bathroom scale double checks her morning weight while at the deli counter. • A lighting technician in the City of Westminster taps an app in the middle of Harrow Street to see which streetlights need to be replaced.
Field service	Serve customers better through routing, status updates, collaboration, or logging.	• A GE service technician retrieves maintenance history for a wind turbine before climbing to the top and can video chat with an engineer once she gets there. • A Dish Network installer with an Android phone is re-routed to deal with an urgent call, then suggests and sells products during an installation. • At QDI, a truck driver accesses customs manifests while at the loading dock, shortcutting a lengthy paper review process.

continued . . .

Table 3-1: Envisioning Mobile Moments in Different Scenarios (*continued...*)

Scenario	Customer or employee motivations	Mobile moments
Work	Access the information and data needed to make a better decision right in the moment.	• A Mondelēz International sales exec dives into the sales history of a flagging supermarket chain before the weekly operating review. • A manufacturing worker on a shop floor pulls up the product schematics or reroutes work without leaving her station. • A business consultant at Deloitte keeps a project moving at a high-profile client right from the soccer field.

To catalogue the relevant mobile moments for your customers, ask three questions (we've written these from the point of view of serving customers, but you can ask the same questions about serving workers):

First, where can you immediately solve a customer's problem? For example, if a Telstra customer receives a notification that she is near the limit on her data plan, she can pay for the next bundle of data directly from her phone to avoid overage charges. The same applies to a traveler seeking an upgrade or a salesperson who needs information in a sales call. This is the no-waiting mobile moment that accelerates tasks with the information and tools needed to act immediately.

Second, where can you eliminate friction or annoyance in your customers' lives? Can you improve something they're already doing another way? Here's where you come up with features like depositing a check with a photo or providing a map of the retail store. This question should unleash a torrent of moments in which you can find, and fix, life's little annoyances.

Third, where can you deliver a new business service? This is the blue-sky path for new mobile moments—and multiplying mobile moments is a great path to profit. As we'll show in chapter 8, this is how entrepreneurs like Russell Hall at Hailo, Tony Fadell at Nest, Ma Huateng from Tencent, or Don Cowley from Proteus Digital Health think about mobile as they create new business models. They imagine where mobile devices create opportunities to radically improve someone's life.

How many potential mobile moments can you find in a brainstorming session or journey mapping exercise? Four? 10? 20? Once you start thinking about where your company intersects with your customers' or employees' daily lives, you will discover a multitude of ways to engage them in a mobile moment.

Determine the Context

As we described in chapter 2, the context of a mobile moment makes using a mobile device very different from using the Web. Knowing where someone is and her likely emotional state as well as her preferences and history gives you a rich data set to design a better engagement. And it's important to get this right. When a Lowe's customer pulls out a smartphone at home, she may be seeking store hours. If she's in the store, she may be comparing prices or just looking for the right aisle. Context informs how you help people in a mobile moment.

Table 3-2: Mapping the Context of Each Moment

Element	Data to gather
What is their situation and location?	Location data: Where are they?
	Movement data: How fast are they going?
	Event data: How long until their flight boards?
	Account data: How close are they to their minimum balance?
What is their emotional state or attitude?	Emotions: In a hurry? Agitated? Anxious? Frustrated? Or happy? Leisurely, leaning back?
	Attitudes: What kind of person are they? Impatient? Relaxed?
What are their preferences, profile, and history?	Preferences: What have they told you?
	Profile: What do you know about them?
	History: What have they done in the past?

Three questions will surface contextual information about the mobile moment (see Table 3-2):

Where is she physically? Location is a game changer because when you know where someone is, you are one step closer to knowing her situation and what she needs. It's the simplest part of context, but also the most powerfully different. If you know that someone wants to send flowers, you can direct her to the nearest location—or if she's already there, suggest a bird of paradise instead of a rose.

What is her emotional state or attitude? You may be able to infer someone's state of mind and adjust your response accordingly. In an airport, travelers are frantic when things go badly. How can Lufthansa help out based on its knowledge of that feeling? In financial services, American Express knows that alerts about potentially fraudulent account activity are scary, so it delivers them in a reassuring way with an ability to respond appropriately, simply, and quickly.

What are her preferences, profile, and history? The more someone shares, the smarter your service should get. If someone is a repeat customer, take advantage of your past transactions and interactions. At United Airlines, for example, the mobile app knows if you qualify for TSA Precheck and if you are eligible to enter the United Club, and it presents those options to only qualified passengers. This is the part that makes mobile moments a complex technology problem, since your core technology systems must now be linked directly to the mobile app.

Taken together, these steps—analyzing customers, cataloguing moments, and determining context—give you an idea of what sorts of mobile moments are possible. But which moments matter most? To make that decision, you need to get into the next step in the IDEA cycle, Design.

Design the Mobile Engagement

Mobile moments are like opinions. Having more of them doesn't necessarily make a customer's life easier.

The Design step helps you solve this problem. It helps you prioritize mobile moments based on their benefit to customers and their value to your company. Let's take a look at how one company approached the design problem: Hertz.

Rob Moore, Hertz's CTO, has been thinking about how to use technology to improve travelers' lives for 34 years. In 2010 he noticed that the first thing a traveler does when landing is pull out her phone and check her email. He led Hertz to be the first rental company to notify a traveler (who had asked to be notified) that her car was available in space K-21 on the third floor of the rental garage. He next moved that notification service to an opt-in SMS service and then to a dedicated mobile app.

Rob then realized that the mobile app was a rich platform for more engagement. He led a team of business, marketing, operations, and technology people to dream up new ways to serve customers. The list of services is now long and getting longer: automatic upgrades to preferred customers, paid upgrades for everybody, automatic check-in or drop off to skip even the preferred customer line, and so on. At each step, he and the team designed the engagement to suit the needs of a busy traveler and to look for ways expand the moments in which the company could serve a customer and make money or save money.

To make your own design decisions, you'll want to decide exactly how to engage your customer and then determine the benefit to that customer and the value to your company (see Table 3-3).

Table 3-3: Engagement Types and When to Use Them

Engagement type	When to use it	Examples
Notify a customer when something happens	Use context to determine which notifications to send, concentrating on events the customer is likely to care about.	United Airlines notifies customers of a seat upgrade. Citibank notifies customers of a low balance.
Respond to a request for information	Connect people seeking information with content or resources through searches and easily accessible action buttons.	Solocal sorts restaurants by what's nearby. The New York Times pushes stories down to a phone or tablet for offline reading.
Complete a transaction	When a customer is ready to buy or commit, use context to make it quick to complete the transaction.	Bank of America enables bill pay with a few taps. American Express lets you accept or reject a questionable charge.
Collaborate with a customer or employee	Communications represent the biggest slice of mobile moments at home and work. Use in-app collaboration to help people stay in touch with you or each other.	Salesforce Chatter lets you answer colleagues' questions. Amazon Mayday connects Kindle Fire users to a customer service agent over video.
Entertain or educate someone	Turn seconds or minutes of downtime into enjoyment with information or video.	ESPN sends alerts about your favorite teams. Netflix streams movies and TV shows. Candy Crush is fun in a spare moment.
Share an experience	Use mobile devices to ease access to social networks. More than half of Facebook and more than two-thirds of Twitter traffic is on mobile devices.	Apple makes it easy to share photos on Twitter. Guinness' Pub Finder lets you rate local pubs and share recommendations.
Capture or create content	Use the smartphone camera where photos are appropriate. You can also make it easy for people to enter text on the spot with voice entry.	Cisco employees log security problems with photos. Yelp users enter text to rate local eateries.

Decide How You Will Engage Your Customer

Rob and team engage travelers in three different ways on their mobile devices: notify a customer, respond to a request, and execute a transaction. For example, Hertz lets people search for cars currently available on the lot to find one they like best. They can then make the switch right from the airport bus and know what space their new car is in as they walk through the door to the car lot.

We have identified some of the key engagement types that many mobile apps use, from notifications to transactions to sharing. The important thing about these engagement types is that you see them through the eyes of your customer; what you do to engage them matches their motivations to interact with you.

Prioritize Based on Customer Benefit and Value to You

Who should your mobile moment serve—your company or your customer?

This is a crucially important question. Automate your existing web interactions and lean heavily on more sales, and you'll create an app or site that is annoying—*and won't be used*. But focus only on the customer's needs, and you may spend an awful lot of effort for very little return—and corporate budgets don't tolerate a lot of that.

The way to choose—the *only* way—is to focus on features and moments that benefit both the customer and your company. This philosophy will focus your efforts and help your team to agree on what's most important to do *now*.

To help, we created a simple Mobile Moment Assessment Tool so you can calculate the scores for the benefit to your customer and the value to your company. Calculating the benefit to your customer builds on Forrester's "levels of customer experience" model: meets needs, easy to use, enjoyable. Because context is so important, we added it as a fourth factor.

Calculating the value to your company encourages you to quantify the return: revenue earned, loyalty gained, expenses reduced, and the like. Based on these two scores and the quadrant they fall into, you can prioritize the mobile moments you need to tackle first (see Figure 3-3).

On this chart, the most successful features fall into the upper two quadrants.

Figure 3-3: The Mobile Moment Assessment Tool

Score from 1 (completely disagree) to 5 (completely agree). Add the factor
scores together to get a total score.

Benefit to your customer	Score
The app or site delivers a service that improves a customer's experience.	
The app or site allows a customer to easily accomplish a goal in seconds.	
The app or site is convenient and enjoyable to use.	
The app or site uses context to deliver a better experience.	
Total benefit score:	

Value to you	Score
The app or site delivers a service that generates revenue or reduces cost.	
The app or site increases the engagement opportunity with customers.	
The app or site greatly improves customer loyalty or experience.	
The app or site improves a business outcome such as referrals.	
Total value score:	

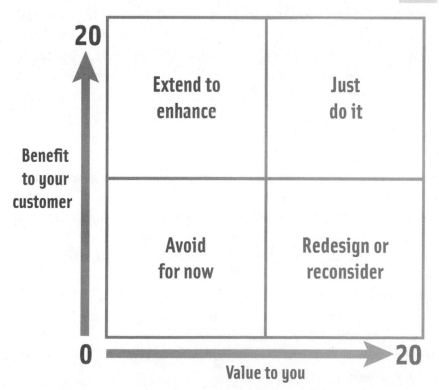

Just do it. If the service you can provide in the mobile moment helps your customer and is valuable to you, then it's a clear priority. Hertz's upgrade feature generates revenue by upselling cars that are already available to customers. Business renters like it because they can expense a nicer car—Hertz likes it because it generates revenue and helps with staff efficiency.

Extend to enhance. If a feature is good for a customer, but not as valuable to you, then you face a tough decision: Is it worth investing in? Because of the pace of competition, we believe you should invest in apps or features in this category as a way to keep up with the mobile demands of your customers—but plan to extend the engagement so it's also valuable to you. For example, the benefit of remote check deposit to a USAA customer is incredible convenience, but it may also reduce the company's check-processing costs.

The bottom two quadrants are features to avoid.

Redesign or reconsider. If the mobile engagement is inconvenient for a customer but could be valuable to you, then redesign it for mobile. This happens all the time as people port web interactions into mobile settings where they're no longer effective. It's also the problem Facebook faced with its first mobile app—a hybrid app using web technology. Few liked it—as an extension of web content, it was sluggish and ill-designed for mobile. The company had to design and build a native mobile app with a mobile-first experience. And it succeeded. In Q3 2013, compared with a year earlier, mobile ad revenue soared from $152 million to $882 million.[1] If you can't imagine what it will take to convince customers to use a feature, then table it until you've gained more experience because apps that don't create simple, easy-to-use benefits for your customer are a waste of effort.

Avoid for now. If the engagement isn't valuable to you and doesn't benefit a customer, then it falls into this last quadrant. Many of your existing website features will show up in this category. Porting them over just for completeness is a path to madness—they'll waste your budget and disappoint your customers. Concentrate on features that matter.

Armed with this analysis, you are in a position to trim the list of mobile moments from the Identify step of IDEA down to a more reasonable three to five moments or features to tackle this time around the IDEA cycle.

But you're not done. Even if a feature is worth including, it may not be worth the total effort required to implement it. To understand this effort—which goes way beyond app creation—you need to look closely at the Engineer step in IDEA.

Engineer Your Platforms, Processes, and People for Mobile

Many people in your company will think "mobile" means "app." Watch out for them. If you're not careful, they'll ruin you.

The delusion that mobile is just an app is a clear path to failure. Why? Because of the engineering required to make apps effective. When you don't involve technology and operations staff and systems, the mobile app often fails because it doesn't use your firm's core platforms and processes. That's why step three of the audit is to assess the impact of your mobile engagement on three vital elements of your company: platforms, processes, and people.

Use a Checklist to Assess the Impact on Platforms, Process, and People

Since you will likely spend 80% of your money and effort engineering your platforms, processes, and people for mobile moments, you need to prepare. For each core system, make a list of the things you need to worry about, then assess whether that thing is *available* to you and if it is *ready* for engagement.

Are your technology *platforms* ready to support mobile engagement? Bring technical experts into the mobile moment audit to identify the back-end systems and the new engagement technologies you need. You will need to know if that technology is ready to support your mobile moment. At American Airlines, the 10-fold increase in mobile logins over web logins meant the technology team had to scale up capacity. There's much more detail on this in chapter 10.

Are your customer-facing *processes* aligned for engagement? In the mobile moment audit, prepare and assess a list of processes like field service, retail sales, marketing operations, or customer onboarding that the engagement will touch. Where will they break down? What changes will you have to make? What new skills will their staff need? Will they support the engagement? At JCPenney, for example, store associates had mobile checkout, but there weren't receipt printers or bags distributed throughout the store to finish the sale and send the customer on her way. We will show how mobile moments change core processes in chapter 11.

Are your *people* ready to win the mobile moment? In the mobile moment audit, determine how you will organize to build the mobile app. Do you have the right skills? Have you combined business and technology staff in a single IDEA team? Do you have an executive charter? At American Airlines, CIO Maya Leibman chairs a mobile steering committee and director of mobile apps Phil Easter runs a mobile center of excellence and an IDEA team. We will talk about organizing to continuously improve mobile moments in chapter 12.

At this point in the audit, you know what mobile moments to target, how to design for the context of those moments, and what efforts you'll need to engineer solutions for those mobile moments. Are you done? Almost. If you're thinking strategically, you'll also want to plan for the data that will come from the back end of your new relationship with customers or employees in the Analyze step of IDEA.

Analyze Results to Monitor Performance and Optimize Outcomes

An application without analytics is like a car without a speedometer. Is it doing what it is supposed to do? Who knows? When budgets are tight and feature requests are flooding in, you need a systematic way to make decisions and to prove to others that those decisions are right. That's where data comes in.

So what will you measure and how will you use the data? The IDEA cycle comes full circle when you collect data that helps you monitor performance and figure out how to optimize outcomes. In many companies, data and analytics are a notable challenge; executives want to master the insights, but the necessary tools and skills seem just out of reach. The mobile moment audit is the right place to identify the data you need and determine if you're ready to use it. Don't put this off until later because, in all likelihood, then you won't ever actually do it.

First, identify the data you need. Consider usage data (data about the app itself), customer data (including people's locations), business data (such as transactions or sales), performance data (such as speed or failed calls to servers), and insight data (other data streams that help you figure out what's really going on). For each category of data, make a list of specific metrics you will be collecting. Then answer the next question: Is it practical to collect this data? And if you have the data, are you ready to use it? This question often reveals subtle organizational barriers to collecting data. But be courageous. Plow on to ask the next questions: Do you have the right expertise in place and the right technology to analyze the data?

. . . .

You're finished with a mobile moment audit. You've brainstormed a universe of possible mobile moments. You've winnowed the list by designing your engagement, then assessing the benefit to your customer and value to your company. With the audit in hand, you've also made a checklist of back-end systems and processes needed to support the mobile moment. Lastly, you've started to identify and build support for collecting and analyzing the data to let you complete the IDEA cycle.

Now what? Now it's time to dive into the details of a specific mobile strategy in sales, marketing, or product development. To start, you need to understand your own customers' mobile mind shift. Next, in chapter 4, we will introduce you to the Mobile Mind Shift Index to help you analyze your customers.

4

. . . .

Measure the Mobile Mind Shift

Build the Mobile Moments
That Your Audience Is Ready For

Some companies have mobile-friendly sites. Some have apps. Then there's E-Trade.

E-Trade was born online. It started along with online services like AOL. When the Web came around in the mid-1990s, E-Trade grew like a weed, exceeding $10 billion in assets in 2000. All along, the company's management recognized that its customers were more demanding than other investors. As far as technology was concerned, they were a very forward-leaning group.

By 2008, E-Trade had an app for BlackBerry devices, an app that for the first time released its investors from being shackled to the desktop.[1] Customers embraced it, especially in the throes of the stock market crash of 2008, an event that created a cascade of how-are-my-stocks-doing-right-now mobile moments. E-Trade followed up with an iPhone app in 2009. Its iPad app appeared on April 6, 2010, just three days after Apple released the iPad.

And just in case its demanding users failed to notice the release of these new apps, E-Trade advertised them with its highly engaging "talking baby" ads. In some of those ads, the baby was tracking his investments on his iPad. Most of those ads debuted during the Super Bowl, at around $2 million a spot.

Now every company that serves investors has investment apps. And the E-Trade apps do what those other apps do, very well—allow you to keep track of your portfolio, get alerts, trade, get quotes, and so on. E-Trade's customers want more, though, and the company has responded. Any investment app will let you buy 100 shares of Apple. But E-Trade's app was the first to recognize your voice—just say "Buy 100 shares Apple," and you're in the market (after tapping to confirm, of course). The E-Trade app even lets you scan a barcode and invest in the company that made the product.

Why bother with all this? Because, as Teron Douglas, E-Trade's VP of product management told us, "All of E-Trade's customers have shifted to mobile." That's pretty close to true. In fact, client trades from mobile accounted for 8.4% of total trades in 2013. Out of more than 19,000 people who rated the app, more than 11,000 gave it four or five stars.[2]

This is an absurdly high level of mobile service, but E-Trade's customers demand it. Do yours?

The Mobile Mind Shift Index

Clearly, something is going on with E-Trade's mobile customer base, and the company has to respond. Your customers may be just this avid, or maybe they aren't. You could guess, or you could ask them. But to truly understand your customers' mobile mind shift, you'll need to benchmark their mobile behaviors and attitudes.

That's just the problem we set out to solve. Forrester Research surveys hundreds of thousands of consumers and workers every year. We're bathed in data. So we took a close look at the data and asked "what really drives mobile engagement?" We were looking for the indicators that mattered.

What we found is fascinating. You can actually see the mobile mind shift as it happens. First, people get a smartphone. They start using it. They increase the frequency with which they interact, and the diversity of locations. They download apps. They begin to expect, and then demand, mobile services from the companies they deal with. And they move through stages—first communicating, then consuming content, and finally transacting.

Think about this, and you'll realize the risks of misjudging your customers. If you assume incorrectly that they're deep into the mobile mind shift and you create a sophisticated transaction app for them, they're unlikely to embrace it in large numbers. Conversely, if they're far along on the shift and you've got no mobile functionality for them, they'll be disappointed, and you risk losing them to some entrepreneur who is ready to meet their needs.

To calibrate and shape your mobile investment, you need a tool that measures mobile engagement. So we created one. We call it the Mobile Mind Shift Index.

While you can't measure someone's state of mind, you can measure his activity and attitudes. That's the insight behind the index. By analyzing consumer surveys from around the world, we have put together a series of measures that allows us to score any group of individuals—customers, employees, athletes, shoppers, stock traders, or citizens—to provide insight for companies that want to interact with them on mobile devices.

Figure 4-1: Mobile Mind Shift Index for E-Trade Customers

Mobile Intensity

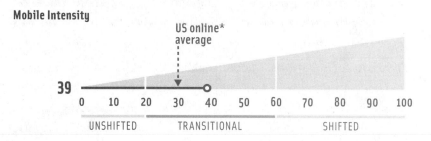

Mobile Expectation

Mobile Behaviors

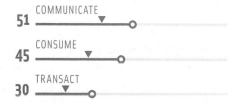

Base: 286 US online adults (18+) who are E-Trade investors
*Base: 8,224 US online adults (18+)
Source: US Mobile Mind Shift Online Survey, Q3 2013

The Mobile Mind Shift Index has three major components (see Figure 4-1). First, there's a Mobile Intensity Score that measures how immersed people are in their mobile lifestyle. Then, there's a Mobile

Expectation Score that measures how strongly people expect companies to deliver mobile services. Finally, there is a component that assesses mobile behavior, with three Mobile Behavior Scores: one for mobile communications, a second for consuming mobile content, and a third for conducting mobile transactions. Take a look at scores for E-Trade customers and how they compare to average online American adults, and you can see why E-Trade found it so urgent to provide sophisticated mobile applications for its customers. We'll explain the details behind this three-component index in the rest of the chapter.

The Mobile Intensity Score

Two simple factors, more than any other, identify people who are making the mobile mind shift:

1. **Frequency of access.** People making the mobile mind shift take out their phones (or tablets) frequently. So we score them on access, with more weight on consumers who use mobile devices more frequently.

2. **Diversity of locations.** People making the shift become increasingly adventurous with their devices, taking them out in different rooms in their homes, outdoors, at work, while shopping, and so on. So we score them on the number of locations in which they use their phones or tablets.

We combine the access and location measures to create a *Mobile Intensity Score*, which we scale from zero to 100. If you have no phone or tablet, or you never use them, you get a zero. If you have both and use them frequently everywhere, you score a 100.

The average online American adult scores 30 out of 100. But behind this single number is a lot of variation.

Age makes a huge difference. People age 18 to 24 score 44 on Mobile Intensity, but those over 65 score only 10 (see Figure 4-2). If you suspected that younger customers are more mobile, now you have proof. The generation coming of age next will be even more mobile than that. They may never even own a computer.

Mobile Intensity Score is also correlated with income, although not as strongly as it is with youth. People with household incomes of $25,000 per year or less score 26, while those making more than $100,000 score 32 (see Figure 4-3). Why? Because people who make more money tend to have better access to technology, which drives the score up, but they're also more likely to be older, which drives the score down. This also shows why you can't just make assumptions about your customer base. There's a lot of variation in mobile intensity, even if you know someone's demographics.

Figure 4-2: Mobile Intensity Score Declines with Age

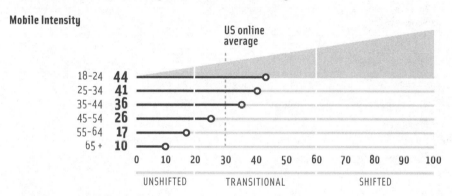

Base: 8,224 US online adults (18+)
Source: US Mobile Mind Shift Online Survey, Q3 2013

Figure 4-3: Mobile Intensity Score Increases with Income

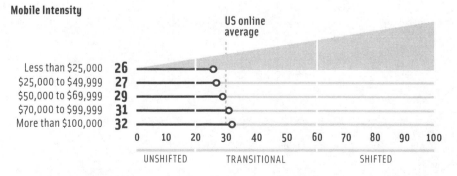

Base: 8,224 US online adults (18+)
Source: US Mobile Mind Shift Online Survey, Q3 2013

We use the Mobile Intensity Score to classify people into four groups. These range from Disconnected (Mobile Intensity Score of zero, don't interact on mobile at all) through Unshifted (greater than zero up to 19 after rounding to the nearest whole number), Transitional (20 to 59), and Shifted (60 or more). While half the population is Transitional or Shifted, these tend to be high-income, desirable consumers—the targets for most mobile apps (see Table 4-1).

Table 4-1: Characteristics of Mobile Intensity Segments

	All US	Discon-nected	Unshifted	Transi-tional	Shifted
Mobile Intensity Score range*	0-100	0	>0 to 19	20 to 59	60 to 100
% of online adult population	100%	24%	26%	29%	21%
% male	49%	51%	52%	46%	46%
Mean age	44	54	47	40	35
Mean household income	$80K	$64K	$86K	$87K	$82K
% with smartphone	54%	8%	44%	76%	84%
% with tablet	36%	5%	45%	42%	51%
% who recom-mend products to friends	57%	43%	53%	61%	70%
Phone apps (number of dif-ferent types)	3.9	0.3	1.9	5.4	8.5
Tablet apps (number of dif-ferent types)	2.6	0.1	2.4	3.2	4.8

Range describes where score falls after rounding to the nearest whole number.
Base: 8,224 US online adults (18+)
Source: US Mobile Mind Shift Online Survey (Q3, 2013)

The Mobile Intensity Score for any group gives you a good idea of just how many of your customers are demanding that you be there in their mobile moments. Why does this matter? Because it can help you convince your boss (or if you are the boss, your company) to get started now, as well as clearly delineate the costs of missing out.

What Mobile Intensity Tells Us About E-Trade

Let's imagine for a moment that you have Teron Douglas' job—that you're doing product management for E-Trade. Should you put a lot of effort into mobile applications?

To answer this question, we can look at E-Trade's customers. Remember, the average online consumer in the United States has a Mobile Intensity Score of 30. Other investment companies like Charles Schwab and Fidelity have scores at this average or below, probably because while their customers are affluent, they tend to be older than average consumers (see Figure 4-4). But E-Trade's customers' score of 39 is significantly above the average for online Americans (or other investors).[3]

Figure 4-4: Mobile Intensity Score of Investors

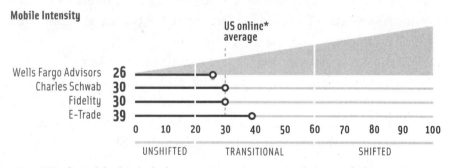

Base: US online adults (18+) who have an investment account with the specific firm
*Base: 8,224 US online adults (18+)
Source: US Mobile Mind Shift Online Survey, Q3 2013

Now look at the segments (see Table 4-2). Almost two-thirds of E-Trade's customers are Transitional or Shifted, higher than any other investment company we track. Even more interesting is *who* those Shifted customers are. The average Transitional or Shifted customer at E-Trade has an income of more than $123,000, compared with $102,500 for E-Trade's Disconnected and Unshifted customers. E-Trade cannot ignore this affluent customer base; they're crucial to the success of the company.

Table 4-2: Segment Breakdown of Investors

	US online average	Wells Fargo Advisors	Charles Schwab	Fidelity	E-Trade
% Disconnected	24%	24%	14%	20%	8%
% Unshifted	26%	30%	32%	28%	28%
% Transitional	29%	29%	34%	33%	33%
% Shifted	21%	18%	20%	19%	30%
Transitional + Shifted	51%	46%	54%	52%	64%

Base: 8,224 US online adults (18+)
Source: US Mobile Mind Shift Online Survey (Q3, 2013)

As a product manager at E-Trade, you would hear this as a clarion call to go mobile in a big way. And E-Trade did. Now you know *quantitatively* why it makes sense for E-Trade not only to build a tablet app, but to also advertise it during the Super Bowl to be sure to reach those Shifted customers.

What does this mean for you? Before investing in mobile, evaluate your customer base. If their average Mobile Intensity Score is greater than 35, you'd better get moving. If their score is 25 or below, you've got a little time to figure this out. And if it's somewhere in the middle, you'll have to look at the other components of the Mobile Mind Shift Index to determine how urgent it is to act.

If you look back at Figure 4-1, though, you'll see that there are two more components to the Mobile Mind Shift Index. And you'll also see that E-Trade customers score well above average on all of them. The full set of components helps determine the appropriate mobile strategy, as we'll describe in the rest of the chapter.

The Mobile Expectation Score Determines Urgency

The mobile mind shift doesn't stop with the Mobile Intensity Score. Recall that the mobile mind shift is the *expectation* that I can get what I want in my immediate context and moments of need. Just how strong is that expectation among your customers? We measure this with a *Mobile Expectation Score*, the second component of the Mobile Mind Shift Index.

The Mobile Expectation Score comes from people's answers to questions about what they expect from companies—mobile apps and sites—and how the quality of those apps and sites influences their engagement with the companies who created them. Like the intensity metric, it's scored from 0 to 100. The average Mobile Expectation Score for online American adults is 44. For E-Trade, it's 59, again, significantly above the score for other investors.

For the most part, the Mobile Expectation Score rises along with the Mobile Intensity Score (see Figure 4-5).[4] If your customers score more than 40 on Mobile Expectation, that score provides additional quantitative evidence that you've got to get moving; not only have your customers made the mobile mind shift, but they are actively judging your company on what it provides.

Figure 4-5: Mobile Expectation Rises with Intensity

Mobile Expectation

Base: 8,224 US online adults (18+)
Source: US Mobile Mind Shift Online Survey, Q3 2013

Let's look at how this metric works in practice. We looked at Mobile Expectation Scores for people who visit media sites online. In general, if you read, you have higher mobile expectations. Even readers of local newspapers online score 50 on expectations, which is above the US average. But the online readers with the highest mobile expectations are readers of *Entertainment Weekly (EW)*, with a score of 56 (see Figure 4-6).

Figure 4-6: Mobile Intensity and Expectation Scores of Online Media Readers

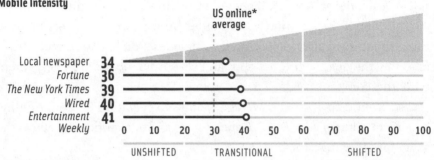

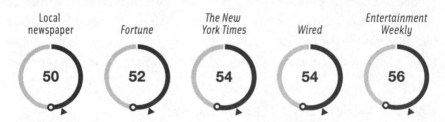

Base: US online adults (18+) who read the specified publication online in the last month
*Base: 8,224 US online adults (18+)
Source: US Mobile Mind Shift Online Survey, Q3 2013

Does *Entertainment Weekly* live up to those expectations? It does. Of course *EW* has an app for downloading, reading, and searching its magazine. But more importantly, *EW* is ready in the mobile moment when you're choosing entertainment with the "Must List," an app that lets you see what the magazine is recommending this week in movies, TV shows, music, books, games, and more. If you spot something you like, you can put it on your own personal "Must List" and then refer back to it when you're trying to figure out what to do for fun this weekend. Since media companies live and die over eyeballs and time spent, *EW* couldn't afford to cede its expectant readers to competitors like the IMDb app in that moment when they're selecting entertainment.

The Mobile Intensity Score tells you whether your customers are ready for mobile interactions. But the Mobile Expectation Score tells you whether their expectations are high; in other words, whether your absence (or an app of poor quality and utility) will disappoint them. If the Mobile Expectation Score of your customers is above average, you'd better be there, because that's what they're expecting.

But what should you do for those customers? To answer that question, look at their mobile behaviors.

Behavioral Metrics Help Define Your Strategy

What features should you include in your mobile applications and mobile sites? That depends on what your customers are used to doing on their devices. If they're just texting, don't expect them to buy a house on your app. Conversely, if they're ready to transact, then you'd better let them do so.

Figure 4-7: Behaviors Vary with Mobile Intensity

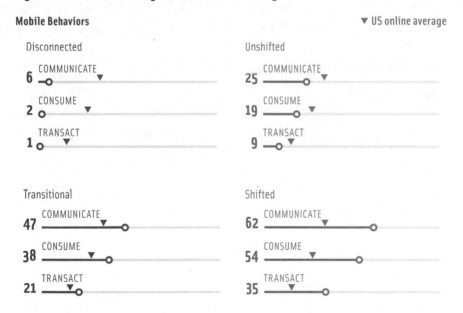

Base: 8,224 US online adults (18+)
Source: US Mobile Mind Shift Online Survey, Q3 2013

That's why we created three behavioral scores for each consumer (see Figure 4-7). One measures their communications behaviors, things like texting and sending email. A second measures behaviors that involve consuming content, like watching videos or researching purchases. The third looks at whether they're transacting on their devices, such as buying things or making travel reservations. Just as with the other metrics, we score people between 0 and 100 on each of the three behaviors.

When we compare these behaviors across Mobile Intensity segments, we see just what happens in the mobile mind shift. People making the shift communicate first, then consume, then transact.

Looking at the segments once again, the Unshifted consumers get a communicate score of only 25, and hardly consume or transact at all. The Transitional consumers are great at communicating, typically using applications like texting, but they score moderately on consuming (like checking on weather) and are just beginning to transact. Even the Shifted consumers, who communicate and consume like champs, are only transacting at a moderate pace. This reflects that transacting on mobile devices is still relatively complex and that many people, even among the Shifted, are just not ready to buy on their phones and tablets yet. Just wait, though, they'll get the hang of it.

How would you use these three scores? Let's take a look at the customers of several retailers (see Figure 4-8).

Figure 4-8: Mobile Behavior Scores for Retailers' Customers

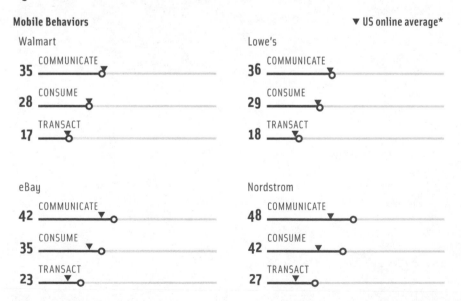

Mobile Behaviors   ▼ US online average*

Walmart
35 COMMUNICATE
28 CONSUME
17 TRANSACT

Lowe's
36 COMMUNICATE
29 CONSUME
18 TRANSACT

eBay
42 COMMUNICATE
35 CONSUME
23 TRANSACT

Nordstrom
48 COMMUNICATE
42 CONSUME
27 TRANSACT

Base: US online adults (18+) who have purchased from the listed retailer in the specified channel in the past three months
*Base: 8,224 US online adults (18+)
Source: US Mobile Mind Shift Online Survey, Q3 2013
Note: Walmart, Lowe's, and Nordstrom analysis for in-store customers, eBay for online customers

How should Lowe's, for example, interpret these scores? Lowe's customers have moderately high scores on Communicate and Consume. Looking at the retailer's app, it has seized one mobile moment: the in-store moment. If you've found a product on the app, it actually pinpoints the location of that product in the store. With a middle-of-the-road Transact score of 18, Lowe's customers are not demanding commerce on their phones . . . yet. But the retailer must keep an eye on these customers and on whether they're getting what they want from competitors.

Not surprisingly, eBay's customers are further along on the Mobile Transact scale, with a score of 23. Of course, eBay is all *about* commerce, so the company felt it had to create a commerce-enabled transaction app. The alerts for items under bids satisfy the eBay buyer's desire to communicate, and with a bar-code scan feature from its acquisition of RedLaser, consuming is also easy. Apparently, it's working; 40% of the dollar value of stuff sold on eBay now includes a mobile device touchpoint of some kind. So far, customers have downloaded its app 186 million times. And when we examined its iPhone app in the App Store in January of 2014, more than 200,000 customers had given it a very strong average rating of 4 out of 5 stars. eBay is now moving on to focus on local commerce with its eBay Now project, which we describe in Chapter 13.

Finally, let's take a look at Nordstrom. Its customers score very high on all three scales relative to other retailers. The Nordstrom app delivers strongly on content, with blogs and an Instagram feed with shopping and fashion ideas. While you can complete commerce on it, it's not clear that mobile buying is the Nordstrom buyer's goal. Nordstrom has been focused on providing mobile devices to sales associates to ease the in-store experience—clearly, based on the scores, its shoppers are ready. But from our analysis of Nordstrom shoppers, the company could also benefit from examining its shoppers' mobile moments—including transactional moments—and delivering more on its mobile app to influence sales.

Putting It All Together—Interpreting Scores on the Mobile Mind Shift

We've described a lot of statistics in this chapter. What should you do with them? Based on our work with clients, we've developed a chart that describes the strategies that apply best depending on your customers' scores (see Table 4-3).

Table 4-3: Your Mobile Strategy Depends on Your Customers' Mobile Mind Shift Index

1. Mobile Intensity Score

Determines whether it is *appropriate* to connect with customers on mobile.

- *Less than 25.* Low Mobile Intensity. Only a minority of customers are ready.
- *Between 25 and 35.* Moderate Mobile Intensity. Move forward or not based on the Mobile Expectation Score.
- *Greater than 35.* High Mobile Intensity. Check the Mobile Expectation Score, then move forward quickly.

2. Mobile Expectation Score

Determines the level of *urgency* to create a mobile application or site.

- *Less than 40.* Low Mobile Expectation. Take your cues from your customers' mobile usage, but, in general, major investments in mobile are not urgently needed.
- *Between 40 and 50.* Moderate Mobile Expectation. Start investing now; many of your customers are already expecting mobile service.
- *Greater than 50.* High Mobile Expectation. Your customers are demanding mobile and will be disappointed in a lack of service. It is urgent that you move forward.

3. Mobile Behavior Scores

Determines *features* that customers are ready for.

- *Communicate Score greater than 30.* A high Communicate score indicates a readiness for features like text messages, mobile alerts, and mobile-ready emails.
- *Consume Score greater than 30.* A high Consume score indicates a readiness for features such as online news feeds, videos, and other valuable content.
- *Transact Score greater than 25.* A high Transact score indicates a readiness for transaction features such as deposits or bill pay, making reservations, or completing purchases.

Note: Strategy decisions also depend on conditions unique to your company, including the expectations set by entrepreneurs and competitors in your industry.

As you review these rules of thumb, here are a few things to keep in mind.

If your customers' Mobile Intensity and Mobile Expectation Scores are low, your customers are not very active in mobile. Moderate your investments and monitor your competitors and your customers. Even when these scores are low, look for opportunities to communicate with your customers over mobile devices. Be prepared to make larger investments as customers become more comfortable with mobile interactions.

If your customers' Mobile Intensity and Mobile Expectation Scores are moderate, check whether the Shifted customers in your customer base are particularly valuable (high net worth, spend a lot, repeat customers, spread word of mouth, or something similar). Invest moderately, and optimize your website for mobile. And keep in mind that customers are learning, so you'll probably need to move more rapidly in the next year or so.

If your customers' Mobile Intensity and Mobile Expectation Scores are high, then your customers expect you to be there. Decide what features are acceptable to customers based on the Communicate, Consume, and Transact scores. Then decide which features are desirable based on a review of the value of those features to your company and to the customer, as we described in Chapter 3. Be aware that if you fail to move, an entrepreneur is likely already targeting your market with mobile service.

The World Is Shifting at an Uneven Pace

One of the best things about working at Forrester Research is our access to global data and insight. Our analysts work in markets throughout the world, and we can actually compare the mobile activities of citizens across many countries. This, combined with our interviews with businesspeople in many of those countries, allows us to paint a global picture of the mobile mind shift.

It's a fascinating picture. Regardless of whether you're a global corporation or based in one region, you need to know what's going on in local markets. While mobile technology is spreading faster, and more broadly, than any digital technology that came before, it's not the same everywhere. Americans are wild for apps. Europeans and Asians in advanced markets are embracing smartphones, but with fewer apps, more mobile sites, and more partnerships with established players. And in developing markets, mobile—and not necessarily on smartphones—is creating an entrepreneurial explosion as entire countries leapfrog the PC-based Internet to embrace interactivity on phones. The Mobile Mind Shift Index makes it possible to measure these variations. Take a look at the Mobile Intensity Scores for the countries where we do surveys (see Figure 4-9).[5] If you're going to do business globally, here are a few insights about mobile behaviors that might be valuable to you.

Figure 4-9: Global Comparison of Mobile Intensity Scores

Mobile Intensity

Hong Kong	33
South Korea	30
United States	30
Metro Argentina	27
Indonesia	27
Metro India	26
Turkey	26
Metro China	25
Sweden	24
Metro Mexico	23
Metro Brazil	22
Spain	18
Canada	17
Netherlands	16
Metro Russia	16
Italy	16
Australia	16
Germany	13
Great Britain	12
France	12
Poland	12

0 10 20 30 40 50 60 70 80 90 100

UNSHIFTED   TRANSITIONAL   SHIFTED

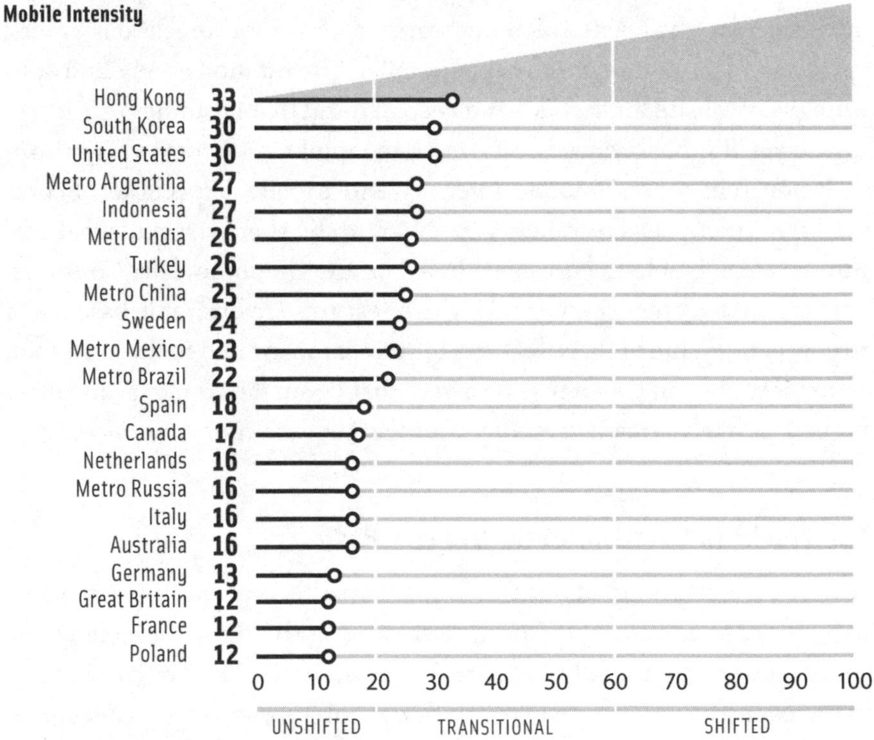

Base: Online adults (18+) in each country
Source: Global Technographics Online Benchmark Surveys 2013 and US Mobile Mind Shift Online Survey, Q3 2013
Note: "Metro" refers to surveys that reach only inhabitants of major cities.

Advanced Asian Consumers Embrace Mobile Activities

There are only four places in the world where more than one in five consumers is Shifted: Hong Kong, South Korea, Metro Argentina, and the US.

Hong Kong already has more smartphones than people. But when it comes to mobile intensity, South Korea may be the most fascinating place on earth. Home to Samsung, the world's biggest handset manufacturer, its subways are filled with people consuming streaming video and video games on over-size handsets. (Mobile game playing is so popular that the government had to put rules in place to limit daily spending on video games.)

While our data from Japan was not available in time for this publication, it's another market where mobile activity rivals Hong Kong and South Korea. By 2016, half of Japanese consumers will have smartphones. Already, Japanese consumers are intense users of their mobile phones on daily commutes that can be up to several hours each day and have embraced mobile content, mobile social networks, and mobile television. Nissan in Japan takes advantage of the heavy usage of the browser by posting fresh, short-form content for consumers to read while commuting. During the recent Tokyo Motor Show, they received 3 million video views. And using just a smartphone, Japanese consumers can even sign up for a mobile-only bank called Jibun Bank, a joint venture between The Bank of Tokyo Mitsubishi UFJ and telecom operator KDDI.

One mobile application that's been popular in Japan recently is Line, a rich messaging app with stickers (small evocative graphics, like emoticons) and Internet voice calls. With the uptake in smartphones, Line grew into a social lifestyle platform that deepens communication among family and close friends with photos, games, timelines and video calls. Today, Line boasts 310 million registered users who send 7.2 billion messages and use 1 billion stickers *each day*. Line generated more than $100 million in revenue in Q3 2013 from in-app purchases such as stickers, in-game purchases, and spending by mobile marketers who create accounts to engage with consumers.

Shifted Consumers in Metropolitan China and India Engage Differently

India's mobile population may have fewer sophisticated devices—in 2013, only 8% of the population owned a smartphone—but that hasn't stopped Indian entrepreneurs from creating mobile applications that work on feature phones as well. With more than half a billion mobile phone sub-scribers, India trails only China in connected consumers. Companies like

Celltick distribute 30,000 mobile coupons daily from local merchants in India to phones of all kinds through its applications LiveScreen and Start. Tech Mahindra offers a mobile job posting service to connect job seekers to potential employers with a healthy conversion rate; it makes recommendations on any phones and offers click-to-call to close the deal.

Chinese consumers in metropolitan areas use their phones less frequently and in fewer places than in many other Asian countries, resulting in a Mobile Intensity Score of only 25. While China has the largest smartphone population in the world, it relies heavily on slower 2G mobile networks today, with many consumers seeking out faster Wi-Fi connectivity in workplaces, malls, and other public places. Mobile coupons and QR codes are popular. Rather than download a lot of apps, the Chinese tend to depend on a handful of services like WeChat, a social networking platform with 600 million registered users where members distribute voice messages, text messages, videos, and photos to their friends. Chinese companies seeking broader reach often design their consumer apps to work within WeChat; the Beijing restaurant ShunKouLiu even allows customers to order takeout food from its microsite in WeChat. As Forrester's Bryan Wang, who analyzes the Chinese market, suggests, "With the high mobile penetration in China, mobile offers a great opportunity for companies to access consumers in many regions, ranging from large cities to smaller villages."

European Mobile Use Is Less Intense

European countries like Germany and France have lower Mobile Intensity Scores. This is a result of both decreased frequency and a lower diversity of locations in which European consumers access mobile devices. Among the factors that hold back Europeans from more intense interactions are lower smartphone and tablet penetration, limits on mobile phone data plans, and a relative paucity of public Wi-Fi zones. But this hasn't stopped some European companies from exploiting mobile. Thomas Husson, a Forrester mobile analyst based in Paris, expects Europeans to move more rapidly on the mobile mind shift. "With growing smartphone penetration rates, the progressive rollout of 4G networks in Europe, and more affordable data plans, I'd expect European consumers to catch up quickly with their US counterparts." This has already begun in Sweden, which scores much higher than other European countries on Mobile Intensity Score.

Australian Companies Are Embracing Mobile Utility

Australia is a hotbed of activity, despite a relatively low Mobile Intensity Score. We'll describe the sophisticated Fairfax Media newspaper applications in Chapter 6. Australian banks are also competing on mobile applications. The Commonwealth Bank of Australia launched an app for new home buyers that used augmented reality to simplify the discovery and consumption of housing prices in target areas, and the bank ended up generating many mortgage leads through the mobile app. ING Direct, a bank, delivered a breakthrough mobile experience that allows banking customers to see their balance without logging in. As a result, 200,000 customers downloaded the app in the first three months, the same number as in the previous three years.

Where Is Mobile Going?

We've seen waves of technology adoption. We saw PCs become universal in the early 1990s, and the Internet become ubiquitous by 2000. The connected consumer and the connected employee are already embedded in the way we think about the world.

The mobile mind shift, though, is accelerating much more rapidly than those previous waves of technology.

In developed countries, smartphones are already half of all mobile phones sold, and they will rapidly become the default mobile device. The irresistible appeal of this device will stimulate people to try more apps and more experiences in more mobile moments, driving the Mobile Intensity Score way up. In the US, we've already seen it increase from 20 to 30 over a six-month period in 2013. As changes in the structure of the European mobile market remove barriers, we expect Europeans to catch up quickly; in 2015, more than half of Europeans will own smartphones.

In Japan, Korea, and China, the rapid expansion of smartphone penetration, especially in urban areas, will create new, unique ways of interacting. China is on a path to surpass 500 million smartphones in 2014, the year this book was published, making it a larger smartphone market than the US and Europe combined. We may see the emergence of new forms of mobile interaction based more on sites than on apps. And because social media participation is so pervasive in Asia, the mobile moments in Asia will increasingly be mobile *social* moments.

But perhaps the largest change will take place in less developed areas like Africa, where mobile banking, mobile health, and access to mobile information could transform whole nations. We estimate that more than half of Africans own mobile phones. Inexpensive mobile devices could create an economic boom by unleashing the creativity and entrepreneurial spirit to a generation of previously Disconnected consumers.

· · · · · · · · ·

The future is now for companies tapping into mobile moments. Starting in chapter 5, we'll show how you can embrace mobile for business advantage in sales, marketing, and product design and how new business models will challenge companies of all kinds, globally.

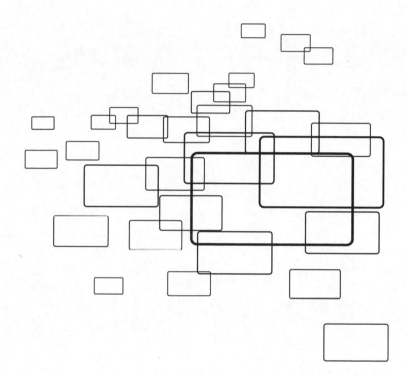

PART II
The Mobile Business Shift

5

. . . .

The Sales Shift

Use Mobile Moments to Influence and Drive Commerce

"Everyone loves being in the wine and spirits business. It's a very stable business. There is always a reason to drink." So says Jamie Arking, CFO of his family's business, the Roger Wilco Discount Liquor Store in Pennsauken, New Jersey. Stability is great, of course. But when it comes to mobile, immediacy is even better. That's why it took a different twist on the sales of spirits to get the Arking family into the spirit of mobile sales.

Jamie's father Elliot and his uncle Joe started Roger Wilco with a traditional storefront. Eventually Joe thought they should consider online opportunities, but Elliot was resistant. "No, that will just increase overhead," he said. Joe's counterproposal (originally from his other son, Edward) was this: "What if we just sold one item at a time [online]?" Elliot gave in, and the brothers launched WTSO.com.

Wines Til Sold Out (WTSO) sells one high-value wine at a discount until it sells out, then moves on to the next item. Unlike most online businesses, WTSO emphasizes urgency over variety. Consumers must buy during the "flash sale" or miss the bargain. Selling one thing online at a time is far easier for the liquor store, which can just slap mailing labels on the one designated wine in the back of the store and ship it to the customer.

While WTSO was successful, customers often missed sales during their work hours, or if they weren't at their desks. Here's how Jamie describes it: "Every *minute* is very expensive real estate for us. We wanted to make sure that everyone had an opportunity to buy. Time is of the essence. When it's on, it's tick, tick, tick." Email can't do that so well. But mobile can.

If you've got the WTSO app, then the minute a sale begins, you hear the sound of clinking glasses. For customers, this sound becomes a Pavlovian cue. The buyer knows it's game time, the clock is ticking, and they have a limited time to buy. (The clink sound also gets the customer's friends interested, leading to more downloads by word of mouth.)

Does it work? One day in 2013, WTSO sold more than 105,000 bottles in a single day. Today, more than 45% of sales midweek and more than 70% of weekend sales are on mobile phones. Not bad for a discount liquor store in New Jersey.

The Impact of Mobile on Sales Is Not What You Think

WTSO is an amazing success story. Can you do what the Arking family has done?

Probably not.

You have now entered the world of mobile's impact on selling. Please leave your preconceptions behind. You are about to learn that when it comes to sales, mobile strategy is often the exact opposite of what you might expect. We're here to guide you through this strange land and to show where the real opportunities lie.

Here are the counterintuitive things you'll learn in this chapter.

Mobile selling is not like eCommerce. Impulse drives much of mobile sales.

Mobile influence is more important than mobile selling. Mobile devices are much more important for influencing sales than closing them.

Mobile is not a channel. If you organize your strategy around the mobile "channel," you'll miss the real opportunities.

Mobile changes everything about selling. It changes what you carry, where you can sell it, and how you price it.

For loyal customers, mobile devices in stores help sell more. People "showrooming"—that is, checking prices on their phones—terrify retailers. But if you connect their mobile devices with your loyalty program, mobile in stores can actually generate sales.

And finally, **mobile can be most helpful in selling big-ticket items.**

In business-to-business situations especially, mobile in the hands of sales staff can supercharge closing rates.

So open your mind to a new way of thinking about sales. We'll explore these concepts one by one.

Mobile Selling Is Not Like eCommerce

eCommerce is about selection, efficiency, and discovery. It's designed for websites where people can linger over things, make comparisons, click for more detail, and come back and check what they've bookmarked. It's like an infinite, clickable store.

Mobile commerce is typically *not* like that.

Mobile selling often succeeds based on an impulse in a mobile moment. See a deal, click a deal, and move on. Tap into this impulse, and you can sell more, as WTSO did. Companies like Gilt Groupe, Rue La La, and Groupon are making money from flash sales, just like WTSO.

Mobile selling has its place. According to projections from Forrester Research, customers in the US will buy $45 billion worth of merchandise and services from phones in 2018, up from $18 billion in 2013.[1] These are often high-margin sales, impulse buys that sellers would otherwise miss out on or sales of expiring inventory (like airline seats). As Bob Kupbens, VP of marketing and digital commerce at Delta Air Lines puts it, "Mobile is like an end cap in a store. It's where you put the impulse purchases."

If you've got an eCommerce group, though, don't just turn it loose and expect to replicate what you've done on the Web. Shrinking your eCommerce site down to a smartphone screen is not what your customer is looking for. Our clients are often tempted by this opportunity and hope to replicate what they created online in 1998 or 2000. For the most part, they can't and neither can you. As Sucharita Mulpuru, Forrester's eCommerce expert, points out, "On the desktop, everyone did the same thing. But your mobile strategy has to be so customized for who you are. You can't just copy someone else and expect to be successful."

As far as selling goes, if you think about it for a moment, you'll realize that in most cases, impulse purchases are *not* the main driver of buying. Many mobile customers may embrace mobile buying, but they all want real-time *information*. So, for many companies, mobile moments are much more about influencing sales than they are about actual purchases.

Mobile Influence Is More Important Than Mobile Selling

How big is mobile's influence on sales? According to Deloitte Digital's Kasey Lobaugh, mobile will influence $689 billion of US in-store retail sales by 2016.[2] And this makes sense: As more customers make the mobile mind shift, they check their devices more frequently—more instinctively—as part of the buying cycle. This $689 billion—in the US alone—dwarfs not only mobile sales, but online sales as well; eCommerce in the same time period is less than half this amount.

Even within a store, mobile can help influence people to buy—or at least help them make better choices. What are people with mobile phones doing in stores? Among online US adults with a mobile phone, 14% are researching products, 10% are reading product reviews, and 9% are comparing store prices. So you're better off making it easy to find information in the store.

One way companies influence in-store decisions is with 2D barcodes that customers can scan to get more information. Electronics retailer Best Buy created 2D barcodes for each item on its shelves. A quick mobile phone scan allows customers to see detailed product information, reviews, and product comparisons. Manufacturers are helping customers find information this way, too. Smashbox (cosmetics) and Ryobi (power tools) use 2D barcodes on product packaging to link shoppers to product demonstration videos to guide a customer's decision.

But tracking mobile's influence across channels can challenge businesses, especially retail businesses. That's the problem that Sona Chawla had to solve at Walgreens.

. . . .

CASE STUDY: How Walgreens Turned Mobile Influence into Cross-Channel Revenue

Sona Chawla is used to finding creative ways around obstacles. Originally from India, she wanted to go to college in the US and study computer science and math. Her parents insisted she choose an all-women's college. Her solution: attend the well-respected women's college Wellesley in suburban Boston but supplement her coursework at MIT nearby in Cambridge—in the end she spent her junior year at MIT, but graduated from Wellesley. To her, the boundary between "women's school" and "co-ed institution" was irrelevant, so she found a way around it.

She needed to see past traditional boundaries when, in 2010, digital photos and mobile devices created challenges in her job as president of eCommerce for Walgreens and its 8,000-plus retail stores.

"When we looked at store and digital, we realized we were optimizing two different things," Sona recalls. The stores focused on selling physical photography products including batteries and accessories. The digital team wanted to sell more digital photo-based products such as greeting cards and calendars. And the digital photo opportunity was growing rapidly. "From our perspective, consumer behavior was changing and our digital team was able to see it," Sona says. "We'd reached a tipping point in a business that is extremely valuable to Walgreens."

So Walgreens found a way to resolve the conflict. It combined the profit-and-loss (P&L) responsibility for photos, both digital and in stores, and put it under Sona's eCommerce group. Once the company's leadership could see the full opportunity, they offered the business to Sona's team. This was possible because she had developed relationships on the retail side of the business; to cement these relationships, she chose a staffer who had spent most of his career on the retail side to run the entire photo business.

In 2011, the photo business shifted as smartphones created a massive surge in demand for digital photo services taken on mobile devices. A business organized strictly by channel—one that treated online, mobile, and stores as separate entities with separate investments and revenue—would struggle to take advantage of that opportunity. But Sona's new organization for the photo unit could.

Even as the phones were generating more photos, they were also generating more traffic and impulse purchases. Phones and tablets represent more than half of the web traffic to Walgreens websites. The company changed its marketing and merchandising mix in the photo business to promote both digital and physical photo products, both in the stores and online. It added features so that people could send a print to Walgreens from other apps, not just from Walgreens' own mobile app. Because Walgreens was well positioned, as Sona puts it, "We changed the trajectory of the photo business." In 2010 less than 1% of the company's online orders for prints were from mobile. In 2013, that percentage had soared to 40%.

Walgreens makes decisions differently because it is organized to do so, without channel silos. Only a business organized in this way can profit from the changes mobile is creating.

Mobile Is Not a Channel

Once you realize that mobile is about influence, you see why it makes no sense to treat it as a channel. That's what Walgreens found out. Mobile *eliminates* channels—it's the fertilizer in the garden, not another perennial flower sprouting. As Deloitte Digital's Kasey Lobaugh says, "[It's] not about connecting the channels, but getting rid of the channels. Channels shouldn't own inventory, product assortment, pricing decisions, or customers." It was only through that kind of thinking that Walgreens could capitalize on the mobile photo opportunity.

Figure 5-1: Mobile Mind Shift Index of Walgreens Customers Who Take Photos on Their Phones

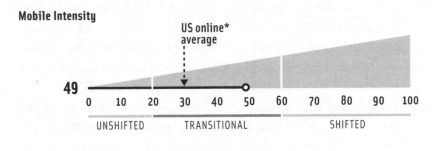

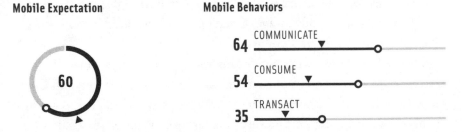

Base: 1,437 US online adults (18+) who have purchased offline or online from Walgreens in the past three months and take photos/videos on their phones at least weekly
*Base: 8,224 US online adults (18+)
Source: US Mobile Mind Shift Online Survey, Q3 2013

Let's take a peek at the Mobile Mind Shift Index of Walgreens customers who take photos with their phones to see why this worked (see Figure 5-1). Their Expectation score is 60, far higher than average US consumers, and they also score very high on the Consume and Transact measures of the Mobile Mind Shift Index. Based on this analysis, and using the rules of thumb we put forth in Chapter 4, Walgreens would have left behind a very large and enticing opportunity if it *didn't* find a way to tap into the mobile photo phenomenon.

Mobile Changes Everything About Selling

For most firms, mobile selling is not about how much you sell through mobile devices or apps. It's about creating mobile moments that lead to *new ways to sell*. Mobile will change the mix of products you sell, where you sell them, and how you price them.

Mobile Expands What You Sell

Start with your product assortment. If you sell direct, you probably sell a broader selection online than in stores, because stores must optimize for the local customer base and shelf space. But mobile bridges the gap between the limited space on store shelves and the vast variety online—it's inherently local, but not limited to local inventory. This often creates a conflict that you'll need to resolve between the people who do the merchandising in stores and online.

Mobile Amplifies Where and When You Sell

Mobile changes the moments in which you can influence a sale. That influence can now happen anywhere. Customers who use the UK app for Autotrader.com, for example, can take a photo of a car and find other people selling cars of the same make and model near them. That turns any moment of seeing a car in the street into a car-selling moment. Shazam lets people hold up their phones and identify (and buy) music, regardless of where the buyer is located. Amazon's mobile app allows you take a photo of any book's cover—in a friend's house, or in a Barnes & Noble store, for example—and then identify and buy it.

Mobile technology also enables sales in non-traditional retail outlets, like pop-up stores, street fairs, or holiday festivals. Square, which works with a seller's smartphone or tablet, makes it easy for merchants to take orders in any location. Whether you're a food truck in a parking lot or a nurse selling flu shots in an airport, you're ready to take a payment.

You can also extend the store, virtually, into the world. One of the most fascinating examples of this kind of thinking is the food and sundries retailer Tesco Homeplus in South Korea. The company recognized that commuters have free time, and that they wanted to use it to shop. So the company put up graphics on transit station walls resembling the shelves of a Tesco store. The graphics allowed customers to easily scan codes of what they wanted—drinks, food, other goods—to build a shopping list and request home delivery, with those bags of goodies arriving just as they got off the bus and returned home. The initial three-month test in 2011 boosted online sales by 130%. By February 2012, Tesco Homeplus had expanded the virtual stores to more than 20 bus stops, and its app, downloaded 900,000 times, was the top shopping app in South Korea.

Mobile Levels Pricing across Channels

Perhaps the most pervasive way in which mobile changes your business is through pricing. *Mobile levels pricing.* According to Forrester Research surveys, consumers using a smartphone in a store are more likely to be checking prices—"showrooming"—than anything else except checking product features. So it's very hard to maintain different prices in different channels.

Jamie Arking at WTSO turned this expectation to his advantage. "Consumers need to feel confident they are getting the best deal," he says. "We do the research for the consumer and present everything we find to them. We give them the lowest available price online from yesterday—it's completely transparent."

Big online sellers keep the pressure up here, especially Amazon. In 2011, Amazon conducted a trial. If a consumer used the company's Price Check app while in a competitor's store, Amazon exploited that mobile moment to lower its price by up to 5% to capture or steal the sale. In this way, Amazon made itself part of the mobile mind shift, and inserted itself into the sales process of its competitors, stealing their mobile selling moments.

While this sort of behavior drives retailers crazy, it's the new reality. You must match competitors' prices, or offer unique products, or generate some other sort of value that enables you to charge more. Target is one retailer that has already moved to an everyday price match strategy amid this more intense competition.

For Loyal Customers, Mobile Devices in Stores Help Sell More

WTSO and Walgreens both succeeded in their mobile efforts by focusing on *helping customers*. One thing mobile does really well is to provide utility in moments of need. That utility can come from applications that empower either the customer *or* the salesperson helping that customer.

This is a bit ironic, because the first thing retailers think of when they think of mobile is showrooming. Talk to a retailer about showrooming, and you'll see a face that recalls Edvard Munch's "The Scream." But, as it turns out, consumers who are using their mobile phones in a store are *more* likely to buy from you, not less likely. According to Deloitte Digital, the conversion rate for consumers using mobile phones in stores is 14% higher than for those without a phone. Conversion rates shoot up by 30% if the consumer is using the retailer's app. Kapow! Take that, showrooming!

To tap into this energy, though, you need to connect with the customer. And the key to this is a loyalty program.

Here's an example from the beauty retailer Sephora. The company wanted to deliver personalized service right in the store. Both customers and salespeople would benefit if a sales associate could answer a question like, "What moisturizer did I buy the last time I was here?" But before the customer reaches the register, engaging them might feel awkward; once she's there, spending time with her may annoy the other customers in line.

Sephora's loyalty program, Beauty Insider, turned out to be the key mechanism it needed to re-engineer in-store interactions because it includes information about customers' preferences, past history, and loyalty points.

The trick was to make this information instantly available when the customer was in the store. Sephora accomplished this by integrating the Beauty Insider loyalty program with Sephora's mobile app and Apple's Passbook. The result: The customer saw her loyalty card pop up on her phone automatically, including points and tier in the loyalty program, whenever she was near a store. That was the first mobile moment, designed for the customer. The second mobile moment was enabled by Sephora's app, which lists previous purchases and a wish list, helpful information for the shopper in the store. And finally, when the customer presents the loyalty card in the app to a salesperson, the salesperson's own mobile point-of-sale device makes it easy to look up the customer's account history and recommend products that work well with the ones the customer preferred.

Loyalty programs are essential to any multi-touchpoint customer strategy, because they identify the customer, her history, and her preferences. "Loyalty and engagement are really important. We want to build relationships with our customer over time, and we want to move her up in the loyalty program," explains Johnna Marcus, director of digital business development at Sephora. "So far, over 1 million Sephora clients have registered for Passbook, and 80% of our Passbook users are active Beauty Insiders or frequent shoppers. They shop twice as much as our average Beauty Insider client." She describes the customers who register through mobile as "materially more valuable" than store-only customers. That's the value of mobile-influenced commerce.

Loyalty is great for repeat business—moving the customer along the path to repeated purchases of a few dollars, or even a few hundred dollars. But what if your customer buys products worth thousands or tens of thousands of dollars? When the purchase requires careful consideration, mobile devices in the hands of sales folks can make a huge difference. That's what the heating, ventilation, and air-conditioning (HVAC) manufacturer Trane found out.

CASE STUDY: Trane's Sales Partners, Armed with Tablets, Close Business Faster

Selling air-conditioning systems is hard. It's even more challenging if you've got a premium-priced, high quality product line like Trane.

Take it from Donna Self, founder of the Independent Trane dealer Lakeside Heating & Air Conditioning. Here's the situation she faces. Customers typically call for an HVAC estimate when they have an air conditioning emergency—a failing system and rising temperatures. When the HVAC salesperson arrives at the door, a panic-stricken housewife greets him. He shows up with a rolling suitcase filled with binders of HVAC products. The worried look on the customer's face deepens. He walks around the home, crawls through the attic, goes out to the truck and works on a quote for 45 minutes, scribbles some notes, comes back to the door, and hands over a business card with an estimate written on the back—probably enough to buy a used Toyota. Then he says, "I can get you something more detailed within a few days."

With a selling moment like that, and in the teeth of a recession, dealers were typically closing only 30% of sales. Smart dealers like Donna created paper-based selling plans (more binders), but that's a lot of work—as Donna put it, she felt as if she were working for "a dime an hour." What was holding things back?

First, in that selling moment, there is an asymmetry of information. The HVAC field salesperson knows a lot more about air-conditioning systems than the customer does. Because those systems are complicated and expensive, they're hard to sell. And second, because a company like Trane relies on a national network of independent businesses to sell, there is no uniform set of selling processes. While Trane can guide the selling process, it can't control the quality of every interaction.

Trane knew it had to improve that selling moment. Its sales team turned to Bruce Tansy, a technology manager with more than 40 years of experience to help solve the problem. Here's how he fixed things, with the help of Cynergy, his digital experience design agency (now part of KPMG).

He *identified* the right mobile moments—including the moment when the survey of the house is complete, and it's time to talk to the customer. Folks from Trane and Cynergy went into the field with Donna's HVAC field service men. They rolled with the trucks, carried the binders, crawled in attics, and observed the interactions between the panic-stricken customers and Donna's service team. They identified the unmet needs of both customers and service people.

Then they set out to *design* a tool to arm every sales and service person to record information about the customer and the site, communicate the value, deliver a great customer experience, and give customers the confidence that they were making the best decision with Trane. They gave the sales and service team an interactive iPad tablet application that replaced the suitcase full of binders. With checklists and load calculators, they could assemble more accurate and comprehensive bids right there and then. They could use tools and videos on the iPad to demonstrate to customers visually how the system worked and to provide alternatives at different price points and levels of quality. This made it far easier to close the deal on-site—a beautiful iPad app is a lot easier to trust than an estimate on the back of a business card. Donna's first impression of the iPad application was that it would make the selling process easier and more organized. "We could look and be more professional. Information was immediately available. It gave us more time to prepare an installation."

Trane didn't stop there. It *engineered* a better selling experience. It equipped the field teams with neat red shirts with the Trane logo. It included checklists on the tablet to collect information key to the installation (like "Don't let the dog into the backyard.") It designed the system with a cross-functional governance team internally that included a dozen dealers from around the country. It invested heavily in marketing and training at its annual sales event to drive interest and adoption, because change, even positive change, is hard for people to accept.

Finally, Trane *analyzed* the success of the application. The iPad tool had an immediate impact on both Trane's bottom line and that of its resellers. The close rate among those using the Trane iPad tool went from 35% to 65%. Revenue among Trane resellers increased by 22% with margins up between 2% and 3%. Making its field sales members smarter had another benefit—by demonstrating additional features, those sales members were able to sell more or increase the ticket price per deal. Product mix per sale increased 16%. The reason: As Trane's Bruce Tansy says, "There is definitely a higher match rate—right equipment for the right problem for the right house. Accuracy has absolutely increased."

And dealers like Donna love it, because her people are always on the go—and now they can sell just as well as they can estimate and install. As Donna puts it, "It takes an average salesperson to the next level, on organization alone. You can't screw up with this program."

Mobile Can Be Most Helpful in Selling Big-Ticket Items

A sales engagement is a crucial point in time. Mobile selling moments make it far more effective. To improve the selling process, Trane and Cynergy followed the IDEA cycle—they identified the selling moment, designed tools based on learning what happens in that moment, engineered their relationships and processes with their independent sales force, and analyzed the result. And it paid off.

By providing real-time, up-to-date information at the moment of need, mobile apps make everyone smarter. In the hands of a salesperson, they make it far easier to communicate complicated information to customers, which makes those customers a whole lot more comfortable as they're buying. That's what happened at Trane. The same sorts of applications are making salespeople better communicators at sellers like Mercedes-Benz dealers and Nike retail stores. A salesperson with a tablet can know what's in stock, demonstrate what works best for the customer, and make complex sales more manageable.

Empowering sales staff with mobile information is even more effective in business-to-business selling situations. Businesses typically buy more complex products than consumers. Just as we saw with Trane, mobile helps sales staff master complex product offerings, understand their buyers with greater depth, and know when to contact buyers for follow-up. Sales staff from Oracle Europe use mobile tools from a company called Qstream to help sell complex software solutions to Oracle's business customers. Summit Media uses a solution from ClearSlide Outside to manage presentations that sales staff make to customers. We anticipate a lot more activity in this space, because business-to-business selling is a natural fit for mobile devices.

The key insight is this: Remove friction from the sales engagement, and you'll speed up the process. While customer applications are vastly different from those used by salespeople, both applications have the same goal—provide real-time options to customers, and remove friction from the sales process. Mobile applications can also make it possible for people who don't typically sell—like field service employees—to create effortless upsell opportunities. (You'll see how that works for Dish Network in chapter 11.)

If you're like many of our clients, before you started this chapter, you might have believed that mobile apps were for eCommerce, mobile devices were bad for retailers, and mobile sales apps were primarily for customers. But as you've seen from these examples, mobile excels at influence, not just sales; mobile plus a loyalty app can make a great in-store combination; and mobile sales apps in the hands of sales staff can transform the selling experience. If you want to sell more with mobile, these insights will make the difference.

. . . .

Of course, not every company sells directly to its customers. But nearly every company has to market. Traditional marketing—screaming to be heard and reach customers—is less and less relevant when we all have access to the Internet in our pockets. Instead, marketing depends on offering utility to customers. That's the topic of the next chapter.

6

. . . .

The Marketing Shift

Tap Mobile Moments to Acquire and Retain Customers

It's a marketer's dream. Imagine that you had a brand that people interacted with frequently—for many of those customers, every day. Imagine that those moments of interaction were mostly positive, reinforcing your brand value. If you were in charge of digital marketing for such a brand, the stakes would be high. Find a way to reinforce that brand value, and you win. Interfere, pester, and over-market, and you lose—and damage the brand in the process.

That's the situation that Alexandra Wheeler was in at Starbucks. Starbucks is one of those iconic brands with a powerful brand image and thousands of touchpoints across America and around the world. As vice president of global digital marketing, Alex is in charge of the overall mobile experience for Starbucks, including mobile marketing. She's been with Starbucks since 2007, working on digital and social connections. She was in this position for the rise of mobile interactions, starting with the iPhone in 2007.

Starbucks was in an ideal position to tap into mobile moments. Today, if you stand in a Starbucks in San Francisco between 7:30 a.m. and 9:30 a.m. on a weekday morning, you'll see a long line of professionals staring down at their mobile phones. Some are reading emails. Some are checking Facebook. Those moments could belong to Starbucks.

"Mobile is probably the most transformative device or experience that consumers have ever had," says Alex. "It's like an appendage, you always have it with you." Alex knew the demands on any mobile brand experience for Starbucks were high, not just because of the impact on the Starbucks brand, but also because its customers were already having mobile experiences with Wi-Fi and devices in Starbucks stores. How could Starbucks effectively take advantage of that?

Enabling mobile payment was a crucial step. In 2009, the company began encouraging consumers to register their stored value and loyalty cards online. With a Starbucks mobile app, customers could connect to and reload their cards. By 2011, Starbucks made it possible for customers to pay with their mobile phones in nearly 6,800 company-operated stores in the US and promoted the payment app with mobile display ads to drive up awareness. "The payment app is magical," says Alex, "since it completely transforms the transactional experience." With an animation of gold stars falling into a Starbucks cup, it reinforces the concept of delight from a Starbucks purchase.

The payment app is far from Starbucks' only mobile program. Starbucks has also had a long business relationship with Apple iTunes. At the start, Starbucks offered one free song each week. Today, it pushes out redemption codes for music, movies, mobile apps, and more through an in-app mailbox. The connection between Starbucks and iTunes is seamless, especially if the customer downloads the new media over Wi-Fi while in the store.

Starbucks has combined content and payment; it now rewards its payment app customers with "Pick of the Week" songs, videos, offers, and other content. These offers are consistent with its brand, which has always embraced music as part of the experience. And people have responded. In 2013 alone, the number of mobile interactions grew from around 2 million per week in January to nearly 4 million per week in June, with around 10 million active mobile users.[1] About one in every 10 transactions now goes through mobile.

Starbucks was also one of the first to launch an MMS messaging program, texting exclusive content, offers, and trivia contests to customers that opt in.

The app, the messaging program, and all of Starbucks' digital efforts provide the one thing that's hardest to get in this digital age—insight into your customers and what they want. Starbucks looks at mobile transactions per store per day and how frequently people reload their payment cards and apps. They can see who is redeeming the Pick of the Week and which picks get the most engagement. Combining this with responses to emails and social media monitoring, Starbucks is now one of the most connected brands on the planet.

Is this marketing?

Well, typical marketing programs—outbound advertising, emails, and the like—need to be repeated to be successful, and much of these programs fail to create a more intimate connection with customers. Improved customer experience, by contrast, is hard to get right, but when you do, it keeps on delivering with customer loyalty. Alex at Starbucks describes her customer philosophy this way: "It is about relationships, not marketing. Our brand is all about moments of connection. That is at the core of the brand." Thanks to mobile, Starbucks knows exactly what its customers are responding to and can build on those moments of connection. That makes marketing a whole lot easier.

The Three Types of Mobile Moments That Marketers Can Embrace

Starbucks had a whole lot of possible moments in which it could engage its customers (see Figure 6-1). Maybe you can tap into this kind of in-the-moment, experience-based marketing that Starbucks has built. Maybe you can't. It all depends on just how direct your relationship with your customers is today. Different marketers must succeed with different types of mobile moments.

In our review of mobile marketing programs, we've identified three types of moments that marketers tap into: loyalty moments, manufactured moments, and borrowed moments. Each is appropriate for a different type of customer relationship.[2]

Loyalty moments are appropriate in cases where the customer already has a relationship with the brand; they're moments in which customers look to that brand on their devices, and the brand has a chance to reinforce that relationship. Starbucks already owned plenty of moments in the store, as is obvious to anyone in line with dozens of others interacting with their smartphones as they wait for their nonfat Venti latte—it just had to grab them by creating a payment app. Financial services, retail, and travel companies, with their direct customer relationships, have a lot of potential loyalty moments in which they can succeed by being helpful, or fail by disappointing customers seeking service or by being too "salesy."

Figure 6-1: Plotting the Mobile Moments on a Starbucks Customer's Journey

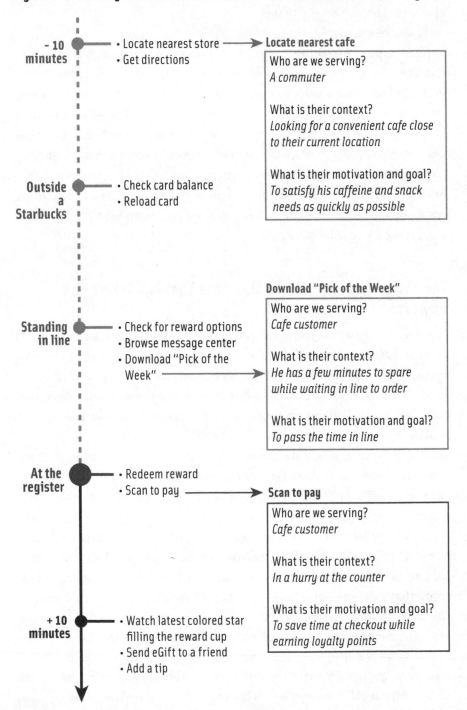

If you don't have any loyalty moments, you can create some. We call these moments *manufactured moments*. They arise from companies creating assets to solve a customer's larger problem. If your brand helps solve a problem—keeping campers warm, removing stains, making dinner quicker to prepare—then mobile creates an opportunity to connect with customers around those problems. Jay Baer, author of *Youtility: Why Smart Marketing Is about Help not Hype,* describes this as "marketing that is so useful, people would pay for it."[3] As L'Oréal's Isabelle Cinquin explains, "you have to understand that this is not about digital marketing anymore. It's about engagement." Even if you can't provide utility, you can still create that engagement—you can manufacture moments by supplying entertainment. We'll explain the clever strategies companies are using to manufacture more moments later in this chapter.

Both loyalty moments and manufactured moments are hard to master, but they pay off continuously in the form of customer engagement. You may not be ready for this level of complexity or investment. Or maybe you're in a part of the world, like Europe or Asia, where customers aren't yet as willing to download apps from brands. If this is the case, you'll have to consider the third type of moment: *borrowed moments*.

Borrowed moments are moments that belong to someone else. Your customer is already on a social network like Facebook, Twitter, WeChat— or on media properties like *The New York Times* app. You can pay to be represented in those channels and create moments that way. Or if you don't want to pay, you can still find ways to be part of moments people spend with third-party applications through content, games, and services placed within these apps. This is a lot easier to pull off than succeeding in loyalty moments or creating manufactured moments. It's also a lot more in line with how marketers already think. Of course, the challenge with borrowed moments is that they don't have staying power—you have to keep paying or posting to retain a customer's attention.

In this chapter, we'll take a close look at strategies for all three type of moments, and the pluses and minuses of pursuing each type.

Making the Most of Your Loyalty Moments

Forrester Research's 2012 book *Outside In*, by Harley Manning and Kerry Bodine, proved that the thing that matters most in a company's success is the quality of the experience that the company provides.[4] Deliver a great experience, and your sales will go up, your costs will go down, and your customer loyalty will improve. Delivering a great experience sounds like an obvious strategy, but it's very hard to do.

If your company already owns moments with customers—if you have a relationship that includes direct interactions—then improving that experience is paramount. Your customer is already looking to extend that relationship with mobile, or will be soon, depending on the Mobile Mind Shift Index of your customer base. If you can eliminate friction, deliver service, and solve problems, you can extend brand loyalty and create a new platform you can own. The challenge is that improved experience in this way is expensive because it requires you to re-engineer and tie into the core systems at your company.

Let's look at an example from USAA, a financial services company that serves 10 million members of the US military and their families. USAA consistently scores among the leaders in Forrester's Customer Experience Index, indicating that it already has an excellent customer experience. How would mobile fit into that experience?

Consider that at USAA, the customer might be an American soldier in Afghanistan, 7,500 miles from home and regularly under threat from hostile forces. This soldier's family depends on every dollar he earns; getting his money in the right place and to the right people might mean the difference between their comfort and their having the electricity switched off.

Neff Hudson, the vice president, emerging channels for USAA, realized that on overseas bases in places like Afghanistan, mobile solved a problem the Web couldn't—it created a dependable connection that could be used in a mobile moment. "We stripped down our site to basic transactions—banking, insurance, and investments. All in, there are about 30 things someone needs to do to manage their accounts with USAA. USAA put all 30 of those things into their first mobile website."

Mobile rapidly became central to USAA's customer experience. "Mobile eliminates requirements in other channels," says Neff. "We realized early on that mobile was core to our business. Mobile is our centerpiece. It's where people start their experience with USAA. And when we back that experience with the world's best member service representatives, we hit a completely different level of effectiveness."

USAA was the first American bank to enable "remote deposit capture" (taking mobile photos of checks to deposit them). Now, as Neff says, "Mobile is driving a fundamental business transformation for us." In 2013, members deposited close to $10 billion on phones alone—money that otherwise would have gone to a local ATM or bank.

These mobile features give USAA many more chances to delight that customer and find new and profitable ways to serve him. The more a customer can do with USAA on that phone, the more he can't imagine going to any other bank.

One great thing about succeeding in these loyalty moments is that it pays off big time for many of the companies that pursue it. The credit union BECU saw a 15% increase in deposits from members using remote deposit capture. United Airlines gets 1% of the $2 billion it generates in ancillary revenue (products and services beyond the regular airfare) through mobile phones. In China, the retailer Carrefour sends out five to seven push notifications per store visit based on its estimates of a customer's location and intent to buy; 15% of the time, customers click through. If you're targeting loyalty moments, make sure you build in business metrics so you can see exactly *how* your app is benefiting your business.

Who Else Succeeds in Loyalty Moments?

Fairfax Media in Australia, owner of the *Sydney Morning Herald,* has embraced its loyalty moments in a big way. Stefan Savva, mobile director at the company, maximizes every moment he has with readers. When he spoke to us in late 2013, he predicted that his mobile audience would exceed his PC-based Web audience in 2014. And he knows exactly what his mobile customers want. In the morning, the site emphasizes quick-hit news that focuses on the useful—financial information and traffic reports, for example. In the early evening, the mobile site delivers more entertaining lifestyle, entertainment, and sports features, during what Stefan calls "me time." At night, it's even more entertainment. As Stefan says, "The more relevant we are, the more chances we have of inserting ourselves into their day." Fairfax is now exploring customizing content and ads to the reader's location. As media consumption moves to mobile devices, media companies must shift their attention accordingly. With a strategy focused on reinforcing loyalty, the *Sydney Morning Herald* is winning in the mobile moment.

Can you create loyalty in a troubling moment? Sure you can. Pascale Vold-man Hutz owns the global strategy for credit and fraud operations at American Express. "Fraud is a moment of truth for our customers," says Pascale. "They expect us to instill a deep sense of security and confidence that we're looking after them." Once a possible fraudulent transaction is detected, the company calls the customer and authenticates him over the phone, using an automated system built by [24]7. After he has opted in, the company sends a text message. The customer can then review the charges and accept or reject them with a single tap on the phone, an experience that would only be possible on a mobile device. Nine of 10 American Express customers who use the mobile service give the experience at least 4 out of 5 stars.

You can even succeed in a disastrous moment. For an airline, the worst days are the days of "irregular operations," when thunderstorms or other travel disruptions mess up dozens of flights. At United Airlines, executing on mobile involves millions of pieces of information changing by the minute, especially on one of those terrible days. When a passenger is running from gate B20 to C1 at Chicago O'Hare International Airport, the mobile phone is the only device he has. Using ethnographic research, United determined just what people needed in the app—including action buttons all within reach of the thumb, because the other hand is dragging a suitcase. It made sure it provided two options for rebooking any flight that was cancelled, making life a little easier for the disrupted traveler. And it undertook a major engineering effort to redesign the back-end systems to power the app. "Customers feel as though they are more in control," says United's VP of eCommerce and merchandising, Scott Wilson. "There has been a step-function increase in self-service with adoption of the mobile app." After 25 app releases, about one every month, the company has attracted 6 million customers to its app; 20% of domestic boarding passes are now on mobile devices.

In the world of the mobile mind shift, delivering a great mobile customer experience is what makes the difference between a customer staying with you or defecting to a competitor or a startup. You already own those moments. If you want to create loyalty, you'd better deliver in them.

CASE STUDY: Clorox Manufactures Moments by Fighting Stains

Unlike USAA, United Airlines, or Starbucks, The Clorox Company doesn't have a direct relationship with most of its customers. Customers think of Clorox once a week when they do laundry and are facing an ugly stain from too many slides in front of the soccer goal. They may trust the Clorox brand, but they don't actively engage much with Clorox.

Amanda Mahan, Clorox's director of digital and content, knew the stain moment wasn't hers—yet. To earn it, she had to *manufacture* a reason for people to interact with Clorox. When she learned that tens of thousands of people were searching on the term "stain"—and that many of these searches were from mobile phones—she realized that Clorox could earn its way into its customers' phones at those moments. When a college student squirts ketchup on his friend's pants or a candidate's dress shirt is showing sweat stains right before an interview, Clorox needed to be there.

Amanda started relatively small, spending less than $40,000 to create the myStain iPhone app and promote it in magazines and with mobile phone ads. As the app gained traction, the team expanded it to Android and translated it into Spanish. Now in a pitched battle with Tide's Stain Brain app, myStain continues to add content and functionality. You can even ask "Dr. Laundry" a question and get specialized advice on cranberry and gravy stains at Thanksgiving. Clorox spends about $50,000 annually to keep the app fresh.

More than 200,000 customers have downloaded myStain. Media coverage and word of mouth have generated millions of impressions. Research shows that consumers are viewing Clorox, a 100-year-old brand, as "hip and fun." More than half of those who use the application share their impressions on a social network.

These mobile moments exist because Clorox manufactured them. By solving its customers' problems, it had created a chance to connect its brand with customers in a mobile moment.

How to Manufacture Moments and Influence

So your customer doesn't touch your product every day. Is that any reason to be absent from mobile? You just need to start thinking outside in—think about your customer's problem. In the case of Clorox, the

customer's problem is not laundry, it's a stained garment. Clorox manufactured its way into a new moment: the stain moment. What moment
can you manufacture? And what context can you use to provide better
service in that moment?

In this section, we'll describe a slew of innovative marketers who
figured out how to make themselves *useful* and earn a moment of their
customer's time. As the author Jay Baer told us, "The better approach to
marketing is to be useful. People will treat you differently; they will treat
you as they treat their friends. We keep useful."

Here's why it pays to be useful.

First, in a crowded world of advertising and media, useful earns you
a permanent spot. Advertising is expensive, and it fades. Useful gets you
friends, and they spread word of mouth. Why not have your customers
spread your brand for you? In his book *Velocity*, Stefan Olander of Nike
predicts, "As advertising evolves, it will provide real answers to real questions, not canned information. It will offer interactions and services that
satisfy real needs, not blanket persuasions. It will create communities that
speak to one another and are not just content with aspirations."

Since it is permanent, you can build on it. Clorox continually updates
its myStain app. You don't have to pay each year to start over—you can pay
to boost the value of what you've got. It's relatively cheap to create an app
(at least compared with paying for media—that initial myStain app cost
less to build than a single prime-time television ad), so you can start small
and work your way up from there.

Finally, and perhaps most importantly, you can create a customer connection where none existed before. Starbucks already had many of its
customers' emails, and USAA knew all about its customers. But Clorox
didn't have anywhere near that level of customer connection until the
app created it. It's leveraging that connection now; even the R&D group
at Clorox wants to know what stains the app users are searching, to know
which kind of products to work on next.

Let's get a look at how a diverse set of companies manufactured
moments by thinking bigger and solving their customers' larger problem.

Outdoorsman and developer Jay Kerr at Columbia Sportswear realized
that his customers wouldn't be interested in an app about outdoor clothing.
Their larger problem was surviving in the outdoors. His response: create an
app called What Knot To Do. To serve Columbia Sportswear's customers,

the app has to work in places where there's no mobile connection, like the top of a mountain. Half a million downloads later, Columbia owns knots, the essential tools of the camper, hiker, and kayaker. All it took was one developer's time and a little PR to manufacture this outdoor moment.

Here's another delicious example of a company manufacturing a moment for customers. It's the moment when you drive by a Krispy Kreme store and see the neon "Hot Light" is on—indicating that hot doughnuts have just come off the line. Krispy Kreme's customers salivate when the Hot Light goes on. But what if you're too far away to see the light? Just download the app. With the help of a clever design by the integrated marketing agency Barkley, Krispy Kreme set up a system that allowed the same switch in the store that turns on the Hot Light to tell a customer that hot doughnuts just became available in, say, Collingswood, New Jersey. If you've downloaded the app and happen to be anywhere near Collingswood, you'll get a push notification. So now that Hot Light can do its marketing work for many miles around. Krispy Kreme CMO Dwayne Chambers has cancelled all of his traditional media buys; as he says, "We need to be careful not to take a brand so simple and make it too complex." After 450,000 app downloads and double-digit increases in same-store sales, the Hot Light app appears to be doing its job.

It's not just for doughnuts and clothing. It works in business-to-business settings, too. Cisco is a tech giant that sells routers, servers, switches, and cloud management suites. Of course it owns the moments associated with running that equipment with an entire suite of apps to allow highly mobile techies to remotely manage the company's products. It's got apps that turn data sheets for network equipment into 3D images that allow network engineers to configure server stacks. But one of Cisco's most popular mobile apps is the Cisco Binary Game—an app that helps you learn and practice the binary number system. It's got hundreds of thousands of downloads—a huge number when you consider the relatively small number of networking geeks in the world. For engineers, these apps qualify as entertainment—and entertainment moments are manufactured moments.

What if you've got a lot of brands? Couldn't managing all these mobile applications get out of hand?

That's the problem that Pete Blackshaw, global head of digital and social media, manages at Nestlé. His facility in Switzerland is the nerve center of the company's digital acceleration team. In 2012, Nestlé had around 100 apps globally, with each of its many brands managing its own budgets and local agency partners. As Pete puts it, "Mobile is a services layer that wraps around our products. Mobile is the connective tissue." But the mobile apps were a mishmash of quality and value. Pete set out to standardize elements of Nestlé's apps, starting with an inventory of existing mobile services that parts of the company had created. He set out to find and spread best practices. Now Pete brings local brand talent to his headquarters and exposes them to tools and techniques that are most effective for Nestlé globally, both for mobile and for other types of digital engagement. The company has standardized packaging elements, including QR codes, to jumpstart mobile apps anywhere in the world. His staff has created training, starter kits, and resources to support the brands. Some elements of Nestlé's mobile apps, like content management systems and analytics, are centralized, while local agencies handle creative and app or campaign development and execution. (We provide more detail on how large companies can best organize for mobile in Chapter 12.)

Apps that manufacture moments for marketing purposes are a lot cheaper than those for loyalty moments because you get to build them from scratch, and they often don't need to tie back into expensive-to-engineer corporate systems. But if you're building an app or site like this, you ought to get going quickly. The categories of customer problems are filling up with apps all the time. You don't want to be on version 1 when your competitor is already delivering version 3.

Now before we go all app-crazy on you, we realize that there are parts of the world where apps aren't as popular as they are in the US. In Europe, mobile overages and roaming charges have lowered mobile intensity. And in China, the connections in cities can be spotty or slow. In places like this, app downloading isn't nearly as common as it is in the US (although that may be changing depending on when you read this). Apps for loyalty moments and manufactured moments may not be an option for marketers in these places—and it may not be an option for you, either, depending on the politics at your company. If this describes you, you may need to borrow your mobile moments.

CASE STUDY: Coca-Cola Borrows Its Mobile Moments in China

China is a fascinating market. Advertising hasn't been around there nearly as long as it has been in the West. The market features voracious consumers and cutthroat competition. Companies need a way to stand out. That was the problem faced by Stephen Drummond, Coca-Cola's senior director of integrated marketing and communications in China.

Stephen needed a campaign to drive brand awareness and sales of icy cold Coca-Cola soft drinks during the scorching hot summer months. The company also wanted to tap into the local culture of gift-giving and personalization.

The Coke China team decided to adapt the highly successful Australian campaign "Share a Coke," which personalized bottles with hundreds of the most popular first names. However, Chinese names are put together differently, and they don't have "first names" as such.

Coca-Cola solved the problem by allowing Chinese consumers to choose nicknames for their digital personas. Coca-Cola put more than 60 different Internet nicknames on 500 mL and 600 mL bottles. To generate prelaunch buzz, it sent custom bottles to hundreds of celebrities and opinion leaders, each with the recipient's full Chinese name etched on the bottle.

The resulting organic social media campaign took flight on a range of Chinese social networks including Weibo, WeChat, and Renren where celebrities are followed by millions of their fans. Coca-Cola sustained the momentum by creating stories to go with each bottle and releasing them periodically to spark social media chatter. As Stephen saw it, this was "the best mass market solution."

The social campaign seeded the marketing campaign. Before the bottles were launched broadly and before the company's TV advertising campaign, the combined social media programs generated 4 billion social media impressions. Sales of Coca-Cola bottles of the sizes in the trial were up 20% from the previous summer.

Coca-Cola extended the campaign to allow consumers to etch a name of their choice on the bottle from 40 specialized vending machines at Coca-Cola events around the country, driving additional buzz and further tapping into the concept of personalized gift-giving.

If you're going to borrow moments, think about how Coca-Cola did it.

Invent something people want to share. And launch it on a social platform that's already got a huge audience sharing their moments.

Leveraging Borrowed Moments

Don't own any loyalty moments? Lack the time or resources to manufacture them? You'll have to borrow or rent them. A handful of popular mobile sites or applications own a phenomenal amount of real estate as measured by mobile media minutes. Domestically in any one country, a few social media providers could provide reach to most of your target audience. In America, you could tap into Facebook or Twitter. In Korea, KakaoTalk users spend more than 200 minutes per week in their application, according to Mobidia. Line users in Japan and WeChat users in China each spend nearly 100 minutes per week.[5] Any one brand's chance of replicating this reach would be the equivalent of winning the Super Lotto.

In many of these markets, it's more effective to tap into these platforms rather than build an app. China is now approaching 500 million smartphones, but most of them are on slower 2G networks, so people connect with Wi-Fi in malls, at home, or in restaurants. As we described in chapter 4, the Mobile Mind Shift Index of urban Chinese consumers shows a lower mobile intensity, with higher scores in communicating, consuming, and transacting (see Figure 6-2). As CEO of Isobar China Group, Jane Linbaden says, "We often don't recommend to clients that they build their own apps. Brands have limited ability to get consumers to come into their own park. Brands need to go to the park where the consumers already are." That's why, in China, it makes more sense to borrow moments on a third-party platform like WeChat. You could even tap into popular local mobile applications like weather and taxi apps, as some Chinese brands have. However you borrow the moments, you still need utility or content that will spread, like coupons or Coca-Cola's personalized bottles.

Of course, the simplest way to tap into borrowed moments is to rent them—to advertise. You've got three options: Get on board with a third-party app or platform that does have mass reach, tap into paid search, or buy display ads.

You can pay to rent moments on third-party apps, but your flexibility is limited because these platforms want to protect the overall user experience. In the US, Lyft, a mobile-only ride-sharing service based in San Francisco, uses Facebook to drive downloads of its app or service. In India, ICICI Bank even allows customers to bank within Facebook. Regardless of how you tap into these platforms, you'll succeed only if you offer something useful, like coupons or services, that will drive interest and click-throughs.

Figure 6-2: Mobile Mind Shift Index of Metro China

Mobile Intensity

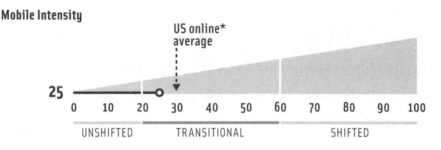

Mobile Behaviors

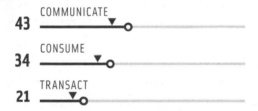

Base: 2,500 Metro China online adults (18+)
*Base: 8,224 US online adults (18+)
Source: Asia Pacific Technographics Online Benchmark Survey, 2013
and US Mobile Mind Shift Online Survey, Q3 2013
Note: "Metro" refers to surveys that reach only inhabitants of major cities.

If you don't want to advertise on other sites or play in social networks, consider search as a means to drive action. A mobile search could be within a browser, a mapping app, or even a third-party vertical app like Yelp. According to Google, one in five searches has local intent. When the search leads to a store visit, four out of five of those visits happen within 5 hours of the search; many also triggered calls to stores. As Jason Spero, Google's global head of performance media, says, "Click to call is often the perfect experience for a 'new moment of acquisition' when a consumer is looking to buy. Local product listing ads are bridging the physical and digital worlds."

Finally, consider mobile display advertising. So far, it's had a poor track record. But that's because people treat mobile ads as miniature web ads. As with everything else in mobile, approaching mobile advertising as you do web ads isn't going to work. But keep an eye on this space. Mobile platforms are going to get better at the qualities advertisers need—the ability to identify individuals and to measure mobile ad effectiveness. Once that happens, mobile ads will become more relevant and less annoying and interruptive, creating borrowed mobile moments that may be far more inviting than today's online ads are.

Mobile Moments Are Now Central to Marketing

When smartphones first arrived, marketers assumed mobile would take its place among other marketing modalities such as print, outdoor, video, and online. But the mobile mind shift means that mobile is now central to experiences. If your brand already offers connected experiences to consumers, you must maximize loyalty moments within those experiences, as Starbucks does. If you don't already have those connections, you can manufacture them, as Nestlé does. And if you can't afford to manufacture connections, you can borrow them, as Coca-Cola does in China. But there's a lot more at stake here than just marketing strategy. The moments that Shifted customers spend with your brand are now central to their assessment of that brand. And for that reason, mobile moments will become central to all marketing strategy.

. . . .

Physical products live in the real-world. So does mobile. The combination of the two improves product experiences, providing product brands with a way to develop new relationships with customers. That's the topic of the next chapter.

7

. . . .

The Product Shift

Enrich Connected Products through Mobile Moments

In Tahoe, Tony Fadell was building the most connected, greenest, most modern home he knew of. It was going to be as connected and modern as he could make it. As the author of hundreds of patents and the leader of the team at Apple that created the first iPod, he was curious, technologically sophisticated, and fanatical about detail. One of those details in particular was galling to him.

The thermostats were unsophisticated.

"What was wrong with them? They were ugly." That's how he described it talking to *Wired* reporter Steven Levy in 2011. "They were confusing. They were incredibly expensive. They didn't have half the features you would expect for a modern thing. None of them were connected, so they didn't talk to each other. I wasn't able to remotely control them. In Tahoe, you want to be able check on the temperature of the house or turn it on before you get there. Because it's really cold in the winter. I couldn't do any of that, and I was like, Why is this?"[1]

So he set out to fix things.

Heating and cooling accounts for approximately 50% of home energy bills. While a well-programmed thermostat can cut a typical household's energy bill by 20% (and 10% of the nation's energy consumption is controlled by thermostats), a lot of people *don't* program their thermostats properly. Why? Because those thermostats are poorly designed. They have lots of buttons that work in ways that make no sense to consumers trained by the mobile mind shift. Even if a consumer figures out how to program the thermostat once, following the little manual (what is this, 1997?), she forgets the counterintuitive steps when it's time to change it.

Trained by mobile devices, we've grown to expect things to be aware of our context and connected to what we do. They ought to accommodate themselves to us, rather than force us to accommodate them. That's why Tony set out to create a product, the Nest Learning Thermostat, that worked more like a smartphone than a thermostat and that saved energy in a more intelligent way.

The Nest thermostat is Wi-Fi connected and mobile-enhanced with a digital display. It has motion sensors—it knows if you're home and adjusts the temperature accordingly. It knows when it's you walking around the room and when it's the dog. Naturally, you can set it up and control it from a mobile app, and you can keep score—how much energy have you used, how much have you saved? And you can tweak those settings any time you want, whether you're standing in front of the thermostat or not. More than 95% of Nest owners use a mobile device (smartphone or tablet) to connect with the thermostat, and many use *only* the mobile device.

The Nest thermostat costs $249, 10 times the price of a typical thermostat, and it's selling like mad. Nest is the number-one selling thermostat at Amazon, Best Buy, and Lowe's. Its Net Promoter Score is an astounding 82, indicating overwhelming customer satisfaction. To date, the Nest thermostat has saved consumers 1.5 billion kilowatt-hours of energy.

What makes a thermostat worth $249?

Because it's not just a thermostat. It's a *connected* thermostat supported by mobile moments. As a result, a homeowner can control it via any device she has, wherever she is. Nest's mobile moments happen anywhere, whether you're at home, on the way home from work, or on vacation. As Maxime Veron, Nest's director of product marketing, describes it, "Consumers expect to be able to do everything from their mobile phones in the moment they have a desire. The success of our product rests equally on the physical product itself and the mobile service."

And it keeps getting better. Nest collects data from customers' thermostats and uses the resulting insights to design, and then download, improvements. Since the product launched, Nest has delivered 25 product updates, all of which were free to customers.

It's not just Nest that is making the product better. After thinking through the issues of customer data and trust, Nest recently introduced a way for its own developers and the coders of trusted partners to build more and better apps that combine thermostat data with weather and energy cost data to further extend the value for customers.

Why is the Nest thermostat worth $249? Because it adds value in mobile moments—the company has layered services on top of what used to be a product that people bought once and used infrequently. Nest's thermostat and its subsequent product, a connected smoke and carbon monoxide alarm, create a multiplicity of moments for customers. And Tony Fadell isn't the only one who sees value in those moments, as became clear when Google bought Nest in January 2014 for $3.2 billion.

Mobile Moments Add Service to Connected Products

Most products are dumb, disconnected from systems that could give them intelligence. They sit there and do their job as best they can. You engage with them only when you have to via their knobs and buttons and displays. But dumb products don't learn. They don't capture and store their data. They don't connect to a universe of services that enhance their value. And they don't help the company who made those products understand how people use them.

Here's the challenge. We live in a commoditized world—no matter what product you've invented or marketed, somebody else is out there trying to create a version that's cheaper. If you want to create products that aren't a commodity, you're going to have to make them smarter. You're going to have to add enough service, and enough value in enough mobile moments, to make people purchase your product over your competitor's.

Tony Fadell realized that a thermostat doesn't have to be dumb. No product does. With ubiquitous wireless access and a $15 chip, any product can connect to services over the Internet—starting with services from the people who made it, eventually adding services from a whole universe of developers who might want to interact with it. And, as we'll show, you can charge more money for these products, create new selling opportunities, and even create value from the data they provide.

All this comes about because you carefully pick the right moments to provide interactions that are smarter. Interactions get smarter because the company behind them harvests, aggregates, processes, and analyzes data to offer a better overall customer experience. And even after people stop fiddling with the settings, products that include mobile moments create peace of mind. People are happier because they know "my parent is ok" or "the house is not on fire" or "dinner isn't burning."

As Google realized, smart, connected products are just worth more than dumb products, and much of that value comes from the systems they're connected to.

You'd Be Amazed at What Products Are Now Connected

If you make a complicated product that already has microprocessors in it (like a car or an industrial robot), you've probably already figured this out. If you're making stuff that's a little simpler, like a stove or lighting system, maybe you're thinking about it. But while you're thinking about it, entrepreneurs out there aren't limiting their imaginations. They're already connecting everything from socks to bandages to turn them into smart products that capture, learn, and teach (see Table 7-1).

First, there are companies vying to create the next big category of devices that enhance the functions of phones or tablets. These include the Google Glass device, a product you wear on your head which includes a camera, a heads-up display, and voice recognition. There are also watches like the Samsung Galaxy Gear smart watch that bring some of the phone's display, apps, and functions right to your wrist.

Then there are a whole host of somewhat less ambitious single-purpose wearables. These include the Nike+ FuelBand and the Fitbit, devices that compete to clip onto your body and track your exercise and movement. Medical device makers have enhanced everything from diapers to glucose meters to track your health or monitor your safety—some are standalone devices, and others connect to your phone. There's even a set of specialized wearable devices for law enforcement officers from Motorola that's designed to stream video, detect running, and know when a gun is drawn from the holster. The devices send information in these mobile moments to a central hub to facilitate better management of everything from a high-speed foot chase to a shootout.

Table 7-1: Connected Product Categories

Type of product	How do mobile moments enhance the product?	Notable examples
Phone adjunct devices	Make mobile functions easier to access through a display, camera, and/or voice control.	Google Glass Pebble (watch) Samsung Galaxy Gear smart watch
Fitness wearables	Collect data through sensors, then offer real-time feedback to athletes as they perform or later on after the performance.	Fitbit Heapsylon socks and anklet Nike+ FuelBand Whistle Activity Monitor (for dogs)
Medical and safety wearables and connected devices	Use health or biometric data to enhance care or detect emergencies through either standalone devices or devices connected as phone attachments; detect or record unsafe conditions or improve decision-making in those decisions	AliveCor Heart Monitor (ECG) CellScope Oto (otoscope) Evian Smart Drop Jawbone Up (monitors sleep quality) Motorola Connected Law Enforcement Officer Netatmo June (sun exposure monitor) Pixie Scientific Smart Diapers Proteus Digital Health (ingestible sensor) Sanofi iBGstar (glucose monitor) SecuraFone Health (skin patch) SoundWorld Solutions Personal Sound Amplifier Withings Blood Pressure Monitor
Connected consumer products	Use Wi-Fi, Bluetooth, or cellular networks to transmit data collected from sensors; improve consumer control of devices and create new mobile moments	AT&T Digital Life (home security) Connected cars Cable and satellite TV set-top boxes Lively (activity monitors for the elderly) Nest Learning Thermostat Nest Protect (smoke and CO alarm) Philips Avent Smart Baby Monitor Philips Hue (lighting) Samsung refrigerators Whirlpool refrigerators
Connected industrial products	Relay performance information to field service teams to optimize maintenance efficiency and avoid breakdowns	GE jet engines, turbines, and locomotives Harvard Engineering street lights Maersk Line shipping containers

Every imaginable type of electrical device is becoming available in a connected format. The Nissan Leaf electric car emails you when it's done charging and lets you turn on the air conditioning or turn off the charger remotely from a smartphone. Samsung makes refrigerators with an Internet display on them, while Nest's smoke and carbon monoxide alarm talks to you and tells you what the problem is rather than simply emitting annoying beeps.

Finally, just about anybody who makes industrial equipment is going to start instrumenting it for mobile control, if they haven't done so already.[2] When the GE wind turbine needs service, it's a heck of a lot easier if it tells you what's going on *before* you make the long climb to the top of the tower.

What do all these devices have in common? They add value because they're not just products—they connect via the Internet to services from the companies that created them. They have APIs—application programming interfaces—that turn these products and services into platforms, allowing independent developers to create additional services for them, making them even more valuable. And because these products are connected, companies can capture and mine the data they generate for insights on how to make new services, improve future products, and create more resonant marketing pitches. All this adds up to more valuable products that escape the commodity trap.

Connected Products Gain Value by Connecting to Systems of Engagement

As you look at the list of products in the previous section, you may get excited. What kind of value could you create by building mobile connections in your products? Or you may be intimidated, thinking, "we have no idea how to do this."

Rather than jumping ahead or hanging back, ask yourself this question: *"If I made my product into a connected product, what would I connect it to?"*

The answer to this question will tell you what to do next. All products have to connect to information systems managed by the manufacturer specifically to create value for a customer. Only after you have conceived what the information system for your product does can you think about the value you can create for customers through your product. The Nest thermostat is valuable because it *knows* how customers use energy in their homes because of the information system behind it. The Fitbit succeeds because it connects to a system that helps you track your progress on health goals. *Every* connected device creates value in this way.

The Three Moments that Matter Most

Face it. These products are slick. If they're going to add value in mobile moments, their product managers must pick those moments carefully. They succeed because their developers start by identifying the customer's larger goal (like saving energy, losing weight, cooking, or conducting law enforcement activities). Then they identify the mobile moments where such a product can save time, save money, improve efficiency, or just add coolness. By analyzing a lot of devices like this, we've identified three types of moments where they prove their value.

1. **Setup.** The first encounter a person has with your product is crucial. Don't just aim for easy setup—aim to delight and show off the product's capabilities. A standout here is the device from Sound World Solutions that helps the hearing impaired. Typically a hearing aid customer would spend $2,000 and then make multiple trips to a specialist to tune a hearing aid. Using a mobile app, Sound World Solutions customers can do this setup themselves. Seven out of 10 of its buyers need no further help from the company or the retailer.

2. **In use.** Apps enable customers to explore the new, exciting capabilities of these mobile-enhanced devices. For example, consumers can create personalized atmospheres in their homes with Philips Hue lighting systems, monitor diabetes markers with iBGStar's glucose monitor, or track sleep patterns with a Jawbone Up. Connected cars add value by notifying people when maintenance is needed and contacting emergency services in a crash.

3. **Maintenance and upgrades.** Products—especially expensive products—can help customers know when it's time to get a new product or upgrade or when the product may wear out. You can put a sensor in Nike shoes that monitors use and communicates with

an app on your phone to tell you when they need to be replaced. Some Whirlpool washers/dryers send alerts to an owner's mobile phone if the dryer is clogged with lint or needs maintenance.[3] And cars, mining equipment, jet engines, and industrial equipment now have hundreds of sensors monitoring performance to detect failure or degradation. In the words of Bill Ruh, vice president of software research at GE, "we have 10 times more sensors in a jet engine than we had 20 years ago."

Think about all those moments—and the system that will power them—and you're on your way to an improved device. And if you're lucky, you'll create something as popular as the bathroom scale that Withings created.

CASE STUDY: Withings and a Host of Developers Create Mobile Wellness Moments

Bathroom scales by themselves don't make people healthier. It's the systems and services they connect to that make the difference.

That was the insight that led Cédric Hutchings, the CEO of Withings, to create a line of connected bathroom scales. Withings is a Paris-based company that is redefining what health and wellness products should be. Like Tony Fadell at Nest, Cédric saw that with a system behind it, an ordinary consumer product could accomplish a larger goal for consumers. But what makes Withings stand apart is how that connected product has become part of a whole ecosystem of partners adding even more value to it.

A Withings connected scale is actually three things all wrapped up together.

First, it's a product that people are proud to own and use a lot. The entire aesthetic of the Withings scale is sleek and modern. It's a connected device that looks like it's worth the value it delivers.

The second element, which you can't directly touch, is the software and systems that work with it. Withings' developers not only build the software that powers the scale, they also build the online systems supporting it that people use to track their weight. Hardware developers, software developers, and product managers at Withings all work together on this in rapid development cycles. In fact, the fastest growing department in Withings contains the developers and staff who make it possible to update the software on the scale, collect the data to extend its capabilities, and deliver new services.

But Withings doesn't stop with just its own services. The third element of Withings' development system is the way it makes it easy for *partners* to connect to this system. And that's where mobile comes in.

LoseIt!, one of the most popular weight loss apps in the world (19 million customers in 2013), can connect directly to the scale and track your weight, right in the app. So can MyFitnessPal, with 40 million users. So can 100 other mobile app providers (as of November 2013). No money changes hands—the companies that make apps like LoseIt! and MyFitnessPal work with Withings because it adds value to their apps, and conversely, this app ecosystem adds value to the scale. Withings gets new customers who hear about the product through the apps. Everybody profits and everybody wins.

These partnerships are also good for Withings because they allow all of its products to work together. Withings now sells a blood pressure meter, an activity tracker, a baby monitor, and even a product that monitors sleep quality. Customers can see all the results on a single dashboard. Cédric's vision is that his products can eventually change the way that people interact with the entire healthcare system: doctors, insurance companies, and chronic disease management.

Because Withings' products are connected, they can become part of a larger system, a quality that makes them ideal in a healthcare setting. This is why Dr. Dave Levin, chief medical officer at the Cleveland Clinic, is using mobile apps and connected products in the Clinic's practice. Whether it's 90-year old patients logging their own medical history on an iPad or a connected scale that warns clinicians of a patient's unexpected and potentially dangerous weight gain, Dave and his team have seen how connected devices make a dramatic difference in health outcomes.

How did we start with a simple scale and end up with a whole system enabling improved health outcomes? It's all about the mobile connection.

Three Ways Mobile-Enhanced Products Pay Off

It's expensive to build connected products. But because they're not commodities, they make it possible to make money in all sorts of new ways. Here are three possibilities.

First, you can extend the value of your products with services. People spend $149 for the Withings Smart Body Analyzer, a bathroom scale, because it does more—it accomplishes broader goals than just weighing yourself. The system behind the scale connects the owner with a slew of services and even other customers, increasing the perception of value. The device and the system keep updating, again improving the value. And then there's the cool factor. "The combination of appealing to both the rational and emotional side of the brain is core to our success. It isn't one without the other," says Nest product strategist Maxime Veron. While most of the services built on these consumer products are free right now, we expect companies to offer paid services as well, once they've built up a sufficiently large customer base.

Second, you can attract partners to make your product more valuable. Manufacturers and third parties will build services on top of those platforms to generate new streams of revenue. The monster example here is the smartphone itself—as of November 2013, Apple has generated more than $15 billion from app sales to more than 500 million consumer accounts and repaid 70% to the app developers to keep the ecosystem working.[4] eBook platforms like Kindle make money delivering content. Philips' Hue lighting systems let people build applications that control those lights—it calls the community "Friends of Hue." There's even a company building a "learn to tango" app to work with Heapsylon's smart socks.

Finally, you can generate revenue from the data you gather. This revenue stream remains mostly in the future now, but keep an eye on it. Once you've got tens of thousands of people using your product, you'll know more than anyone else about their behavior. Not only can you improve the product based on this data—you can sell it in the aggregate. Nest helps utility companies see how consumers use energy. TiVo, for example, sells program analytics based on the aggregated behavior of the people who use its digital video recorder. In the future, we expect consumers and enterprises will pay for data that helps them understand the relative health, wealth, strengths, and weaknesses of different user groups.

While building these higher-priced, more networked products may be worth it, product companies must go about things differently. The product development organization itself must change, with product design acknowledging the need to create services and ongoing support for systems of engagement before any given product launches. If you're going to get serious about this, you'll have to do it the way Philips does: systematically.

CASE STUDY: How Philips Develops Products with Engagement Built In

Philips is a diversified company headquartered in the Netherlands. The company makes light bulbs, baby monitors, electric shavers, air purifiers, coffee makers, and a full line of other lighting, consumer lifestyle, and health and wellbeing products. All are subject to commoditization. So the company is investing in ways to improve those products with mobile devices and connections.

Thibaut Sevestre is innovation manager for the information technology department at Philips in the Netherlands. Working with a variety of groups—Philips Design, Philips Research, Philips Innovation Services, and the company's Consumer Lifestyle Digital Innovation program—Thibaut has helped develop a systematic process for building connected products.

They start by understanding core customer needs. They learn these with market research, ethnographic research, and social co-creation sites, leading to an understanding of key mobile moments and their associated context. With these techniques, they learned, for example, that mothers using Philips products want far more than to feed their families—they're seeking to nurture their families with well-balanced, diverse, innovative, nutritional meals.[5] And moms are multitaskers—they want to create these meals even as they're helping with homework, collaborating with a colleague at work, or watching their children play outside. A mom like this is primed for a mobile-enhanced product.

Analyzing these mobile moments enabled Philips to create a prototype called the HomeCooker neXt, a cooking appliance that uses mobile devices to offer remote monitoring and control. The cooker sends notifications or texts to the home cook when the pot needs attention—a stir, more salt, or the carrots. If the cook fails to respond, the cooker turns down the temperature to avoid burning dinner (or catching the house on fire). Philips will extend the value of the product by working with content partners to offer recipes, nutrition planning, and cooking lessons.

The HomeCooker neXt is just one of five new product concepts launched by Philips in the fall of 2013. Creating these products requires a cultural shift. Product engineers are accustomed to delivering complete, finished products, while for these mobile-enhanced products, they must continue enhancing the products with regular updates based on what they learn from customer usage data. As Thibaut says, "We are not an Internet giant like Google or Facebook," but the company must learn to think like that.

Philips applies what it learns from delivering one product to the development process for other products. It's developing new product architectures: not just electronics, but embedded software and cloud-based systems supporting mobile applications. Those apps must continue to evolve as phones improve and change; a customer doesn't want to have to throw out the home cooker if she switches from iPhone to Android. Philips now has a team of engineers dedicated to embedded platforms. Another team focuses on the mobile application platform.

Even more than a startup like Nest, Philips needs tools that work across diverse product categories. Thibaut is now working to connect everything from coffee makers to baby monitors to air purifiers. He helps business units transform their products and create services that improve their value over time.

What Product Teams Do in the Mobile Mind Shift

Philips' experience clarifies some elements of the product development process for connected, mobile-enhanced products, a process that resembles software and Internet development more than traditional product development.

You must assemble and empower a multifunctional team to build connected products. Hardware designers work on the look and function of the product, software developers build the applications and the technology platform it connects to, and product managers make sure the product stays on track to solve the customer's larger problem. The team is more complex and diverse than a traditional product team, and it works differently. What's most different is the pace of development.

First off, products ship earlier. We've all become used to companies like Google releasing products before they're done ("beta" versions). Connected products have to be more done than this, because you can't change the hardware after the product ships. But the *services* don't have to be in their final form, because the company can enhance a connected product's software and back-end services after it's installed.

Increasingly, product developers roll out what's known as a *minimum viable product* (MVP).[6] An MVP accomplishes the goal of the customer—it tracks your exercise, cooks your food, or monitors your blood sugar—with services and some style, to support the higher price tag it carries. Companies that ship MVPs know that they will improve them and that ideas for those improvements will be generated from the people who first use the product. As Stefan Olander, vice president and general manager of digital sport at Nike, puts it "Get going. Then get better."[7]

Software development for websites and applications is undergoing a revolution, from huge complex projects and infrequent releases to the continuous, agile development cycles happening now. This same technique is a critical element of building and enhancing connected products powered by software and technology systems, as we describe in detail in Chapter 12. It's not possible to know every last feature and function up front. You have to learn as you go, often in two-week "sprints" where the entire product team—hardware, software, and product managers—come together to choose features, build software, and test capabilities. An effective agile team fixes bugs on this schedule and releases new software features several times each year. Product managers also need to think differently about the business architecture. Products and their supporting systems become platforms on which services, partnerships, and whole product ecosystems can be built.

These elements of the new product engineering—ship minimum viable products, improve with agile development, and think of products as platforms—will transform product development. With this new approach, you can increase the price you charge for the product. It's more than a good idea. It's the path to higher profits for product companies.

These principles are even more relevant for industrial products. Mobile is a natural enhancement to many instrumented systems, from wind tur-bines to industrial robots. But would you believe even streetlights benefit from mobile moments?

· ·

CASE STUDY: The Clear Benefits of Mobile-Enhanced Streetlights

At Christmastime 2012, the City of Westminster staged a holiday celebra-tion. At 4 p.m., just as Jermyn Street was growing dark, singer Katherine Jenkins tapped a button on an iPad to light up the scene for the holidays. This wasn't stage lighting at an opera. It was street lighting and Christmas trees on a London shopping street. And the whole thing was Dave Franks' idea.

Dave Franks has been a street lighting man for 30 years. Dave keeps 14,000 streetlights in the City of Westminster burning brightly to keep people and property safe from harm. Some of his streets have been contin-uously lit since 1807, when a German entrepreneur living in London first turned nighttime into day on London's Pall Mall.[8]

In the beginning, street lighters went around every evening with a lighting wand to turn on the gas and ignite the gas filaments in each street lamp one by one. Eventually, street lighters became experts in managing electric lights for safety and efficiency. But the three bugaboos of a street lighting man's life remained: the cost of power, maintenance efficiency, and keeping the lights on for safety.

Dave realized he could solve all three problems at once by both con-trolling and collecting data from the lamps remotely from a mobile phone or tablet app. He convinced the city council to spend £3,250,000 on the Smart Lights Project, upgrading the lights to save the city more than £400,000 every year.[9] While the energy savings funded the project, Dave actually sold it by telling the council leader to look outside as he turned the lights on with his phone. As he told us, "In street lighting, it doesn't get much sexier than that."

With the help of a firm called Harvard Engineering, Dave unshackled street lights from mechanical switches and manual inspection processes and connected them to the Internet over a wireless network. In doing so, he put control over the city's lights into the hands of maintenance staff, first responders, and celebrities.[10]

A maintenance crew can see at a glance on a tablet which streetlights are about to burn out (because the voltage spikes) and pre-emptively replace the bulbs. That's far better than waiting for a citizen to complain that a street light is out. With a few taps on a smartphone, a police officer can turn the lights on full blast if a street brawl is underway. And a celebrated musician can ring in Christmastime in a mobile moment.

Industrial Products and Mobile Moments Were Made for Each Other

What happens with streetlights can happen with any industrial equipment. A ship captain at Maersk can see the location and manifest of 18,000 shipping containers on its 20-story cargo ship right from the con. A chocolate maker at Tcho Ventures can change settings on lab equipment in her factory, because machines are instrumented for mobile control. And a wind turbine technician from General Electric can diagnose a problem with the unit at the far end of a line of 30 wind turbines and pull the right tools and parts from the truck before climbing to the top of the tower.

The more expensive the equipment, the more valuable the mobile-enabled service is. General Electric understands expensive equipment. This industrial giant builds some of the biggest machines on the planet: power-generating turbines, locomotives, jet engines, and oil and gas extraction machines. In all of them, putting the remote controls into the hands of machine operators and maintenance staff pays off in higher efficiency, lower maintenance costs, and safer equipment.

· · · · · · · · ·

If you add services to a product that gives you a direct relationship with a customer then you open the door to new revenues and maybe even a new business model. Withings and Nest charge their customers more money for the product and potentially an enhanced service. And we've also seen how connected products can extend relationship with partners through APIs and the value inherent in the data they generate. In the next chapter, we will discover just how far reaching mobile moments are in changing the business models for product and for service companies.

8

· · · · · · · · ·

The Business Model Shift

Mobile Moments Create New Business Models

"**U**nder Armour is not just a company. It's a locker room created by the country's greatest coaches where everybody is dedicated to 'making all athletes better through passion, design, and relentless pursuit of innovation.'"

The words roll off Chip Adams' tongue because he practices them as chief performance officer of the fitness apparel company Under Armour. Driven by the vision of founder and CEO, Kevin Plank, Under Armour has pursued its mission by creating great products that appeal to a defined group of customers, marketing them broadly, and selling them through retailers. With 2012 revenues of $1.8 billion, Under Armour has become familiar as athletes of every ilk don its performance apparel to feel cool in the midst of their workouts or strolls through the mall. But like most consumer product companies that sell through retail, Under Armour rarely has a direct connection to its customers.

Not so, Nike, Under Armour's fierce competitor. Since 2006, Nike has been harnessing the mobile mind shift to serve its customers directly. Beginning with its Nike+ iPod sensor and app and continuing with many other apps, Nike has built direct relationships with 18 million runners tracking their workouts.[1] Nike now knows more things about these dedicated athletes than any market research company could tell them.

Athletes are some of the most Shifted people on the planet. As a group, athletes' and particularly young athletes' Mobile Mind Shift Index is much higher than the general population (see Figure 8-1). Not only are they more Shifted; they communicate, consume, and transact on their mobile devices at much higher rates than the general population. The high Communicate and Transact scores of athletes indicate their readiness to share results and do business over mobile devices. Athletes are also avid users of smartphones while exercising. Among athletes with smartphones, 26% use them when exercising; that number rises to 33% among athletes ages 18 to 40. Only 12% of non-athletes with smartphones do. Athletes are ready for a direct relationship in their mobile performance moments.

Figure 8-1: Mobile Mind Shift Index of Athletes Ages 18 to 40

Mobile Intensity

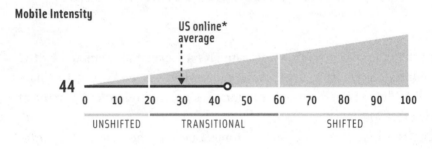

Mobile Expectation   **Mobile Behaviors**

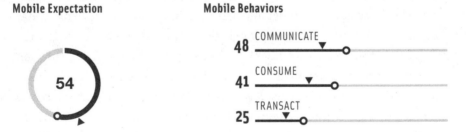

Base: 2,072 US online adults (18-40) who play sports or exercise in their spare time
*Base: 8,224 US online adults (18+)
Source: US Mobile Mind Shift Online Survey, Q3 2013

Nike is not the only innovator tapping into athletes' mobile mind shift. A new category of mobile fitness apps, including Strava and MapMyRide, serves athletes using any smartphone in their mobile moments. The advantage of these fitness apps is that they are built on an open cloud platform, so an athlete can connect them with data from any wearable device or mobile app. With an open platform, Under Armour could pursue direct connections to customers *and potential customers.* But how could Under Armour get an edge on that platform?

This is where Robin Thurston comes in. Robin is a hyper-Shifted athlete who is also the CEO of MapMyFitness, the company that builds the mobile fitness apps MapMyRide, MapMyRun, and MapMyWalk. As a former professional cyclist, Robin started the company because he was looking for a better way to find the best cycling routes anywhere in the world. And because Robin still rides between 8,000 and 10,000 miles a year, he's as passionate about his mission as Kevin Plank and Chip Adams are about Under Armour's.

Cyclists with a smartphone and MapMyRide in their pocket find routes, track their performance, log personal records, and compete with friends and other athletes doing the same segments. It's like running a virtual race against yourself and anybody else that slogs up the same hills you do. The pinnacle of achievement is to be the fastest up the hill—or at least the fastest in your network.

In 2013 MapMyFitness had 21 million registered users, up from 13 million in 2012. And 9 million of those customers are active every month. When Kevin met Robin in 2013, he realized he had found his direct connection to athletes in their mobile moments.

Under Armour purchased MapMyFitness in December 2013 for $150 million.

MapMyFitness' business model is digital. It sells subscriptions for athletes that want to share routes broadly or compare their statistics over time. It sells advertisements. But Robin's real business model innovation is bigger than that: He is making MapMyFitness into an open "fitness cloud" that any company can use to serve athletes in their mobile moments. A fitness cloud, like a social network for athletes, is an Internet-hosted platform for storing fitness data, managing personal accounts, establishing social connections, and hosting new devices and applications *from any company.* When your mission is making all athletes better, you have to pursue every advantage and be open to every device and application, especially those from other companies. Hundreds of gadget, gear, and service companies already use MapMyFitness' software to enhance their products and services.

MapMyFitness' business model is thus more than digital—*it's mobile-native.* It wouldn't exist without mobile moments.

So when Kevin Plank met Robin Thurston, it was a match of common missions and diverse business models. As Chip Adams explains, "If we both focus on every athlete and their needs, good things will come. Any money will be a byproduct of doing the right thing."

With MapMyFitness in its portfolio, Under Armour can enhance its existing physical products business model. The direct relationship with tens of millions of athletes gives Under Armour new data about how its customers and potential customers use apparel and footwear in sports. Simply being able to correlate weather conditions with running sessions sheds new light on the requirements of performance clothing. MapMy-Fitness has this data from its athlete customers. Under Armour can use this information to create better products and find ways to market them directly to athletes.

Under Armour also now owns a new mobile-native business model completely in line with its mission. Just like an entrepreneur, it can help drive the mobile mind shift by delivering new services into athletes' mobile moments.

Mobile Moments Affect Every Business Model

You can't ignore the impact of the mobile mind shift on your business model. If your company is not present in that mobile moment when a customer is considering your product or service, then *you don't exist.* Heartbroken is the firm that leaves a mobile moment unguarded for some entrepreneur or competitor to steal.

You can use mobile moments to *enhance, extend,* or *invent* a business model.

We've shown how mobile moments *enhance* existing business models: through sales, marketing, and products. In chapter 5, we told you how Walgreens and WTSO create new selling opportunities in mobile moments. In chapter 6, we showed how companies like Starbucks and Nestlé use mobile moments to serve customers, attract more, and gather valuable intelligence about what they need. Similarly, we expect Under Armour to use MapMy-Fitness to enhance its current business model—selling clothing.

We've also told you how to use mobile moments to *extend* your existing business model. E-Trade is giving control to its customers in mobile investment moments. USAA extends its banking service through mobile moments. Nest, Philips, and Harvard Engineering make their products more valuable through mobile moments.

Other companies are extending their business model by acquiring startups obsessed with mobile moments. Web-centric Facebook bought a mobile-native business model when it acquired Instagram for $1 billion. Facebook did this because Instagram understood the mobile photo-sharing moment better than anybody else at the time. Aetna bought mobile app maker Healthagen and its iTriage app to help members find medical services before it becomes an emergency.[2] Google bought the mobile traffic and navigation service Waze for $966 million to acquire its crowd-sourced route-optimizing service for drivers stuck in traffic, and then bought Nest to extend its reach from the Web and the phone into devices in your home.[3] Even Walmart has bought a mobile startup.

What's motivating these giant purchases? It's fear of being left behind as more customers shift and expectations for service in a mobile moment expand in the face of the entrepreneurial onslaught.

But the really exciting opportunities come from not just enhancing or extending business models, but *inventing* new business models to make money in a mobile moment through services, distribution, or entertainment. In this chapter, we will help you find mobile moment opportunities in your own business model. And that's just the beginning. The mobile mind shift over the long haul creates fundamental shifts in payments, services, infrastructure, and the economy itself. (We'll talk more about those in chapter 13.)

One of the most important sources of new money in a mobile moment is delivering new services. That's what Russell Hall did.

CASE STUDY: Hailo Connects Taxi Drivers to Passengers in a Mobile Moment

Just three years ago, the taxi market was a travesty of inefficiency. Have you ever waited in the rain for a taxi to pull up and rescue you? Do you wonder why there are never enough taxis when you need them most? Taxi drivers are similarly frustrated. They often waste half their day just waiting for a ride. Taxi stands, radio dispatchers, and mobile phones changed nothing—taxis just didn't work.

Russell Hall was one of those people wondering why the taxi market was so messed up. And he should know. Russell is a London taxi driver. He's married to a London taxi driver. He's the son of a London taxi driver. Russell has taxi in his cockney soul. He's also an entrepreneur. In 2009 when Londoners began carrying iPhones in droves, Russell and some taxi buddies mused over a cup of coffee why they were sometimes fareless in Leicester Square when passengers were queued up for rides in Piccadilly Circus.

Russell saw that the car service economy was out of balance. The cars were never where the passengers needed them. The traditional solution was to regulate pricing and availability and establish passenger and driver queues outside hotels and train stations and with radio dispatch. It didn't work.

Russell formed a team to fix the problem, launching Hailo in London in 2011 to offer a new matchmaking service and business model for rides for hire. He invented a new business model that could only exist in a mobile moment. Today Hailo has 42,000 drivers picking up passengers every 4 seconds in one of 14 countries around the world. Here's how it works.

Both drivers and passengers carry mobile apps. When a passenger is looking for a ride, the Hailo app on their smartphone uses GPS to show them a map where the taxis are right that instant and how long it will take them to get there.

The passenger clicks the app. The taxi driver immediately gets a notification on his Hailo app and decides if he wants the fare. If so, the driver responds and Hailo tells the driver the location of where to pick up the passenger. When the driver shows up, on average in just 2 minutes, the passenger is ready. At the end of the journey, the app records the transaction. Passengers can pay effortlessly with a credit card, or, in several cities in Europe, with cash if they prefer.

Drivers and regulators are key to Hailo's success. Hailo's customers are drivers—not passengers. If drivers don't like the service, then Hailo has no business model at all. And because taxis are a regulated industry, Hailo has learned to work out details with both drivers and regulators in Japanese, Catalan, French, and Gaelic, as well as English.

It's simplicity itself. The dispatcher function is gone. In the US, the payment service is automated. And Russell didn't have to build a custom radio network or staff a call center or buy a lot of servers. Instead, Hailo harnessed tens of billions of dollars of other company's capital investments in taxis, wireless networks, and cloud computing servers and software to operate its car service with a minimal number of employees.

Hailo makes money in a very direct way: by taking a transaction fee from every ride it matches in a mobile moment. But Hailo's customers, taxi drivers, also make more money by borrowing Hailo's mobile-native business model to increase the number of rides they provide. When you create convenience in mobile moments, there's plenty of opportunity to make money.

Mobile-Native Business Models Make Money Directly through Mobile Moments

Entrepreneurs and innovators like Robin Thurston and Russell Hall are inventing new services and business models every day to make money in a mobile moment. Some of those services exploit the physical context of a mobile moment. They build a physical-digital connection through location services, QR codes, near-field communications chips, and Bluetooth links. For example, Shopkick's mobile app guides people into and through a store, then rewards them further when they purchase a promoted item.

With the advent of Apple iBeacon in iPhones and iPads in late 2013, location services got a whole lot more precise. This technology connects when you're mere feet away from something you care about. Apps using the iBeacon technology could reward customers with a coupon when standing in front of a TV at Best Buy, guide a museum goer through an exhibit, or unlock a house as a homeowner walks up to the door (undoubtedly with a passcode for protection).[4]

Services are one way to make money in a mobile moment. Entertainment and distribution are two other ways. Any time someone is willing to pay for value in a mobile moment is a place to build a new business. We have sorted through hundreds of mobile startups and identified six options for making money directly in a mobile moment (see Table 8-1).

Entertainment exploits one of the most innovative new business models in the mobile mind shift: in-app purchases. This model exploits the impatience and enthusiasm of gamers in their mobile moments.

Table 8-1: How to Make Money through Mobile Moments

	Description	Examples
Advertising	Place ads or roll videos in a mobile app or site. Opportunities improve with enhanced location and personal context information. Forrester forecasts that brands will pay $25.7 billion for mobile ads in the US in 2018.	• Facebook expects to make more than half its revenue in 2014 from mobile ads. • Flipboard charges brands for placement in premium magazines and individually curated magazines. • Twitter and Google rely on advertising to support services on mobile devices.
Subscriptions	Charge a monthly fee to continue using the service or to use an enhanced version of the service. Many subscription models carry a long tail of freeloaders; it's fundamental to the freemium business model.	• Dropbox and Evernote charge a monthly fee based on storage needs. • Netflix charges a monthly subscription for movies on demand. • The New York Times sells subscriptions to its mobile newspaper.
App purchases	Sell games, productivity tools, and business applications in an app store. (Apple and Google take 30% of app purchases.)	• Adobe charges $9.99 for its Photoshop Touch on Android tablets. • Mojang charges $6.99 for its Minecraft game on iPhones. • Apple charges $9.99 for its iWorks software on iPhone and iPad.
In-app purchases	Sell services, content, products, or enhancements from within a mobile app. Typically, pay a fee to the app store (for example, Apple's US take is 30% off the top). This is a pure mobile moment-based business model.	• King charges game players during the game for more Candy Crush Saga lives. • Intuit's TurboTax Snaptax charges $14.99 to file a 1040 EZ form. • AliveCor charges to analyze the results of an electrocardiogram (EKG).
Transaction and referral fees	Charge per transaction for digital services like payments or physical world services like taxis or retail delivery. Charge for referrals for things like movie tickets and restaurant reservations.	• Square and PayPal charge sellers a transaction fee for mobile payments. • Hailo and Uber collect a transaction fee for taxi rides. • Hipmunk and FlightStats gain referral fees for airplane bookings through their app.
New mobile products	Build new mobile products that extend the mobile moments in a person's day, from wearables to medical devices.	• Google Glass puts a mobile screen and interaction in front of your eyes. • The Samsung Galaxy Gear smart watch moves controls onto your wrist. • The LifeScan glucose meter connects through Bluetooth to track blood sugar.

Most game makers have made their money selling games. On mobile, some, like Minecraft publisher Mojang, still do. But gaming companies like Cmune and King have mastered the art of advertising and in-app purchases. King, maker of the extraordinarily successful Candy Crush Saga, made $633,000 every day in July 2013 by charging players for more "lives" so they could advance through the levels without waiting 30 minutes for another free chance to continue playing.[5]

Cmune, a global massively multiplayer gaming company based in China, is taking in-app purchases a step further by tapping into the Chinese culture of gift giving. Within a Cmune game, a gamer cannot buy weapons, he can only rent them by making ongoing payments or receiving gifts from others. Gamers send a "supply drop box" gift to a friend's mobile phone for free. This creates a mobile gift moment. As CEO Ludovic Bodin says, "gifting creates an acquisition loop." The recipient opens the virtual gift box and can play the game and send a gift back. If a gamer wants to play more, he has to either pay or recruit more friends. Only about 5% of players spend real money on in-app consumables or rented weapons, but with a giant gift-giving user base, that's real money.

Another way to make money in a mobile moment is aggregating and distributing content or service to a mobile device. Flipboard is another example of a company that aggregated something valuable and distributes it directly into a mobile moment.

CASE STUDY: Flipboard Renders Beautiful Magazines Complete with Full-Color Ads

For 100 years, the magazine industry thrived on great content presented in a great format supported by great advertising. Curling up with *Time* Magazine or the latest issue of *Vogue* was a privilege of being a grownup.

Then came the Web.

The Web destroyed the magazine experience so beautiful in print. Nobody curled up with a laptop. Nobody found blinking ads blatantly riffing off your last search beautiful. Nobody took pleasure in slow-loading pages. Web magazines became pixelated shells of their printed beauty.

Mike McCue knew he could do better than that. Mike and his partner, ex-Apple engineer Evan Doll, set out to start a new company in 2010 after experiencing the intuitive touchscreens and visual beauty of images on iPhones. They challenged each other, asking, "Knowing what we know now, if we could build the Web from scratch for mobile, how would we build it differently?" The result is Flipboard, a social mobile magazine. Flipboard has made the Web beautiful.

Consuming content on Flipboard is completely different from seeing it on the Web. In Flipboard, you experience digital content like magazines in full visual fidelity with gorgeous images, including full-color ads. And you flip through pages in a completely natural way just as you would a magazine. You can curl up with *Vogue* on Flipboard for your tablet or iPad and flip through the pages just as you would a magazine.

But because it's digital, *it's your Vogue*. You can pause and share stories with friends. The ads you see appeal to your personality and desires in a *Vogue* moment rather than just reflecting the last site you visited. And it's not just premium content from established publishers like *The New York Times* or *Fast Company*. Anybody can create a personal magazine based on posts from their Facebook and Twitter connections. Or weave *Wine Spectator* stories together with other vineyard and vintage content to curate— and share—his own wine connoisseur's magazine.

Here's how the business model works.

Flipboard distributes content to customers all over the world. (Currently, half its users are outside the US.) They typically start by setting up their own feed based on their favorite news and entertainment sources and Facebook and Twitter connections, but they have access to more than 6 million magazines curated by people on Flipboard. Robert Scoble, a popular blogger, has more than 300,000 readers of his curated Flipboard magazine.

Advertisers can buy full-page ads on a "share of voice" basis in publisher content on Flipboard. One clothing retailer buys a double-digit percentage of the ad space in *Details* magazine on Flipboard, for example. In addition to full-page ads, brands run curated magazines with original content, stories, and photos from other sources and catalogue-style products sections with price tags. More than 100 brands have launched campaigns on Flipboard, including Levi's, Cisco, Estée Lauder, Gucci, Lexus, and Target.

Flipboard tracks the reach of brand magazines and, over time, will be able to analyze influence as well.

Flipboard's goal is to convert more of the $500 billion global advertising market to mobile devices[6] as well as grab a share of the mobile Internet advertising market, which will reach $25.7 billion just in the US by 2018.[7]

How to Think Like a Mobile Entrepreneur

Flipboard makes money through advertising, Hailo by matching passengers and taxi drivers and collecting a transaction fee, and MapMyFitness by reselling its open fitness cloud as well as subscriptions and advertising. They have found ways to be close to customers and bring them something valuable in a mobile moment. You can do this, too. Follow three steps: Protect your mobile moments, think like a disruptor, and use the IDEA cycle to develop new business.

Protect Your Mobile Moments

Entrepreneurs and innovators are after your mobile moments. In the moments that should by all rights be yours, what competitors are coming after your customers? Is Hotel Tonight referring your best customers to another hotel? Is Square taking your payment transaction fee?

Identify the mobile moments where you are at risk and decide for each how to respond: abdicate or act. You may assess the risk and decide to abdicate. Maybe the moment isn't worth pursuing right now. You may not have the internal support you need to push mobile commerce into your stores or the engineering resources to deliver a meaningful engagement in that moment. You may decide the moment is short-lived and not worth the investment or that you don't know enough about what to do to move forward with confidence. If you decide to act, move on to thinking disruptively and exploiting those new moments.

Think Like a Disruptor

Mobile moments unlock a trove of service opportunity, data collection, and advance notice into things your customers care about. In addition to the question we described in chapter 3—where can you improve a service or eliminate friction or annoyance in your customer's life?—ask these three other questions that reveal new opportunities for mobile moments.

What moments do you already own and how can you turn them into money? This is where the new business opportunities lie. Travel companies like Hertz and United Airlines already use the mobile moments they own to sell upgraded cars and seats—or offer them to frequent travelers to earn their gratitude. Telstra offers customers near their data or voice limits additional mobile service packages and now does 10,000 transactions like this every week. The Insurance Australia Group serves customers once every eight years, on average, when they file a claim. It's a rare moment, but one poised to turn into a deeper engagement that might lead to an upgrade or new policy purchase.

What could you do if you had earlier notice or new insight into customers' needs? Location information is a powerful predictor of someone's next step. And so is data on their physical world habits. Grocery iQ customers use a mobile app to create and manage a shopping list. Over time, the app learns what a customer buys regularly to auto-fill a weekly list and makes recommendations for new foods. Grocery iQ collects data on which items are most used and that cluster together—valuable data for a grocer or consumer packaged goods (CPG) company.

Who owns the process to find mobile moments that disrupt your business model? You may have an internal innovation group, or you may want to start one. Companies like Walmart, Target, and Staples are flocking to Silicon Valley to set up innovation labs and tap into the entrepreneurial energy, talent, and disruptive ideas of startups. Or the ideas may lie in your service organizations. Who better to know what customers really want than those who serve them every day. For example, when the traffic to your website shifts from a computer to a tablet, what new services could you imagine providing now that you know your customer is trying to reach you while roaming around the house or city?

Use the IDEA Cycle to Develop New Business Models

Once you've started to think like a disruptor, you can use the IDEA cycle to start to shift your own business model.

The internal resistance to change can be fierce, particularly if the mobile app diverts customer traffic or attention away from a traditional channel such as the store or the Web. To overcome that resistance and create the right momentum in your mobile mind shift, find a willing audience and deliver something vital and useful quickly. You've seen how companies like American Airlines and USAA start with a minimum viable product, develop in cycles, and learn as they go. They didn't tackle the entire business model shift in a single iteration of the app. You should start small, too.

And remember, if you serve only the customers in your existing markets you'll miss out on two-thirds of the population ready to engage you in a mobile moment. Today, a billion people have a smartphone device. By 2017, three billion people will—and almost two billion of them won't have a computer.[8] Mobile devices in the hands of three billion people are a massive delivery system for new services in every market, including yours. This system is particularly valuable in developing economies that struggle to provide services like banking, healthcare, and education to rural citizens.

. . . .

CASE STUDY: Vodafone Delivers Mobile Payment Services to Herders in Africa

The western plains of Kenya look today much as they have for the past 2,000 years. The Masai people herd goats and cows on the same open plains inhabited by zebra, wildebeest, and impala. They live in huts without running water or electricity, let alone telephone lines or Internet wiring. No banks. No credit cards. No way to save or send money. They are unbanked.

Claire Alexandre understands the issues of the unbanked. Claire is Vodafone's head of commercial and strategy for M-Pesa, a mobile payment service available in some countries in Africa and Asia, and she spent two years working with the Bill & Melinda Gates Foundation on initiatives to improve the lives of impoverished people around the world.

An unbanked economy is a cash economy. It's inefficient, bogged down with corruption, and fraught with peril. Workers fret about carrying money home to their families on a bus. Commerce suffers as truck-driving distributors carrying Coca-Cola and toothpaste are robbed on the narrow roads that crisscross the plains. In a cash-only economy it's harder to lend money or pay wages or eliminate graft or collect taxes. These problems make setting up banking services a national economic priority. But how, in a land where in many places, there is no infrastructure for financial services? Claire knew she could do something about it.

Because while rural Kenyans may be unbanked, they are not unphoned. As far back as 2005, Kenyans have used mobile phones to talk, to text, and to work effectively. For example, in 2008, Kenyan game wardens tracked marauding elephants by text message on a radio collar so they could intervene before a hungry bull elephant savaged crops and became the target of angry farmers.[9]

Vodafone's payment service M-Pesa uses the wireless network and local agents to help customers make small payments using their mobile phones. In Kenya, M-Pesa, which is operated by mobile operator Safaricom, now serves 19 million customers using agents in 85,000 retail locations.

Here's how it works.

Mobile subscribers put money in their account through cash deposits at one of the M-Pesa agents. They can deposit as little as 12 cents. Subscribers can then transfer money to a family member or even themselves to avoid carrying cash on long trips. Safaricom collects a fee from each transaction. On the billion dollars customers transfer every month, those transactions add up. M-Pesa accounted for 18% of Safaricom's service revenue in 2013.

Claire and her partners at M-Pesa and Safaricom have worked diligently to expand the services M-Pesa can offer, including small 30-day loans and bill payment. Retailers can now pay distributors electronically. The local beverage distributor can now more safely travel from Nairobi to Mombasa. Consumers can borrow money and pay for goods in shops. And in Kenya, Tanzania, the Democratic Republic of the Congo, or Mozambique, unbanked but phoned rural citizens can now transfer and store their money safely.

Mobile Moments Will Disrupt More Business Models over the Long Haul

Vodafone's M-Pesa is one example of how mobile devices bring whole new classes of service to life. Orange and India's Reliance Communications are two other major companies using mobile devices to revolutionize economies. We believe that mobile devices and networks will create radical change even in developed economies over the next 10 years.

Business models are always in flux. One indication of the importance in keeping up with market and technology changes lies in the rapid refresh of the list of the biggest companies in the world. Between 2002 and 2012, 70% of the Fortune Global 500 turned over.[10] Technology is one of the biggest change agents in the world, and mobile technology one of the most powerful influences on people.

The impact of the mobile mind shift on your business model is probably subtle at first—pressure on pricing, a disappointed customer expecting to find you on their phone, a competitor amping up convenience services. But over time, the subtle shift of power to customers in their mobile moments of decision and purchase will erode portions of your current business model. We'll describe the ultimate impact of those changes in chapter 13.

· · · · · · · · ·

Mobile moments disrupt the way you sell, market, and build products and services, and even sometimes change your business model. But your hold on customers in their mobile moments of need will be flimsy unless you are prepared to execute on their desires. And that takes a massive overhaul to your internal platforms, processes, and people. This is where the hard work and the big investments lie. That's what the rest of this book is about. We start by showing you in chapter 9 how the mobile mind shift affects your employees.

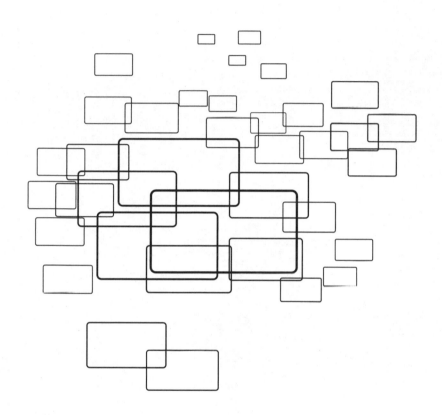

PART III
The Mobile Systems Shift

9

· · · · · · · · ·

The Workforce Shift
Empower Employees in Their Mobile Moments

"I'm tired of being the one who has to say no," said Rebecca Jacoby in the fall of 2007.

Rebecca is the CIO of Cisco Systems, a $49 billion high technology company operating in 94 countries. For years, Cisco employees, like most other employees, had been forced to use a corporate computer and the occasional BlackBerry smartphone. But now they wanted to use their own tools: personal iPhones for work and mobile apps like Dropbox to store files, Evernote to take notes, TripIt to track travel itineraries, and Expensify to capture receipts. They also wanted to get work email on those phones.

Rebecca realized the company had to do an about-face. If employees thought they could be more successful with mobile apps on personal phones, then she needed to figure out how best to support them.

So she made the decision to offer a bring-your-own-device (BYOD) program for Cisco's entire workforce.

The traditional workforce technology model relies on a monoculture of Microsoft PCs and BlackBerry phones. This makes it easier to manage and secure corporate applications linked to databases locked away on servers in the corporate data center. A bring-your-own-device program blows that model up. Suddenly, business applications have to run safely on anybody's mobile device. Corporate data has to be piped over the Internet. Security becomes a quagmire of complexity. And deciding which employees get reimbursed for phones and data plans turns into an HR hassle, particularly in countries like Switzerland where the laws about personal data protection are strong.

So Rebecca and Sheila Jordan, who was a senior vice president in Cisco's IT department at the time, crafted a bring-your-own-device program and a multi-year application migration program. Employees today can select from 100 applications and implement Cisco security protocols on their personal mobile devices in a few steps that they can typically finish in six minutes. Today, Cisco supports 69,000 employee-owned smartphones and tablets, including 16,000 iPads. Wonder how they do it? By embracing five operating principles:

1. Deliver application services that work on any device. Cisco embraces cloud technology with a device-independent security model.

2. Manage workforce technology like a product. Cisco appoints a general manager responsible for each service—such as mobile, collaboration, or video communications—and holds that person accountable for employee adoption and satisfaction metrics.

3. Allow business groups to determine their own reimbursement policies. This flexibility allows variability by business role and country of employment; some business groups might buy phones and monthly plans for every employee, while others might only reimburse a small contribution or nothing at all.

4. Build social learning and sharing into every service. Rather than support all these devices themselves, Cisco's technology group encourages people to support each other on its internal social network

5. Give employees responsibility and make them accountable. Employees using personal devices for work must sign a contract confirming their responsibilities and Cisco's "right to wipe" the device to remove corporate information.

Rebecca and Sheila knew that their trust that employees would do the right thing was working when one of Cisco's employees called in a panic one day: "I've lost my phone. Please can you wipe everything off it? My personal photos and my banking app are on that phone." This guy knew that it was safer to wipe the phone and start fresh. He trusted that Cisco was looking out for his best interest.

Rebecca is far from finished. Cisco's teams are busily finding and deploying a full set of mobile applications so employees can do everything they need on a smartphone or tablet, in essence to be able to carry their office on their hip.

Information Workers Have Made the Mobile Mind Shift, but Employers Haven't

Cisco is a leader. Its workers are sophisticated and mobile; keeping them, and keeping them productive, means embracing the technology they like best, including mobile devices. That's why Rebecca and Sheila took on the task of embracing a bring-your-own-device program, with all that entails.

You might think your company's workers aren't like this, but they are. Your employees also want mobile devices when they work because it means freedom from the office and the flexibility to get work done anywhere. But too often your employees can't be truly mobile at work. In fact, employees have much more freedom to be mobile in their personal lives than they do at work.

This is a very big deal. Globally, there are roughly 615 million information workers today. By 2016, we expect 865 million information workers globally.[1] That's a lot of productivity that mobile could improve.

To see just how mobile employees are at work, we created a *Mobile Work Score* for the Mobile Mind Shift Index. This score runs from 0 to 100 depending on how many mobile devices an employee uses in how many locations. When you see this score in comparison with our other Mobile Mind Shift scores, the contrast is stark (see Figure 9-1). The average Mobile Work Score for online American adults who are information workers—workers that uses some kind of computer or device every day for work—is a paltry 18 out of 100.

If you are in technology or are responsible for making employees productive, how should you interpret these scores? First, see the pressure coming from the Mobile Expectation Score, which is higher for information workers than for average online American adults. That score means that people have a deep and personal incentive to be mobile in every aspect of their lives, *including work*: They expect work apps on their mobile device.

Figure 9-1: The Mobile Mind Shift of Information Workers

Mobile Intensity

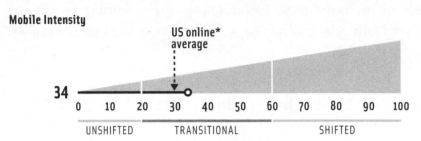

34

```
0   10   20   30   40   50   60   70   80   90   100
        UNSHIFTED      TRANSITIONAL        SHIFTED
```

US online*
average

Mobile Expectation

48

Mobile Behaviors

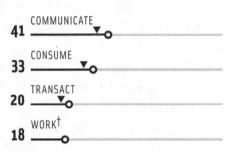

COMMUNICATE
41

CONSUME
33

TRANSACT
20

WORK†
18

Base: 4,324 US online adults (18+) who are information workers
**Base: 8,224 US online adults (18+)*
Source: US Mobile Mind Shift Online Survey, Q3 2013
†Note: "Work" mobile behavior score calculated for information workers only

Figure 9-2: Mobile Work Scores for Types of Information Workers

Mobile Work Behavior

▼ Average work score for
information workers

WORK
Individual Contributors   **13**

Team Managers   **25**

Senior Managers   **35**

Base: 4,324 US online adults (18+) who are information workers
Source: US Mobile Mind Shift Online Survey, Q3 2013

Second, notice that not everybody is quite so immobile at work. The Mobile Work Score ranges from a low of 13 for individual contributors to a high of 35 for senior managers and above (see Figure 9-2). Senior managers need to be productive anywhere; we know that. Why not give that same power to all information workers? They are already working everywhere (see Figure 9-3). Why not let them work productively?

Figure 9-3: Mobile Devices Take Work out of the Office

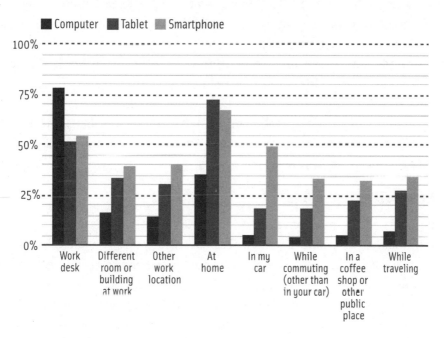

"Where do you use the following devices in a typical week?"

Base: US online adults (18+) who are information workers and work on the specific device
Source: US Mobile Mind Shift Online Survey, Q3 2013

How can you do this? You must provide three things to your mobile workforce.

First, a mobile workforce wants a mobile toolkit. Smartphones and tablets are better than computers for employees that are inherently mobile in meetings, customer visits, travel, and doing anything that's not chained to a desk (particularly for employees that consume more than create content). That means your mobile workforce wants almost every business app in their pocket, not just the few you provide today.

Second, *every job* improves with better information access. With smartphones and tablets, people that have traditionally worked offline are now becoming people empowered by mobile moments. And it's not just the process jobs like sales and field service that we will describe in chapter 11. It's all jobs. Even the farmer spreading fertilizer based on satellite positioning and in-soil measurement.[2]

Third, mobile devices break down the artificial boundary that the office puts on the workday. Ted's grandfather, James Horsfall, who ran the Connecticut Agricultural Experiment Station for 25 years used to say it this way: "Your time is your own, but your brain belongs to the Station."[3] In other words, don't ask me if you can leave work early on a personal matter. Just get important things done wherever you are. Mobile devices and applications extend this beyond the realm of scientists to every employee and turn work from a place you go into a thing you do.

These forces drive the mobile mind shift at work and the rise of new categories of applications.

The Employee App Gap

Why can't you do most of your work on your phone or tablet?

In theory, you could. These devices have the power you need, but the vast majority of the applications that employees need to get things done are still available only on corporate PCs. In many companies, the technology organization still bans even basic apps such as opening email attachments on personal devices. Imagine trying to get through your daily email if you couldn't open an attachment!

This leads to what we call an *app gap*, in which employees want applications to do real work on a mobile device but find those apps aren't available.

Who will fix the app gap? Companies try, but they move slowly. Entrepreneurs like Evernote move faster, and they help people solve these problems themselves.

CASE STUDY: Evernote Plugs an App Gap in Note Taking

Phil Libin has a better way to remember things: put them in an Evernote where they will exist *for you* forever no matter where you are. And by things, Phil means everything: your shopping list, business to-do list, client meeting notes, website links, video clips, photos, calendar invitations, even your handwritten notes in a paper journal.

"It's the oldest idea in world—use technology to help you remember," says Phil, the CEO of Evernote. From cave paintings to mobile note-taking, Phil's philosophy holds true: "Any time you need that memory, we want to make it available."

In 2008 Evernote, led by Phil and founder Stepan Pachikov, created a simple note-taking app that worked very well on any computer, browser, or mobile device. Today, Evernote is helping 80 million customers plug the note-taking app gap by serving people in their mobile moments. Evernote also partners with product companies like 3M and scanner-maker Fujitsu to merge electronic note-taking with the physical world of paper and scanners. After years of viewing paper as "the enemy," Evernote now strives to help its customers keep "the elegant parts of paper" and augments paper notes with Evernote features, like taking a picture of the note so you can find it forever on your mobile device.

Even Moleskine, the famous paper notebook company, wants to work with Evernote. Why? According to Moleskine co-founder Maria Sebregondi, it's because, "we move back and forth between the physical and digital worlds. It's how our lives are made up." Her goal is to serve her customer's note-taking moments wherever they fall.

Evernote has mastered one of the secrets of the mobile mind shift: Serve *an individual* in her moments of need *both physical and digital*, and she'll come back again. If she wants to take notes in a Moleskine notebook or on a Post-it Note, but search and find them in her Evernote, Evernote wants to help.

Start to Plug the App Gap by Following Your Employees' Lead

Evernote is but one example of an application designed for mobile moments at work. Google Docs, SlideShark, and Skype are others. Employees using applications like these can work anywhere on a smartphone or tablet, often at their own expense. In fact, 53% of North American information workers spend their own money on a mobile device or app for work.[4] This is an example of a pervasive trend: the consumerization of IT.

One way to plug the app gap is to follow your employees' lead. See which mobile applications they're already using, then look for ways to add the business and security features you need. In many cases, there's a starter version of the app for free to individuals and a more sophisticated paid corporate version that allows a company to manage usage and security. Better yet, technology managers can embrace apps that solve both personal and work problems, and allow employees to keep the two parts neatly separated. Like Dropbox.

With 200 million users as of November 2013, Dropbox is growing at the same pace that Facebook did.[5] Mobile moments give Dropbox its ignition. As cofounder and CEO Drew Houston told us, "I remember the day I got my iPhone. It had a glaring omission. There was no way to get or save my files." Dropbox fixed the problem with a mobile app that synchronizes files between a customer's phone and Dropbox. Put a photo, document, or video in your Dropbox in the cloud, and you can get to it from anywhere on your computer, phone, or tablet. And now, developers from other companies have built more than 100,000 apps that use a customer's Dropbox to store and retrieve files. To assuage technology managers, Dropbox makes it easy to keep personal and work files separate.[6]

Table 9-1: Apps That Bridge Work and Personal Activities

Purpose	Apps that do this
Note taking	Evernote, Microsoft OneNote
File share and sync	Box, Dropbox, Google Drive, Microsoft OneDrive
Videoconferencing	Skype, FuzeBox
Travel	TripIt, Hipmunk
Expenses	Expensify, ExpenseIt
Presentations	SlideShark, Apple Keynote
Collaboration	Google Docs, Huddle, JoinMe
Project management	Smartsheet, Trello

We believe that this is the future of business applications. People don't artificially divide their brains when they walk in and out the company door. They shouldn't have to artificially divide the tools they use to live and work. You and your workers should embrace tools that work like that (see Table 9-1).

Use the IDEA Cycle to Find Mobile Productivity Moments

Apps like Evernote and Dropbox can't do everything workers need to do. You already have corporate applications running on PCs that your company maintains to make workers more productive, such as customer relationship management systems, financial software, and transaction databases. If you really want to improve the productivity of your Shifted employees, you will need to invest in some custom-built mobile applications.

If you're going to build apps for employees, use the same planning method that you would use for a customer application—the IDEA cycle. But this time, it's the IDEA cycle for information workers. Start with a mobile moment audit for employee applications:

1. Identify the mobile moments embedded in the workday.

2. Design mobile engagement based on the benefit to employees and to the firm.

3. Engineer mobile apps in the cloud.

4. Analyze how employees work to optimize the impact.

Step 1. Identify the Mobile Moments Embedded in the Workday

How can you identify employees' mobile moments? Take a look at how this works in the wine and spirits business.

The typical owner of a typical wine store is an expert merchandiser— she knows how to sell wine. She could do better if she had a system to track what's selling. That's where Constellation Brands, purveyor of Ravenswood and Robert Mondavi wine, Corona Extra beer, and Black Velvet whisky, steps in to help.

When a Constellation Brands salesperson walks into a wine store, she comes armed with a tablet application that helps explain why a particular brand responds well to an end cap promotion, what the product mix is for the most successful wine sellers in the region, and what the year-over-year performance of that particular store has been. That data transforms the conversation from "how many cases do you want?" to "how can we maximize your profit?"

That tablet application is based on Roambi, the application we describe in Chapter 1. Anushil Kumar, Constellation's VP of information delivery, adapted it for his sales team. The application has been so successful for 150 sales reps on the national accounts team that commercial leaders and sales staff in other parts of the business are lobbying to get in on it. Even executives in operations review meetings use it to drill into the trouble spots to identify and solve problems.

If you're looking for mobile moments, you should ask the kind of questions that Anushil did at Constellation Brands.

First, where can we solve an employee's problem? While employees often find their own solutions, you shouldn't let this stop you from helping them out. It's what Anushil did with the Roambi app: bring data into the sales engagement. Many desktop moments, particularly those dedicated to searching, reading, or reviewing, can become mobile moments. You just have to look for them.

Second, where can we solve a business problem? This is where you need to bring business people responsible for productivity and revenue together with technical people that understand mobile moments. When a field technician is at a job site, how can you inject data into the visit to help her complete the work the first time? We'll learn how Dish Network did this with a field service app in Chapter 11. You can do the same for situations where people do manual tasks such as collect receipts or file paperwork. Can a photo taken with a phone accomplish the same goal?

Develop the discipline to find the mobile moments hiding in plain sight. You'll make your people and your company more productive.

Step 2. Design Mobile Engagement Based on the Benefit to Employees and to the Firm

Employees' mobile mind shift carries with it the expectation that an app at work will be as easy to use as an app at home. If it's not, they won't use it.

But for the traditional major suppliers of enterprise software, the user experience has typically been an afterthought. The challenge is especially difficult with mobile. Just as with a consumer application, a mobile employee application needs to be simple and intuitive. It must use the employees' context—especially their location and what step they need to take next—to tailor the data and interface to require the fewest clicks. Designing a great mobile engagement requires you to relentlessly pare back the functionality you expose.

How can you determine which mobile apps to build and what mobile functions to include? Use a modified version of the evaluation matrix we developed in chapter 3 to evaluate employees' mobile moments. Prioritize the apps and particularly the features that bring the most value to the firm and to employees (see Figure 9-4). In that way, you will align the firms' goals with your employees' motivation in the mobile moment.

If the service you can provide in the mobile moment helps your employee and is valuable to you—like email, file sync and share, or field service—then it's a clear priority. If the application is good for your employee, but its business impact is unclear, then you may be better off trusting the employee to use the app she chooses. If the application is valuable to your company but your employee finds it clunky to use, then you must redesign it for mobile first. And finally, if the mobile moment isn't valuable to you and doesn't help your employees, then no matter how tempting it might be, forget about it—prioritize other features instead.

Armed with this analysis, you are in a position to trim the list of mobile moments and apps from the Identify step of IDEA down to just the ones most valuable this time around the IDEA cycle.

Step 3. Engineer Mobile Apps in the Cloud

To empower employees on mobile devices, you should run the systems that power their applications in the datacenter of a cloud provider. There is no better way to serve the needs of employees in their mobile moments. Traditional on-premises communications and document collaboration tools can't keep up with the demands of your mobile workforce. Google, IBM, Microsoft, and salesforce.com have built cloud-hosted platforms engineered for your mobile workforce. For them, the race is on to convert your company to the cloud.

Figure 9-4: Evaluate Apps and Features on a Value Matrix

Score from 1 (completely disagree) to 5 (completely agree). Add the factor
scores together to get a total score.

Benefit to your employee	Score
The app or site delivers a service that improves an employee's experience.	
The app or site runs on employees' preferred smartphones and tablets.	
The app or site helps an employee accomplish a goal in seconds.	
The app or site uses context to deliver a better experience.	
Total benefit score:	

Value to you	Score
The app or site greatly enhances an employee's productivity.	
The app or site eliminates many steps or simplifies a process.	
The app or site provides everything an employee needs to complete a task.	
The app or site improves an employee's work/life balance.	
Total value score:	

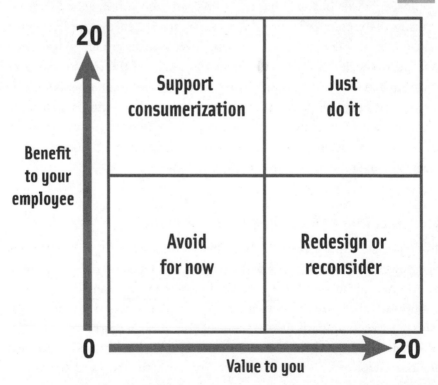

Spanish bank BBVA adopted Google's email and collaboration service to help 110,000 employees in 26 countries collaborate in the mobile moments of their day. In the words of José Olalla, CIO at BBVA, "We were looking for a technology that would transform our business operations, not just make our workers more efficient. [Google Apps] will introduce a new way of working where employees have access to all the information they need with just one click, no matter where they are, and can reap the benefits of using advanced collaboration tools."[7]

In the next three chapters, we will describe the three engineering tasks necessary to support these apps: building platforms, transforming processes, and organizing people. The challenge of building great mobile apps is just as important for employee applications as it is for customer applications.

Step 4. Analyze How Employees Work to Optimize the Impact

How are your employee apps doing? Where are people getting the most work done, and where are they bogging down? You won't know unless you measure the results.

Cisco measures adoption and satisfaction for its corporate technology services. At one large US government agency, the CIO conducted an employee survey before and after deploying Google Apps to find out what the problems were and whether the new system of engagement solved them. Without this kind of data analysis, your technology department is just guessing if the technology you buy for employees is successful.

Analytics are just as important in measuring the performance and effectiveness of mobile apps at work as it is for consumers. We'll learn more about how to implement these analytics in the next chapter. One healthcare provider selling in-home rehabilitation services used the metrics from a mobile app to see, for the first time, when salespeople meeting with a patient and family didn't lead to a sale. They suddenly had visibility into *all the sales activities*—not just the ones resulting in a deal. Why? Because the mobile app logged the visit automatically. Previously, salespeople had only logged the visit when it resulted in a sale. Armed with this information, the sales management team could identify which hospitals or discharging physicians or times of day or salespeople were most likely to generate business, then apply the lessons learned to improve sales.

How Mobile Work Changes Your Culture

What happens when your people use mobile applications—yours or their own—to change the way they do their jobs? They become different. They have different expectations, both of themselves and of you. They change the culture of your company.

We've identified three ways that culture changes as a result of mobile—a bias toward direct action, a trend toward organizing spontaneously, and the information-empowerment of every employee. Let's take a deeper look at each change.

Mobile Devices Create a Culture of Direct Action

Mobile devices fuel an intense level of get-it-done-now behavior. With a mobile device, any employee can get the data, find help, get an answer, share a result, and get something done right in the moment.

There's no better example of a culture of direct action than what has happened with the US Department of Defense's non-military disaster response group.

In a disaster—like Haiti after the 2010 earthquake or the devastated Tōhoku coast of Japan in 2011—you've got chaos. Hundreds or thousands of aid organizations are rushing in to help. Communications networks are spotty, and mobile devices, not computers, are the key information asset of people in the field. This is the environment for which the Department of Defense designed the All Partners Access Network (APAN).[8]

Jerry Giles, an APAN technical director for the US Department of Defense, spends a lot of time developing technology systems for use in disaster areas, so he knows mobile devices are ubiquitous in countries like Bangladesh, China, Haiti, and Nigeria while laptops are not. Jerry explains that mobile devices "are basically the humanitarian response operator's primary sources of information, coordination, and communication" during disaster operations. In 2011, he introduced APAN Chat to make APAN "responsive to any device" in a mobile moment. Recently APAN chat was used to support the Nigerian Navy's battle against piracy; most of the coordination and direct action happened via the APAN Chat site on mobile devices over slow networks. Today, 50,000 military and civilian workers from 1,500 different organizations use APAN's social networking tools, document storage and search, mapping, translation, and support for mobile devices to coordinate their unclassified information sharing and collaboration.

In Haiti, the APAN Community used a software platform from a company called Zimbra to coordinate the US military response with 300 aid organizations. In the field, thousands of aid workers and military analysts in the remotest areas uploaded 3,500 images of problems to help direct food and medical aid to the villages most in need. In one case, a hospital staff person indicated that beds were available for patients through a post on the APAN Community, which enabled the US military and relief organizations to redirect hundreds of patients to the hospital for treatment.[9]

Your business is not a disaster area like Haiti after the earthquake. But your people are making decisions right now. They could be moving faster and acting with more confidence, with access to more data, from wherever they happen to be. Your mobile-enabled staff will learn to act more quickly and directly, just as the military and aid workers using APAN have learned to do.

Employees Collaborate and Self-Organize

People collaborate better when they can collaborate on any device.

To see how effective this can be, look at what happened at Tijuana Flats, a company that includes 100 Tex-Mex restaurants. That means 100 places where scheduling shifts for cooks, cashiers, and servers can set the tone for the entire restaurant.

The typical top-down assignment where managers set schedules can create resentment. Employees often want to swap shifts; managers who need to approve waste time chasing down employees rather than spending time with customers.

Things are different now because Darrin Heisey, the company's technology director, brought in a mobile application called HotSchedules to replace the spreadsheets and paper schedules the restaurants had been using. HotSchedules launched an iPhone app in 2009 and soon after supported Android and BlackBerry phones. That's perfect because many of Tijuana Flats' young staffers may not have a computer, but they live on their smartphones. Managers post the schedule. And because employees carry HotSchedules in their pockets, they can immediately find their schedule, swap shifts, and find substitutes right on their phones. They self-organized. The workers are more productive and happier. And happier workers mean happier customers.

Every Employee Becomes an Information Worker

As computers have spread into the workplace, many workers in large companies became information workers. Customer service, sales, research, product development, marketing, finance—all these jobs are now mostly accomplished by workers at computers. But in the mobile mind shift, *every* employee can be an information worker, using the computer in her pocket to get things done. This has a repercussion: You need workers that are comfortable with technology—even in field jobs.

Take the ground crews at China Eastern Airlines, a fast-growing company that carries 250,000 passengers on 3,000 flights every day. When Kevin Cia Yang, the company's CIO, arrived in 2009, the 8,000 ground crew members responsible for luggage, water, refueling, and passenger support had fixed assignments for gates and times. If flights didn't arrive on schedule, the crew might either sit idle or be overwhelmed.

Kevin saw that putting smartphones in the hands of 8,000 ground crew members could improve efficiency and safety. China Eastern Airlines now uses a real-time dispatch process to service an airplane with the right combination of staff to handle all the tasks when it actually arrives at the gate. After completing the service, the staff members update the status on their smartphones and declare their availability for the next flight. According to Kevin, "mobile changes the timing of every job. We still have to roster staff on shifts, but we don't have to program them for the entire day, not even every hour of the day. We allocate staff in real time."

Kevin didn't stop with the ground crew app. He implemented a similar system for maintenance staff, so China Eastern now knows exactly how long a maintenance task took. This information is a rich database they can analyze to find and fix ongoing problems to minimize the time a plane spends on the ground.

Today, China Eastern has 300 mobile apps across every part of its business: marketing and sales, in-cabin and on-ground service, flight operations, engineering and maintenance, and back-office tasks. Kevin says, "The demand for mobile services continues to pour in. We have a road map for the next three years. It's a business transformation. We always start with the process, not the app."

What China Eastern learned about field workers applies to many other workers that would not be traditionally considered "information workers." In manufacturing, a shop floor worker may use a tablet to program a machine tool for a specific task. A repair technician working in the cockpit of a Caterpillar D7 bulldozer can inspect the 3D manufacturing drawings to identify a problem in a hidden control linkage using a Siemens computer-aided-design tool running on a tablet.

When mobile employees are also information workers, they can bring the full power of your business information and systems outward to serve customers and inward to improve your process and operations.

Just as computers and the Internet flattened organizations by making it easy for information workers to communicate and exchange information, mobile devices and wireless networks extend that power to every employee. As a result, the traditional responsibilities of a command and control hierarchy will continue to change, as we've seen in disaster relief with APAN and with restaurant workers at Tijuana Flats. This is a good outcome for you because it puts more of your empowered workforce in a position to work directly and collaboratively together.

. . . .

We've shown you how to serve employees in their mobile moments. Now that we have laid the foundation for the mobile mind shift in your business, we will show you how to engineer your business platforms, processes, and people. In chapter 10, we will tell you how to engineer your technology platforms for mobile moments.

10
. . . .

The Platform Shift

Mobile Moments Require a New Technology Strategy

Imagine you sell men's suits at Nordstrom. You've spent years building relationships with customers who value your opinion on the latest Canali jacket cuts and silk ties. But now, instead of chatting with you about ties while waiting for a fitting, your customer fills that time checking on everything on his mobile phone—and continues to do so during the checkout process. You've lost your opportunity to connect with that customer.

Nordstrom's mission is service, selection, quality, and value. Making customers wait in line at the counter isn't fulfilling any part of that mission. But since 1901, when Nordstrom was founded as a shoe store on a misty Seattle street, waiting in line has been the only way to complete a sale. Until one day when it wasn't.

In the mobile mind shift, store associates expect to have the critical information about customers and products right at the point of service where it matters most. If Nordstrom could build a mobile point-of-sale system with that valuable information, store associates could improve the customer experience—and maybe business performance as well—by remaining connected to a customer throughout each interaction.

In 2010, Nordstrom initiated a mobile checkout project for these aims, hoping to launch in time for Nordstrom's summer anniversary sale just eight months away. It was a daunting task, but one that John Mayfield, a 30-year technology veteran and a vice president in Nordstrom's IT group, felt ready to help solve.

For decades, Nordstrom has viewed technology—like financial tracking, inventory management, and staff time sheets—as a cost of doing business. As John puts it, "we're a fashion retailer, not a technology company." Mobile checkout would require something new: an investment in new technology that could better serve customers when, where, and how they like to shop.

We described mobile checkout for Alex and Ani in chapter 2. But in the case of Nordstrom, keep in mind that we're talking about a 112-year old company with technology systems built up over many years, not a retail startup building from scratch. What happened at Nordstrom was surprising, even to John Mayfield: A single mobile app triggered a mind shift in how Nordstrom views the risk of new technology investments.

With the full support of leadership, Nordstrom and its technology development partners engineered and delivered 6,000 mobile point-of-sale devices to employees in 117 stores in time for the July anniversary sale event. The company needed to put mobile devices into store employees' hands so those workers could check out customers anywhere in the store, whether in a fitting room, while considering one last pair of shoes, or while relaxing on a bench after a hard day's shopping.

Nordstrom uses Apple iPod devices encased with a credit card reader from Infinite Peripherals for the employee application. Nordstrom manages the iPod devices with software from a startup called MobileIron. The devices use Wi-Fi that Nordstrom had already been deploying for customer use. But don't forget the hard part: engineering the systems that drive the application. Nordstrom hired Infosys to tie in its existing transaction and point-of-sale systems to accomplish that goal.

If that seems like a lot work, it was. But it was worth it. In Nordstrom's Q2 2012 financial results, the company pointed to a 15.3% rise in same-store revenues compared with the year before.[1] Better in-store customer service and experience through the mobile-enabled workforce was critical.

Nordstrom set out to arm its sales staff with mobile devices, but ended up building a platform for a new way of doing business. According to John, "everything changed: people, culture, risk, process, tools, and technology. We changed our mindset: It's okay to move faster and take more risk." It wasn't just Nordstrom's customers that were making the mobile mind shift. It was the executive team and the whole company.

Four Technology Requirements of Great Mobile Moments

Why did "everything change" at Nordstrom with the advent of the mobile point-of-sale system? In particular, why did the approach to technology change? At Nordstrom, and at every company we've seen win a mobile moment, the technical staff used a new set of technologies that are markedly different from the investments companies had made to that point. The technology experts in these companies keep four principles in mind to win the mobile moment.

First, the application must be *intuitive* to a first-time user. The design thinking starts with a human interaction, not a database. The goal is to help someone accomplish something immediately and with no training. This takes a very different mindset and an entirely new approach to putting information and transactions into people's hands. It starts with a deep understanding of a person and his context, as we described in chapter 2 and chapter 3.

Second, the application is *task-oriented*. It must deliver just enough information and action buttons to help someone take the next step. A mobile moment is brief and purposeful. To enable success in this moment, the data and business process must be "atomized" to serve up only what's needed at that moment. No extra clicks and no wading through screens and data fields to accomplish the goal.

Third, the experience must be served in a customer's *context*. Because you know where someone is and a lot about his preferences and previous actions, you can spoon up information to help him take the next most likely step on his way. This information, content, or insight may come from your internal systems, or it may come from a business partner or a service provider like Google or Adobe.

Fourth, the technology platform needs to *flex and scale* to the demands of the customer's schedule and expectations. There is an inherent volatility with technology in the hands of customers. They use the apps at all hours of the day; they do not schedule upgrades months in advance. This leads to spikes in demand and usage.

Your Technology Isn't Ready for the Mobile Mind Shift and its Unintended Consequences

For 30 years, companies have been building the technology systems to power PCs on employees' desks and then websites on customers' PCs.

They built software to connect these tools to the big corporate systems of record that manage things like inventory and customer records. The result of all this activity, in most large companies, is a technological chaos of complexity, redundancy, and antiquity. *It's not ready for the mobile mind shift.*

The technology you invested in to power PCs and the Web won't stretch to handle mobile moments.

Your complex transaction systems aren't designed to deliver simple mobile experiences. These systems were built for employees sitting at desks all day tending complex processes, not for casual customers taking action in seconds on a mobile device over a spotty wireless network. They don't handle the intuitive, task-oriented, contextual requirements of an app used in a mobile moment.

Your technology capacity won't handle the surge in transaction volume. Your systems are designed for a placid and predictable load. Successful mobile applications can drive a tenfold increase in logins and transactions. USAA had to extend and re-extend its capacity because its mobile app generated six times the transactions than the company had expected.[2] Can your systems handle the demands? One banking CIO fears a meltdown in the core transaction systems of the bank should the stock market tank.

Your separate applications will make it hard to deliver new services. For example, if your customer database is disconnected from your inventory and order management systems, you can't customize an offer or a price based on a customer's loyalty and preferences.

Your content systems and processes will hold you back as you stretch them into new engagement scenarios. In the mobile mind shift, people won't wait for your web content to download, and they won't tolerate a clunky content experience.

Your siloed data will fail to address the real-time demands of engagement analytics. In the mobile mind shift, analytics can't be an afterthought—it must be built into the entire system of engagement.

These unintended consequences can sink your mobile moments. The mobile mind shift demands innovation. The complexity of your current business applications and legacy technology architectures won't support that innovation. You need a new technology approach, one designed for mobile moments.

CASE STUDY: Concur Engages Business Travelers on a Cloud Technology Platform

Steve Singh knows about the challenges of building technology platforms for great mobile moments. He learned them honestly by moving his entire company and its customers to a cloud technology platform.

Steve is CEO and co-founder of Concur Technologies. Concur helps businesses and government agencies manage their corporate travel bookings and expenses. Concur's technology platform, which Steve calls the Concur Travel and Expense Cloud, is designed for the demands of mobile moments: It supports applications that make it easy for travelers to focus on a few tasks and complete them quickly. Travel and expense (T&E) software is by its nature complex, but at Concur, the complexity remains behind the scenes in the servers, not in the user interface because busy travelers and business expense managers have no time to puzzle out complexity. To make this work, Concur invests 40% of its research and development budget in the applications and 60% in the cloud technology platform that provides the services.

The success of the strategy and technology platform is reflected in the rapid growth of his company, from a startup in 1993 to more than $540 million in revenues in 2013.

Concur's cloud technology platform delivers four benefits. First, because the Concur software running in the cloud is the same for every customer, developers working on it can fix problems continuously and roll out new services daily. Second, the Concur service is integrated with a wide range and growing list of travel providers such as airlines, hotels, car services, and trains to deliver a complete travel experience. Third, Concur's cloud platform is ready to meet the spikes in demand that happen when weather turns stormy and delays cripple the air travel system. Finally, this modern T&E cloud prepared Concur for the needs of business travelers—the most mobile people on the planet.

Concur layers business traveler and expense management apps on the front end of all that sophisticated cloud technology. Today, Concur's T&E Cloud integrates with dozens of apps, both from Concur itself and from third parties. With all those apps and clients using the T&E Cloud, Concur has access to a lot of data. The company has baked data analytics deeply into its platform and strategy. The travel and expense data spun off the 20 million business travelers it serves gives Concur a powerful analytics engine to help managers optimize expenses and personalize the travel experience across the entire travel ecosystem.

One of the most popular apps that integrates with the T&E cloud is TripIt, a popular mobile-first app that help travelers manage their itinerary on the go, get to the right gate, rebook on alternative flights when faced with a travel delay, and even change their ticket to save money when TripIt alerts them to a cheaper fare. TripIt has almost 10 million users today, and that number continues to grow.

Steve liked TripIt so much that he bought the company. With the T&E Cloud behind TripIt's user base and interface, he knew he could grow and improve the app and its capabilities.

Concur needed both halves of the technology to get things right—sophisticated and complex software and analytics running in the cloud and simple, speedy apps in the palms of a traveler. But it's the T&E Cloud powering the whole system that makes the difference. Great mobile moments can only happen when they're built on a powerful, continually improving platform like this.

The Mobile Mind Shift Demands a New Technology Approach

As Steve Singh and John Mayfield discovered, the technology that companies use now was never engineered to serve customers in their mobile moments. John C. McCarthy, a Forrester analyst who has been studying corporate information systems for more than 25 years, says, "If you want to succeed in mobile, you need to build a whole new digital platform." In the mobile mind shift, you will need a radical overhaul of your entire approach to technology (see Table 10-1).

Both Concur and Nordstrom have learned that mobile requires investments in the systems of engagement that focus on people and their context and tasks, not on internal processes or databases.

The technology platforms for mobile moments are different from the traditional systems of record that companies use to run their businesses. Systems of record, the transaction systems that companies use to manage their back office and core operations like Nordstrom's inventory system or American Airlines' reservation system, were designed to be rock-solid indicators of truth in a business. But these systems—and the business processes they support—are *not* optimized for the speedy, frequent, and granular tasks that people with mobile devices demand.

Table 10-1: The Mobile Mind Shift Will Drive a Radical Change in Your Technology

	In the PC and web eras	In the mobile mind shift
What does the technology do?	Help office employees and committed customers serve themselves on a PC or browser	Proactively serve customers and employees in their immediate context and moments of need
When do you care about technology?	As an afterthought to your business requirements	Throughout a project because technology is a critical enabler and component of the execution
Who is responsible for the technology?	Your IT department	Your technology management organization and employees in business groups
Where does the software run?	On servers and software in your datacenter	Increasingly, as software services on cloud platforms run by other providers

In contrast, mobile apps focus on people, not internal processes. They draw on mobile, social, cloud, and analytics technology to deliver service directly into a customer's context. Google Now can warn that you will miss the train unless you walk a little faster down Park Avenue. That takes technology that can deliver on what a customer expects on his mobile device. And that means a fast response on any mobile device, on any network, in any context.

Elements of Technology Strategy for Mobile Moments

Building a mobile app and grafting it onto your existing transaction systems won't close the engagement gap. To win the mobile moment with its unique requirements, business executives and technology managers must fund, create, and manage a next-generation technology platform to deliver engaging experiences in a mobile moment. Four elements form the foundation of that strategy: 1) master a slew of new engagement technologies; 2) build a cloud-based integration and delivery platform; 3) simplify retrieving data from your existing transaction systems; and 4) implement a comprehensive analytics capability.

New Engagement Technologies

For years, your company has been investing in some of the technologies behind mobile moments, like cloud delivery and mobile apps. Other technologies are brand new. Still others are emerging. They all gain new importance in the mobile mind shift because you must stitch them together to deliver the best service possible in a mobile moment. Here's a list:

- **Devices.** Device sensors and radios generate a deluge of data about what someone is doing. You can know someone's retail location or even what aisle he's standing in, as long as you've earned his trust so he shares that information with you. Bluetooth and Wi-Fi connections make it easy to extend the data a device can gather through wearables or connected products like the Nest Learning Thermostat.

- **Mobile apps.** Mobile apps excel at interactive experiences on devices. With an app, you can offer your customers deeply engaging experiences, even if they are offline away from a wireless network. The million apps in the app store will become 10 million apps as the mobile mind shift really kicks in.

- **Mobile websites.** Mobile web interfaces are a welcome mat for customers visiting from any smartphone or tablet. If you don't know what kind of device someone is using, or if you expect your engagement model to be discovery and occasional use, then a mobile website may be preferable to an app.

- **Content management and delivery systems.** In the mobile mind shift, you will have to optimize content and content delivery to a huge variety of devices and networks. Already around half the traffic to sites like ESPN.com, BBC.com, and NYTimes.com comes from mobile devices and apps of all kinds.[3] You will need a new content system to handle the complexity and more granular view of content components that are assembled on the fly.

- **Social network links.** Real life is social. Mobile moments exist in a social context. A mobile engagement that lacks social sharing is incomplete. For example, TripIt gives you the option to post updates into your Facebook or LinkedIn network, or you can use the app to share travel information with your family, friends, and colleagues directly.

- **Feedback.** You would rather be able to help someone in his moment of need than have him snarl his disappointment in a tweet. For consumers and business customers alike you will need a way to find out what's working and chat with customers who need help. Amazon is a gold standard here with its Mayday video chat in the Kindle Fire tablet.

A Cloud-Based Integration and Delivery Platform

Mastering the technology is not enough. You also need a better way to deliver service. To deliver speedy service over that last "mobile mile" of a wireless network in a system integrated with both internal systems and external partners, you must invest in a new architecture for your mobile platform. That architecture includes these elements:

- **Engagement platform.** The software platform to operate the Web needed three tiers: a browser, application server, and database. Mobile delivery demands a more complex four-tier software architecture that we call an "engagement platform."[4] Forrester analyst, Michael Facemire has this advice for CIOs: "Adopt this new four-tier engagement architecture and hand your business leaders a guarantee that the technology will support the demands of the mobile moment. Reject it and watch your brand fail under the mobile load."

- **Cloud delivery.** You can't deliver a snappy mobile experience if the data sits on a server on your corporate network. The direct Internet connections that cloud providers offer are your best insurance against a bogged-down experience. As a bonus, cloud providers take care of operations and can handle big swings in demand.

- **Third-party services.** You can't possibly host all the software services you need to create a valuable, intuitive mobile experience. You will instead rely on location services, analytics, mapping, and payment services that are easy to link up with. TripIt integrates with more than 2,000 third-party services through its open APIs.

Simplify Your Existing Transaction Systems and Improve Access to the Data

We've described new technologies and architecture—what about the data they connect with? The third component of the mobile technology strategy requires you to simplify your core transaction systems and improve the access to your data. In the airline industry, for example, core transaction systems like reservation systems and loyalty databases are the backbone of the business. They run on mainframe computers that are as risky to touch as the white-hot core of a nuclear reactor. But they also hold the information that travelers need in their mobile moments (see Figure 10-1).

This is why the Engineer phase of the IDEA cycle is so important (and why the cost is so high): These are the systems that make it possible to accomplish something in a mobile moment. And that's expensive; one major consumer brand has asked the board of directors for $150 million to build an "engagement services layer" to support mobile moments. Like that company, you will need to invest in:

- **Atomized processes.** Avon recently wrote off $125 million in a failed implementation of an order management system to support mobile sales.[5] It failed because the sales staff—which, in the case of Avon, are your friends and neighbors—found it too clunky to use on a tablet at the dining room table. One big problem was the mismatch between the complex system of record and the tiny amount of information an Avon sales representative needs in that mobile moment. In the mobile mind shift, companies and the vendors who support them must atomize their complex systems into the bits of data and action that people need in a mobile moment.

- **API management.** It's impossible to extend your mobile engagement with new services unless you create APIs (application programming interfaces) to your back-end systems and put them in a catalogue for developers to use. These APIs provide access to the critical data customers need and let you rapidly assemble new services, offers, or applications without having to rewrite the individual pieces. Randy Tomlin, SVP of AT&T's 26,000 U-verse service reps, exclaims that APIs are "magical" because they make it easy to use the data everywhere.

Figure 10-1: Mobile Moments Require Data from Core Transaction Systems

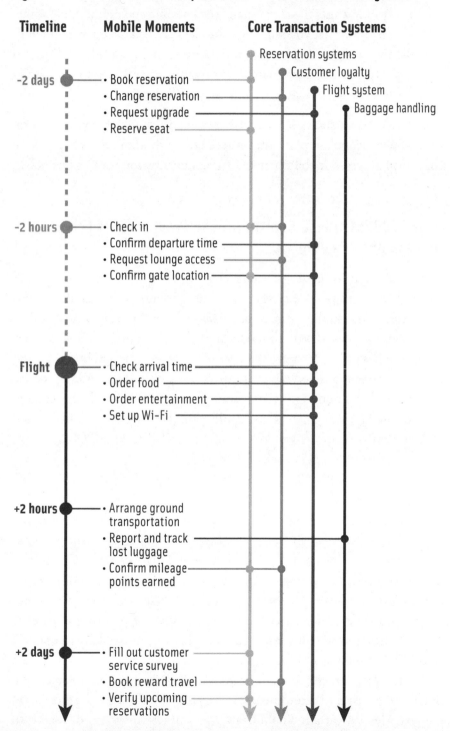

- **Security and privacy.** Privacy is the bugaboo of mobile interactions. Everybody wants the convenience of a mobile app. But nobody wants to feel afraid that you will abuse his data. To establish trust and handle the complex mechanics of data protection, confidentiality, and security, you will need to include a security analyst and privacy advocate on the IDEA team building the application.

Before we introduce you to analytics, the critical fourth component on your mobile technology platform, let's see how one online real estate service company harnessed mobile analytics to significantly improve its business.

CASE STUDY: Chinese Realtor Anjuke Creates More Leads through Better Analytics

Anjuke's 80,000 Chinese real estate agents needed more leads. They don't get paid unless they sell houses or rent apartments, and that starts with leads from interested buyers. Some leads come in by telephone or office visits. But in mobile-crazy China, leads also come in over mobile devices.

Anjuke has offices in more than 30 cities. Leads from mobile apps and sites on smartphones and tablets are a growing part of its selling process. But there weren't enough leads coming in. Before turning the company's 100 mobile developers loose building new features, Anjuke needed to know which features would pay off. It needed to know what, when, where, and why shoppers click or don't click.

That problem fell to Philip Kuai, who runs Anjuke's product and mobile analytics group.

He started with ethnographic research to catalogue how consumers used Anjuke's service. Then he developed a set of hypotheses on what consumers really wanted to do in their mobile moments. For example, did they prefer a tablet or smartphone? App or site? Did they click more often when they were in the neighborhood than on an evening commute? Did they prefer to swipe to see pictures of a listing or click a "next" button? At what times of day were listings most likely to convert to clicks and then to visits?

Philip instrumented the mobile apps and site to see what people were doing and develop a better understanding of their physical and emotional context. He also gathered data from the transaction system of record to improve Anjuke's understanding of conversion rates, from click to lead to sale. Philip's analytics team monitored every feature and button to see where the action is. He worked with the development teams to do A/B testing—testing two versions of the app to see which worked better.

Philip's analytics team learned that location-based search is essential. If a prospective homebuyer is in a neighborhood, he will view at least five properties, far more than if he is on a train. So he improved location search.

The team also found that clicks were 10 times higher on a tablet app than on the tablet website. So it revised the mobile site with an app-like interface for the tablet website. That increased conversion on the tablet site by 200%.

Sometimes you have to be clever to understand what analytics tell you. As Philip told us: "We ran into a problem we couldn't figure out at first. We knew mobile traffic was high in the evenings especially during the evening commute, but our conversions were lower. It didn't make sense." Philips' team dug into the analytics and discovered a simple, but profound insight: There were 20% fewer listings in the evening *and* they were lower quality listings. Why? Because ads that get clicked a lot cost more for the agents. When they hit a daily threshold set by the listing agent, they are automatically taken down. So the most attractive listings were being "turned off" in the evening. Anjuke rebalanced its pricing model to keep higher value listings on the site longer.

Using all this data to revise the application worked out better than even Philip could have expected. In Q2 2013, the combination of mobile phone and tablet traffic was 33% of the total traffic to the service. Six months later, more than 50% of Anjuke's traffic originates on mobile phones and tablets.

Analytics Is the Fourth Component of Your Technology Platform

All of Anjuke's insights came from implementing a comprehensive analytics capability in both the front-end apps and sites and the back-end systems. The data that spins off of a mobile moment—who is doing what from which location for how long—lets you look into the mobile moments and decode the mystery within.

Mobile analytics delivers four benefits. You can use the data you gather in real time to personalize the content you send to an individual or change the next information they see. You can track what's going on with all your customers at that very moment. Your IDEA team can monitor the uptime and performance of the app to intervene when it turns sluggish. And your analytics team can mine the database for new insights, as Anjuke did. These benefits come from implementing two essential technology elements:

- **Data capture.** Start by "instrumenting" the mobile app and technology platform to capture the data you need to know what's going on, from logins and response times on various mobile device types to content and transactions accessed. This "who/what/when/where" data is invaluable for monitoring what's going on in real time and tracking trend lines that will lead you to build better apps or upgrade back-end capabilities. Your application is not ready to deploy until you're ready to capture this operational and engagement data. Established vendors like Adobe, Google, IBM, and startups like Factual and Mixpanel can help here with cloud services.

- **Predictive analytics.** Once you've captured data, you can harness it to improve the mobile moment through better offers, customized interfaces, and smarter design choices about what functionality to expose where. This is where data scientists—people that can unearth the stories buried in data—play a crucial role. At Microsoft's Yammer, professionals skilled at data analysis provide an independent perspective on which mobile app capabilities work best and why. It's too early to prescribe a recipe for success with predictive analytics, but there is enough evidence from companies like Amazon, Google, and Netflix to show that this developing technology will be essential to winning in the mobile moment.

The CIO's New Mandate: Champion the Technology Platform That Supports Mobile

You cannot possibly engage customers in their immediate context in their moments of need without the right technology platform in place. Someone must step up and provide that technology. That person is the business-focused CIO.

A business-focused CIO drives the shift in corporate technology departments away from operating "information technology" to managing "business technology" that helps companies win, serve, and retain customers.[6]

Your technology management organization must assemble the suppliers and technologies you need to support mobile, provide or source the designers and developers to build applications and APIs, and host and operate the system of engagement. We have compiled a short list of things to stop doing and start doing in your technology management organization to be ready for mobile moments (see Table 10-2).

Table 10-2: A CIO's Stop-Start List for the Mobile Mind Shift

Stop doing this	Start doing this	Examples of what to do
Stop counting exclusively on your own servers.	Start looking at cloud or SaaS providers with a deep commitment to your market.	Work with the cloud giants Amazon, Google, IBM, and Microsoft or a smaller cloud vendor.
Stop using waterfall development methods.	Start using agile techniques to build software applications.	Combine business, design, development, and operations people into small teams.
Stop insisting on building everything yourself.	Start looking outside your firm for solutions and best practices.	Work with new mobile engagement providers like Cynergy, Mobiquity, and SapientNitro.
Stop hiring pure IT leaders to run technology teams.	Start hiring business leaders with a passion for technology.	CIOs Diane Bryant at Intel and Rebecca Jacoby at Cisco came from business roles.
Stop investing in web-only architectures.	Start investing in four-tier engagement architectures.	Work more like Netflix, rather than using a closed technology stack like many eCommerce teams.
Stop treating analytics as an afterthought.	Start building data collection—and analysis—into your core engagement process.	Dish Networks uses analytics to look for ways to improve the field service of 11,000 technicians.

The Mobile Technology Platform Shift Requires a Big Budget

Engagement is expensive. That's why your marketing, sales, service, and product teams are funding engagement technology from their own budgets—because the CIO's discretionary budgets are insufficient to expand the firms' technology capability that fast.

How expensive is it to build systems of engagement that support mobile? Morgan Stanley plans a $400 million investment over 10 years. Nike expects to spend as much as $200 million over the same period. We've already mentioned the $300 million that Home Depot is investing. Even a simple booking app can cost a major hotel chain more than $5 million a year, without including the upgrades it needs to back-end systems of record. Add those in, and the cost could easily surpass $7 million in a single year.

As technology budgets go, those are pretty large investments. But a single sales executive can justify spending more than $30 million on mobile engagement because his staff touches customers. Would you have expected your head of sales to request a capital allocation for 16,000 iPads as one global pharmaceutical company recently did? When presented with the cost of provisioning those tablets with regulated content, applications, training, and service, the sales executive didn't balk. He had already spent almost $14 million on devices and data plans. His team carries a $48 billion sales number, so it was an easy decision for him to make to fund another $18 million in applications and support.

Table 10-3: The Cost of Mobile Engagement and Operations for an Employee App

	Cost in thousands of dollars	
	First year	Subsequent years
Supported staff	16,000 sales reps	16,000 sales reps
Tablets	$8,000	$4,000
Content system	$3,480	$3,480
Mobile data plans	$5,760	$5,760
Training and support	$1,920	$1,920
Sales application	$9,600	$9,600
Other business apps	$3,840	$3,840
Total annual cost	$32,600	$28,600

If the payoff of empowering 16,000 sales reps with a tablet app and interactive content fine-tuned for physician engagement is even a 1% increase in sales, that's $480 million in additional revenue for the company. That covers a lot of cost (see Table 10-3).

The point is that while the technology of engagement is expensive and out of the grasp of many CIO budgets, it's small change for a business executive trying to accelerate the company's growth by even 1% or save a percent or two in labor costs. Both of these financial goals are a practical result of the investment in systems that power mobile moments. That's why it's important for business people and technology people to work together on the IDEA cycle. (We'll describe how the IDEA team works to generate these results in chapter 12.)

· · · · · · · · ·

Because technology is embedded in your mobile engagement strategy and execution, it's the single most complex and transformational element of your systems shift. But it's not the only thing you'll have to overhaul to serve customers in the mobile mind shift. You will also need to engineer your business processes and the way your employees work, particularly those that directly touch customers. We'll look at that next in chapter 11.

11

· · · · · · · ·

The Process Shift
Transform Business Processes through Mobile Moments

Start with 11,000 field technicians. Give them a smartphone and a beautiful app. Will you improve your service?

Not if you still run your dispatch and service processes on paper work orders.

You need to redesign your business processes if you want mobile devices to make them more valuable. That's what Erik Carlson was determined to do.

Erik is executive vice president in charge of operations at Dish Network, a satellite TV operator serving 14.1 million subscribers across America. Field technicians are Dish's primary customer touch point. If a service engagement goes well, Dish looks good. And if it goes poorly—well, customers have long memories and plenty of neighbors to influence.

When Erik was asked to lead the field service organization, Dish was, as he puts it, "working with rocks and chisels," running the field service operation on paper and manual processes. Erik had little visibility into what was going on in the field. Every day, 11,000 field technicians would pick up a truck and paper work orders, then pull out the map book and get started. Once in the truck, the field tech was hard to reach. And if she faced a problem, she was on her own. The result? Too many disappointed customers and too much overtime pay.

Erik needed a better way.

One day in 2008, Erik ran into Mike McClaskey, Dish Network's CIO, and a water cooler conversation turned into a "we invented fire" moment. They resolved to rethink Dish's entire approach to field service, empowering field technicians with a mobile device so they could complete the service efficiently on the first customer visit.

Mike and Erik started by installing push-to-talk phones, GPS location trackers, and ruggedized laptops with wireless Internet access cards into every truck. Their goal was to put all the information a field technician needs—customer information, installation details, and service transactions—into the tech's hands on the job. They were off and running.

But after a few years, the implementation ran into snags. Why? Because laptops aren't really mobile devices, they're portable computers. Technicians left the laptops in the trucks where they did nothing to improve the interactions with customers. There were no mobile moments.

Four years later, they found a better solution in the Samsung Galaxy Note, a smartphone with a screen big enough to show all the information a field tech needs but small enough to fit into a uniform pocket. They also implemented a new dispatch and service system from a cloud platform vendor called TOA Technologies. Because TOA's technology platform ran in the cloud, it was relatively easy to connect to the new Samsung phones, and Mike could deploy and secure it over AT&T or Verizon's networks.

Technicians with these new phones transformed field processes, surpassing all expectations. With the upgraded system and the new mobile devices, Erik and Mike improved productivity—the number of visits per day—by 10%. And they did it with 15% less overtime cost. They replaced three devices and a $2,500 toolkit with a single $200 Android phone. They also eliminated 5% in fuel costs through TOA's intelligent route planning. Because technicians could do more on their own with the information right there on their smartphones, there were fewer calls to the office and Dish was able to cut the back-office field service staff by two-thirds. And best of all, they significantly upgraded the one personal experience that customers have with Dish: the home visit.

Better service is great. But sales are even better. Erik's empowered team of field technicians now sells new services while on the job—hanging a TV on the wall, fixing a Wi-Fi problem, or installing a new speaker system, for example.

How did Dish Network achieve all these benefits—higher productivity, lower cost of operations, better customer engagement, and service upsell opportunities? By redesigning its field service process around more productive mobile moments.

How the IDEA Cycle Applies to Business Processes

Although Erik and Mike wouldn't have described it that way, they were using the IDEA cycle to progressively improve Dish Network's field service. In doing so, they found a new way to accelerate and improve complex processes. They didn't just automate the old process. They redesigned the process to take advantage of mobile technology and systems. The secret? Using mobile moments to simplify tasks dramatically (see Figure 11-1).

Companies will spend $189 billion over the next seven years to redesign business processes for the mobile mind shift.[1] Any time an employee engages a customer, she is fulfilling a step in some business process: retail checkout, business sales meeting, store inspection, field service event, and so on. These employees are part of the mobile mind shift. They are ready to act in their moments of need at work, too. You just need to support them with the right platforms and processes. Just as mobile customer applications can make customers happier and more loyal, mobile employee applications can make workers and processes more effective and efficient. And as we saw with Dish, more effective and efficient processes usually lead not just to cost savings, but also to better customer experiences. For Dish, this meant a steady and impressive rise to the top of the TV service provider category in the Forrester Customer Experience Index, with scores increasing from 56 in 2010 to 74 in 2014.[2]

In previous chapters, we've concentrated on how to use the IDEA cycle with customers and your workforce. We've talked about identifying mobile moments, designing mobile engagement, engineering new mobile solutions, and analyzing results—and how to repeat the cycle for a steady stream of improvements.

The process is similar when redesigning processes. Here's what the four steps look like for a process application.

Figure 11-1: Plotting Mobile Moments for a Dish Network Field Technician

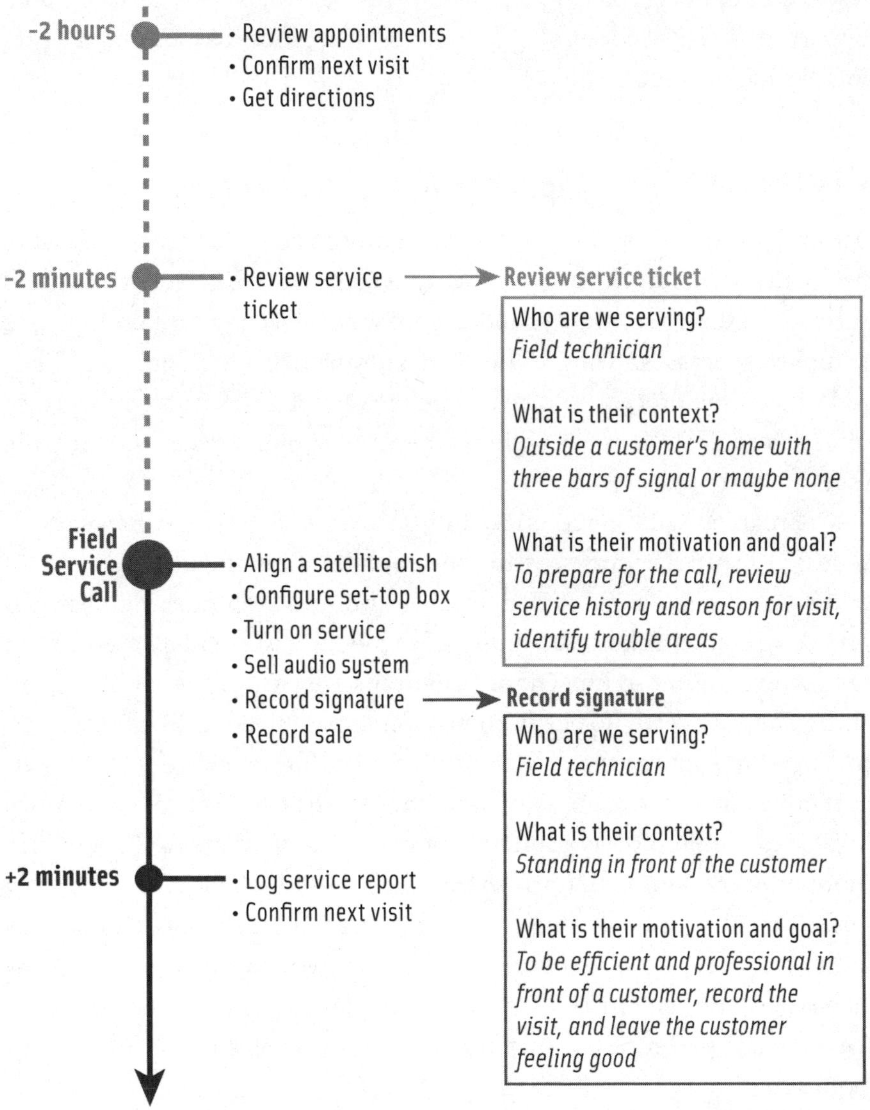

-2 hours
- Review appointments
- Confirm next visit
- Get directions

-2 minutes
- Review service ticket → Review service ticket

Who are we serving?
Field technician

What is their context?
Outside a customer's home with three bars of signal or maybe none

What is their motivation and goal?
To prepare for the call, review service history and reason for visit, identify trouble areas

Field Service Call
- Align a satellite dish
- Configure set-top box
- Turn on service
- Sell audio system
- Record signature → Record signature
- Record sale

Who are we serving?
Field technician

What is their context?
Standing in front of the customer

What is their motivation and goal?
To be efficient and professional in front of a customer, record the visit, and leave the customer feeling good

+2 minutes
- Log service report
- Confirm next visit

1. **Identify the mobile moments embedded in each process.**
   Reconceive the entire process. Throw out the old notions of how the process works. Think outside-in. Any time an employee could pull out a mobile device to take action or act with confidence is an opportunity for a mobile moment. Just as with customer apps, knowing the physical and situational context of the moment will

help you simplify and accelerate the task and thereby transform the process.

2. **Design the mobile engagement to improve each task.** What can an employee accomplish in the mobile moment? What actions or information would empower an employee to take action? Just as with customer apps, an employee needs just the right information and functionality to take the next step.

3. **Engineer your systems to take action in each mobile moment.** Just as with customer apps, you need to align your back-office processes and technology platforms to serve the mobile moment. You will have to "atomize" your business process: break it up into discrete components that accomplish a single goal with the fewest clicks.[3]

4. **Analyze data in real time to make it immediately useful.** With a customer app, you need real-time data so you can customize an offer or deliver a better experience. For employee apps, real-time data makes it possible to give managers a data dashboard showing the current situation with employees and their work. If trouble is brewing, a manager can intervene in just that place.

In the rest of this chapter, we'll show how the steps in the IDEA cycle work in the context of corporate processes like sales, inspections, and field service.

Identify the Mobile Moments Embedded in Each Process

Erik and Mike at Dish Network started with the tasks a technician does every day and worked backward. What does a technician need after pulling up at a house? Or while up on the roof? Or with a customer? Erik, Mike, and their teams rode around with field technicians and climbed up on rooftops to find the moments of engagement that make or break customer visits.

They looked for ways to inject digital intelligence into every physical task. As a result of the insights they gleaned by analyzing their technicians' processes, they made it possible for technicians to get the customer to sign for completed work, right on the screen of the smartphone. Technicians can pull up an arcane configuration sequence for a new set-top box or point the phone at the sky to line up the dish antenna with a satellite. They can even use Google Translate to communicate in a foreign language if needed. Erik and Mike went further to ask what steps in the process they could eliminate. If a technician can now complete a task in the field, what other steps—or people—does that make redundant?

You can do the same thing. Bring your mobile process IDEA team together to explore the universe of possible moments by looking at the tasks on a process timeline: before, during, and after the service. Be sure to include representatives of your own equivalent of a field technician as well as your technical, business, and design staff. Answer three questions to make sure you've considered all possible mobile moments:

1. **Where can we simplify a task by eliminating manual steps?** Dish field technicians can capture and log a customer approval signature on their Samsung devices, so they don't have to file paperwork in the evening and Dish can turn on the service immediately. Any time someone has to pass a piece of paper to someone else or sit down at a computer to enter information is a potential mobile moment. For example, Trax, an audit and shelf monitoring solution, enables CPG sales employees to check compliance and report non-adherence from the aisle of a grocery store with one click. The employees can prepare and follow up immediately on a mobile device rather than in a manual step on a computer that evening.

2. **Where can we streamline a process by completing a task in a mobile moment?** A Dish Network technician can align a dish antenna with a satellite by using the DishPointer virtual reality app, even with the wrench still in hand. That can save a trip back to the truck to pull out the field manual. The technician can also pull up the information to deal with a complex configuration right from the basement control panel. These resources help complete an installation on the first visit. Similarly, a technician working atop a GE wind turbine tower can use video chat to show an engineer back at the shop the problem, often eliminating the need to traipse 350 ladder rungs back down to the truck.

3. **Where can we improve the engagement quality when employees serve customers?** Using mobile devices and apps, Erik Carlson at Dish empowers field technicians to sell service improvements

on the spot, generating not just sales but also happier customers. Banner Engineering has done the same thing for its distributors' sales teams. With an iPad full of product information, a sales rep can immediately answer a customer's questions about how a new sensor will work on the manufacturing line. Giving employees the information they need to solve a customer's problem directly improves the quality of the engagement.

Design the Mobile Engagement to Improve Each Task

Once you've identified mobile moments, you need to design the engagement to help an employee accomplish a task immediately in the context of that moment. Dish accomplished this by working closely with TOA Technologies, its field service management technology platform supplier. Together, they pared back the information and action buttons they put on every screen to make it as simple and intuitive as possible. Mike's goal was never to have to train a technician how to use the app.

He knew that technicians would leave the mobile device in the truck unless it fit in their pocket and was immediately useful. A useful application is designed to:

- **Take one action at a time.** This sounds simple, but what separates the efficiency of a mobile moment from the complexity of a typical process application is that with a mobile device, you can predict what an employee needs to do in that moment—capture a signature, aim a satellite dish antenna, or log a service update. Cynergy, for example, relentlessly refined tasks for an app it created for a major wireless company, making it drop-dead simple for a busy retail store associate to learn about a new service offering or see where she stands against her monthly quota.

- **Use context to eliminate keystrokes.** Because the app knows which customer a sales rep is visiting, it can automatically pull up the correct sales history. That's an example of using *customer context* to eliminate keystrokes. You can also use *physical context* to simplify an app. Using the GPS in a tablet, GE's wind turbine maintenance app knows which of the 200 turbines in the field a technician is standing next to. It uses the location information to pull up the right maintenance history. Use all the contextual information you have, but particularly the physical location and transaction history, to pull up the right information automatically.

• **Relentlessly improve the task experience.** Just because you've built the app doesn't mean that you've greatly improved the process or task completion rate. Even small changes can make or break a mobile moment. At one pharmaceutical company, for example, sales reps were uncomfortable at first pulling out the iPad to show a physician the clinical results because they found it hard to find the right material. When the IDEA team moved all clinical results to a single place in the app, the problem vanished.

Engineer Your Platform to Serve Up One Task at a Time

We told you about systems of engagement in chapter 10. We're now going to describe how this technology platform helps you transform your business processes by serving up one task at a time.

Here's your challenge. If you work at a large company, you've probably got tens of thousands of employees who want access to your data systems to participate in the processes that make up their jobs. Consider the challenge of building the technology platform to support 11,000 field technicians at Dish Network or 19,000 flight attendants at Delta Air Lines.

Over the past 40 years, companies have spent trillions of dollars building complex applications for employees sitting in front of a computer. These applications are not designed for mobile. They're too complex. Employees on the go need just enough information and a single action button to complete the task, not complex screens and onerous data entry.[4] They've been trained by the five-star consumer apps that they use at home.

You will have to re-engineer the APIs to your core data systems to serve up just the right amount of data and action for each mobile moment. You need cloud platforms to serve information to a variety of devices faster, and you must also re-engineer the way the systems work together. If you just shrink down the web interface to tiny dimensions, you'll find the software can't deal with the demands of the mobile moment.

Let's take a look another field service example, because it is rich with insight into how to engineer the processes and platform for mobile moments.

Randy Tomlin, senior vice president of field operations for AT&T's TV, phone, and Internet service called U-verse, had to engineer an entirely different technology platform to help his 21,000 field technicians hit a two-hour time window for each customer visit.

Six years ago, Randy set out to revamp the technician-customer engagement to install broadband and television services. He wanted U-verse to "have the right moment with the right technician for every one of our 10 million customers." He knew that giving tablets to technicians was key to that mission. "We had to make it easy for a technician to initiate a step and have it cascade through six or eight back-end systems before coming back with a single answer."

The problem was those "six or eight back-end systems." That software wasn't designed to serve up tasks in a mobile moment. When he realized that software was the critical component of hitting the two-hour window, Randy decided that he had to become a technology guy. (Only a technology guy says things like, "we do all our testing in the cloud" and "I love APIs" and "innovation is now an ecosystem.") So he made friends with the technology department.

Randy and his new friends in the technology department broke the service process down into discrete tasks then stitched together what a tech needed in each mobile moment using new APIs: 23 of them for field technicians and three more for managers.

They also instrumented the entire process to collect data and gave field managers a data dashboard on an iPad with real-time status updates.

The results were phenomenal. U-verse now hits that two hour window so often that field service is a major contributor to AT&T's success in television. U-verse TV was ranked highest in overall satisfaction in the North Central region where it operates, according to the J.D. Power 2013 US Residential Television Service Provider Satisfaction Study.[5] And it has gained so much efficiency that it can now make one additional service call every day. That means Randy can serve 15,000 *more customers every day*. Not only that, by giving local managers tablets with real-time visibility into what's going on in the field, Randy's managers are saving *90 minutes per day* in manual tasks.

What should you take away from AT&T U-verse's engineering success with field service?

First, know that this is hard. Randy says that he is the North Star to keep everybody on track. Randy got support to upgrade the back-end systems to support the mobile apps from the very top of the organization.

Second, "atomize" your business processes into the discrete tasks. Don't let back-end complexity sap the life from your mobile employees. Simplify things by serving up just the information and actions they need in each moment.[6] Under the relentless redesign of mobile moments, processes become tasks (see Table 11-1).

Lastly, build software APIs that expose just what's needed in that moment. Each API handles a tiny slice of the process and handles it robustly over wireless networks.

Table 11-1: How Mobile Moments Turn Processes into Tasks

	Processes on a PC	Tasks on a mobile device
Assumption	An employee has minutes or hours to sit down and focus on the application.	An employee has a few seconds to accomplish a task on the go and move on.
Design goal	Give an employee a comprehensive application and train her to use it.	Help an employee complete a single task as efficiently as possible with no training whatsoever.
Device	Desktop or laptop computer with a dedicated application using a keyboard and mouse	Mobile device, often a small tablet or a large smartphone, with a touchscreen interface
Key challenge	Knit together multiple systems to cover a complete process in a comprehensive application.	Expose the tasks in discrete APIs that can be stitched together to serve a worker's immediate context.
Key technology	Business process management (BPM) and middleware	BPM and middleware plus APIs and analytics

Analyze Data in Real Time to Make It Immediately Useful

Here's how AT&T's Randy Tomlin describes the visibility that comes from his mobile-enabled workforce and how he can see problems developing as people go about their workday: "Of the 26,283 things happening that day across the nation, you can see the 200 hot spots where trouble is brewing.

And as a manager, you can stop worrying about things because you can see trouble before it starts. That's a great improvement over the old technique of moving colored pins on a bulletin board back in each local dispatch center."

A business that works in real-time solves problems faster because managers can fix a problem as they see it forming on the horizon. When your employees are carrying mobile devices from task to task, you gain visibility from three sources of real-time data. First, location: You always know where your people are. Second, transactions: The system records each action; whether it's a Dish Network customer's signature or sales information sent to a Banner Engineering prospect, the system can serve up the next logical action to the employee. And third, usage data: The app records which activities and features are working and getting used and which are wasteful and need to be redesigned or scrapped.

All three sources of data yield immediate benefits if you put them into a data dashboard for your operations managers. But they also are valuable as databases you can mine to optimize a process over time. Dish Network, for example, collects location data to improve its service routes over time. Trane collects content analytics to prioritize its investments in marketing content.

You will have to work your way ever closer to the analytics competency that AT&T and Dish Network have achieved. If your sales force is skittish about being watched from afar, then you can't light up the analytics on where they are and what content they are showing a customer on day one. You'll have to slowly earn their trust that you are collecting data to make things better for them. That's how things worked at Delta Air Lines, where flight attendants now have new tools to serve travelers in their mobile moments.

CASE STUDY: Making Delta Flight Attendants As Empowered As Their Customers

Like the other airlines we've described in this book, Delta decided to begin its mobile transformation with the traveler experience. As Bob Kupbens, vice president of marketing and digital commerce at Delta Air Lines, explains, "Now every bit of information available to our employees is also available to our customers in real time. You can confirm that your bag made it onto the plane. Or what carousel to find it on at your destination." To do this, Delta has opened up its transaction systems to its travelers. Today 90% of Delta customers traveling locally check in digitally, and nearly 20% check in on a mobile device.

Customer mobile applications have a curious side effect. Delta's customers are now smarter and in a better position to travel successfully. That puts new demands on customer-facing employees. So Delta expanded its mobile strategy to empower its highly mobile workforce. Delta gives baggage handlers a mobile scanner to track bags as they go up the belt into the belly of the plane. Its pilots carry a lightweight Microsoft Surface tablet with the operating manuals and flight paperwork that they formerly lugged around in 40-pound leather flight bags.

And in July 2013, Delta Air Lines gave 19,000 flight attendants Nokia smartphones. These devices help flight attendants serve 160 million travelers annually in the air and work more efficiently. With mobile technology, a Delta flight attendant can better engage an anxious traveler with information that eases her anxiety or solves a problem.

With the help of Avanade and AT&T, Delta is building three kinds of mobile apps to improve the everyday process of being an employee in the sky. First, the smartphone replaces the on-aircraft payment systems. Flight attendants use a familiar device and interface to take a passenger's credit card to pay for a beverage or a meal or an in-flight product.

Second, flight attendants get the same apps that travelers can get on their mobile device, enhanced with information for all connecting flights. This enables flight attendants to serve customers instantly with the same systems that power the customer apps.

Third, Delta has made common employee services available on the smartphone. This saves a flight attendant time. They can pull up shift information or ask another flight attendant for a swap wherever they are, including at 35,000 feet using the airplane's Wi-Fi.

There is a higher-order benefit to all these mobile applications: *A mobile device is a platform for service innovation.* Delta's advertising tag line is "Keep Climbing." It aims to deliver a quality travel experience to every traveler. So Delta plans to build more apps. For example, it might be able to marry the passenger manifest with the loyalty system, so a flight attendant could offer a personalized service, from a quick "Thank you, Mr.

Schadler, for flying Delta," to "I see you travel with us frequently. Can I offer you a better seat or a complimentary beverage as a thank you for your loyalty?" Once it's all on a mobile device, higher levels of service become available in the palm of the flight attendant's hand.

Here's what Delta has really learned: One of the most powerful forces at work is the force of customer expectations. Once a customer's expectations are raised, the entire company must respond. Once Delta began investing in mobile customer apps, mobile employee apps became the next logical step.

Use Mobile Moments to Transform *All* Your Business Processes

Mobile enablement is not just about customer-facing processes.

From how we've described the changes at Delta, Dish, and AT&T, you might think employees that interact with customers are the main beneficiaries of mobile engagement. They are. But it doesn't have to stop there.

Any place an employee works away from a computer is a place where a mobile moment can transform a task. Let's look at four short examples to give you a sense of the range and comprehensiveness of mobile moments at work: training employees at restaurant chain Red Robin, capturing photographs of problems at Cisco Systems, handling in-store stocking and sales globally at Mondelēz International, and making chocolate at Tcho Ventures.

Red Robin Turns Tablets into a "Yummm University" To Train Employees

Red Robin Gourmet Burgers sold more than 16 million pounds of beef to 81.5 million guests in 2012. Running a restaurant efficiently at that scale means building systems that work well in every restaurant and for every employee. When Red Robin rolls out a new recipe or drink to 30,000 employees, it must make sure the new recipe tastes great in every restaurant.

Red Robin needs to train 500 new employees every week, and most of them are better acquainted with YouTube, Facebook, and iPhones than classrooms and manuals. To meet that challenge, Chris Laping, CIO and SVP of business transformation, needed a better training process, one that would appeal to younger employees used to learning on the fly.

For Chris, this felt like an opportunity made for tablets. On a tablet, Chris can serve up training materials and make learning a social and video-rich experience. He called the solution Yummm U. Using the Yummm U app, employees can learn in their downtime or when coming on board. They pull up videos that teach new techniques, interact with games and simulations, take quizzes to record progress, and ask questions of experts back at headquarters.

The tablet app helps new employees come quickly up to speed, and it gives veterans a quick way to learn a new process or technique. The program has been a huge success. Since launching the program, Red Robin has reduced turnover in the first critical month by 10%. But Chris isn't done yet. He just christened a program to encourage employees to make videos of their best ideas. His operations team will share the best videos with everybody and, in some cases, invite an employee to reshoot a video professionally to make it part of the training program.

Cisco Captures Photographic Evidence of Incidents and Facilities Problems with Smartphones

Cisco Systems has a large team of people dedicated to the physical security of its more than 75,000 employees and 23 million square feet of facilities. That's as much space as a small city, and Roger Biscay has to keep track of it all. Roger is not your typical facilities and security executive; he is Cisco's vice president, treasurer and global risk management, a former banker, and the executive responsible for Cisco's $47 billion in cash. In addition to taking care of all that cash, Roger also runs a very efficient global safety, security, and business resiliency operation helping protect Cisco's physical assets and 489 facilities worldwide.

One of the keys to that efficient operation is capturing pictures of incidents including attempted break-ins, vandalism, and other physical damage. Roger's global security team not only needs to take photos, it needs a secure place to store them where they will stand up to the scrutiny of a legal or insurance challenge.

The staffers on Roger's security team register their smartphones, then take photographs of problems with a certified mobile app from a vendor called EvidencePix. The app automatically uploads the photos with the right location data, time, and device information to EvidencePix's secure cloud. Once there, the photos remain in a tamperproof digital lock box until they are needed to file an insurance claim or address a legal challenge. Roger's security team also uses the photo process to trigger a maintenance repair or even an escalation to Cisco's physical security force that handles building security.

Thanks to the app and the system behind it, what was once an ad hoc part of the security and facilities job is now a structured, policy-driven activity.

Mondelēz International Empowers Sales Teams Globally with Tablets

How do you grow faster if you sell Oreo cookies, Cadbury chocolate, and 50 other snack food brands in 165 countries?[7] How do you empower 45,000 people in your global sales force to sell efficiently into hundreds of thousands of individual retail outlets?

If you're Mondelēz International, the global snacks company formerly known as Kraft Foods, you replace a thousand separate sales operations with a single global sales process.

That's the challenge Mondelēz International's CIO, Mark Dajani, and his team are tackling. They have to figure out a way to put just the right information into the hands of sales reps at the mobile moment when they talk to the owner of a small retailer: what products, what sales history, what promotions, and so on. A tablet or smartphone with the right sales data and content is key to the solution.

Mark faces a challenge that AT&T and Dish Network don't: He needs a solution that works on any smartphone or tablet in any country globally. He can't buy every employee the same mobile device. And it has to run on any network: slow, fast, or missing. Mark has chosen to use cloud platforms for sales, email, content delivery, and analytics apps that work on every carrier's network in every country in which Mondelēz International does business. The core application is designed to support the key steps in a sales call performed by a rep in the field as she visits a retailer.

Mondelēz International is still early in this global sales process transformation, but it has seen early success in markets as diverse as Indonesia,

France, the United States, and Australia. For the first time, the company can set goals for each individual store and measure progress against those goals. By injecting the right information directly into mobile moments in the selling process, it can scale up the success it has with a few large retailers to every individual retailer.

With mobile devices and a technology platform in place, Mondelēz International can add training services, more analytics, catalogues of point-of-sale display units, and much more. As Mark says, "we are build-ing a platform that takes work to where our people are every day. We are just getting started with this transformation."

Tcho Uses Mobile Moments to Improve Chocolate Quality from Farm to Factory

Tcho Ventures makes chocolate. Not just any chocolate. Heavenly choco-late for cooks and connoisseurs. From its perch on San Francisco's Pier 17, around the corner from Fisherman's Wharf, Tcho relentlessly improves the process for making chocolate, from growing and harvesting to produc-ing and distributing, to create the most delicious and socially responsible chocolate possible. It had better. The competition for heavenly chocolate is unrelenting.

Chocolate maker Brad Kintzer uses mobile moments to improve the quality of Tcho's chocolate, from farmer's field to factory floor.

He improves chocolate at its source—on the trees in Ecuador, Peru, the Dominican Republic, and Ghana—by helping farmers build a tiny laboratory from readily accessible parts: a turkey roaster, a counter-top coffee grinder, and thermometers. He and other Tcho chocolate makers then train farmers using Skype on a mobile device how to taste and test the quality of the cacao beans as they ferment and dry. Brad explains that "direct connectivity saves us a lot of time—the more we can articulate what we are looking for, the easier it is for us to purchase the right crop."

An essential element of the process is a cloud-hosted evaluation service from a company called Cropster designed to run on mobile devices. This ser-vice gives farmers in their home countries, like Peru, and Brad's team in San Francisco a way to work together, simultaneously monitoring fermentation parameters (during the process that turns raw beans into chocolaty flavor morsels) and tasting a particular cacao batch so the farmers learn to judge the right blend of chocolaty, fruity, citrus, acidic, and bitter characteristics.

Farmers using Tcho's test lab program have improved their growing and fermenting process so much that they beat out 125 Peruvian growers to earn the top five awards for chocolate quality in 2012.[8]

Brad loves mobile moments for a second reason: His chocolate makers can keep a watch over a 20-hour production process on their iPhones. Tcho employees can use an iPhone to control the company's lab with a remote monitoring and control application. The company connected thermometers to its chocolate grinders and added video cameras so chocolate makers can see what's happening in the lab. No longer does a chocolate maker have to drag herself into the factory at 2 a.m. just to check the viscosity of the chocolate slurry. Instead, she can roll over and in a mobile moment make a small adjustment based on the data collected over the past few hours. This data also enables Tcho to analyze and optimize the production process.

In this way, mobile devices bring information and control to where workers are: In the field, at the fermentation pavilion, in the lab, on the production floor, or home in bed. The result is better chocolate through better processes delivered in mobile moments.

Use Mobile Moments to Transform Business Processes

All the companies in this chapter have invested in mobile devices to improve how an employee works and how they work with customers. There is a lot of operational science behind process redesign, and you can work with your process transformation team or pay consultants a lot of money to help you design efficient processes.[9] But before taking on that huge expense, you can get started simply by using the IDEA cycle and focusing on mobile moments. Keep four things in mind as you traverse the universe of possible apps you could build for employees executing the processes of the firm:

1. **Start with mobile moments: Where can you take direct action?** Business management author Michael Hammer famously decried: "Don't automate, obliterate."[10] He was thinking of how software systems could improve back-office processes. As we saw

with Dish Network's satellite alignment and digital signature apps, an employee can take direct action on a mobile device. The hard work is identifying where a mobile device can help someone cut out steps and take immediate action. That's why ride-alongs, persona development, and closely observing people at work are so important.

2. **Consider the impact on your employees: Will they use the application?** You can't foist a crappy app on an employee and expect her to use it. So spend the time and money to design an app that completes the task in the simplest way possible. Use the mobile context to put the right data on the screen with no typing. If you use the device's location to accomplish that, employees will embrace your apps rather than resisting.

3. **Consider your technology platforms: Can they serve up discrete tasks?** Most systems are too complex for a mobile moment. We predict that as companies resurface transaction systems and implement new systems of record to drive them, corporate systems will undergo the biggest technology refresh in history. We will collectively spend $1.3 trillion, more than a third of the total technology economy in 2017, on mobile technology and systems.[11]

4. **Instrument the app for real-time visibility: What data do you need?** Collect and store more data than you think you will need just to get in the habit of analytics thinking. Once you develop the muscles for data analysis, you won't stop until you have a full dashboard with visibility into the current status and a dedicated team of data scientists to find patterns in the history that translate into efficiency (like route planning) or insight (as in knowing what kinds of field technicians sell the most services in the home).

. . . .

Platforms and processes are just two parts of your engineering effort. The last major change you must navigate to win the mobile moment is how you build mobile apps and sites. In chapter 12, we will show you how major companies like ING Bank use agile development techniques and organize and manage people to build and continuously improve mobile apps and sites.

12

. . . .

The People Shift

Engineer Mobile Moments with an IDEA Team

Max Mouwen has learned that the mobile mind shift is inexorable. His customers at ING Bank in the Netherlands expect more every single month. When Apple introduces a new iPhone or upgrades the look and feel of its operating system, customers expect that his mobile banking app will take advantage of the new features immediately. If a competitor lets people deposit a check by taking a picture of it, his customers wonder when they can do that, too.

It takes a relentlessly productive team to keep ahead of customers' expectations. It takes teams using an agile development process to continuously build, test, and deploy new capabilities.[1]

Agile development has transformed how Max's team builds applications for its banking customers. Max Mouwen has been the director of online banking at ING since 2011. In that time, the functionality of ING's consumer banking app has grown, from showing balances to making payments to tracking savings to viewing credit card transactions. In more than 5,000 ratings in the Apple App Store, the app has consistently averaged 4 or 4.5 stars. Max credits that success to the agile approach his team uses to make constant improvements.

Here's how the agile process works for ING's mobile app.

At ING, the agile team of twelve people building the mobile app is made up of developers, designers, and business people *working continuously together*. This close working relationship keeps the technology people highly aware of the business goals—in this case, to build banking services that keep customers coming back frequently on their mobile phones. It also keeps the business people in touch with the cost and complexity of designing and developing a mobile app with direct links to the bank's data and transaction systems. The combination of business and technology skills keeps the team focused and aligned.

ING's agile teams are supported by a steering committee of eBusiness, marketing, and technology directors that meets monthly. The mobile steering committee prioritizes the long and growing backlog of requests coming from every part of the bank, always focusing on banking services over marketing. The success of this strategy is reflected in two key metrics that ING has built into the application and process: 1) Mobile banking customers log into their accounts six times a week, three times as often as ING's web banking customers; and 2) those customers consistently rank ING higher than other customers do on Net Promoter Score.

Armed with a long list of prioritized requests, the agile team then breaks them down into sets of features they can develop and test in three-week time slices called "sprints." At the start of each sprint, the technology, design, and business people on the agile team, together, select just the features they can design, build, and test in three weeks. Before the team releases those features to customers, they get other employees to test the features. The big payoff of three-week time slices is that the team can rapidly deploy and *learn*. The team can minimize the time they spend building a feature that nobody likes. The mistakes are small and get fixed immediately; the successes are quickly noted and the team builds upon them.

Sometimes the team can't fully develop a feature in a few weeks. If the feature requires extensive changes to link into a back-end transaction system, the business people on the team understand that and are ready to scale back or reprioritize features while developers continue work on the back-end changes needed for the next round of improvements. Some things just take more time; that is a fact of life that the business people on the agile team understand and support.

Finally, the team knows that the mobile app is only part of the engagement. To help a customer take action in his mobile moments, the bank must also engineer its *processes* for things like changing an address or processing a credit request. Like the technical teams, the customer process teams have adopted the agile playbook and are changing processes in three-week bursts. As Max explains, "We now use *business sprints* to quickly improve our customer processes." As a result, the mobile team and the business process team can coordinate their releases so the process is ready to go when customers first experience the moment. This is where the magic happens: technology people, designers, and business people come together to deliver a great service in a mobile moment.

Organize for Continuous Improvement

Just like Max, you're going to find that the mobile mind shift forces you to focus on relentlessly improving your app. Customers are constantly discovering new and valuable things to do on their mobile devices. They expand their mobile moments and expectations every time they notice a new app from an entrepreneur or new capabilities from Apple, Google, Microsoft, or device makers. What delighted your customers a few months ago becomes table stakes today and will be humdrum next year. You must deliver something quickly if you want to be there in your customers' mobile moments. But you must *also* continuously improve it with new capabilities based on new insight. That's the key to the IDEA cycle: a commitment to continuous improvement.

Jeffrey S. Hammond, a Forrester analyst who has been studying or practicing software development for more than 20 years, says, "Development velocity is the key to success. That's why successful mobile teams use development sprints, continuous delivery, and fast feedback via analytics to give customers what they want, as fast as they possibly can."

The organizational unit that delivers this continuous improvement is an agile team of design, technology, and business people that develop apps together. There is not a single consistent way that companies organize to support their agile teams. But companies as diverse as ING Bank, InterContinental Hotels Group (IHG), Starbucks, Dish Network, and American Airlines all organize their people for mobile moments around three elements: IDEA teams, agile development methods, and a mobile steering committee (see Figure 12-1).

Figure 12-1: Setting Up Your Mobile Organization

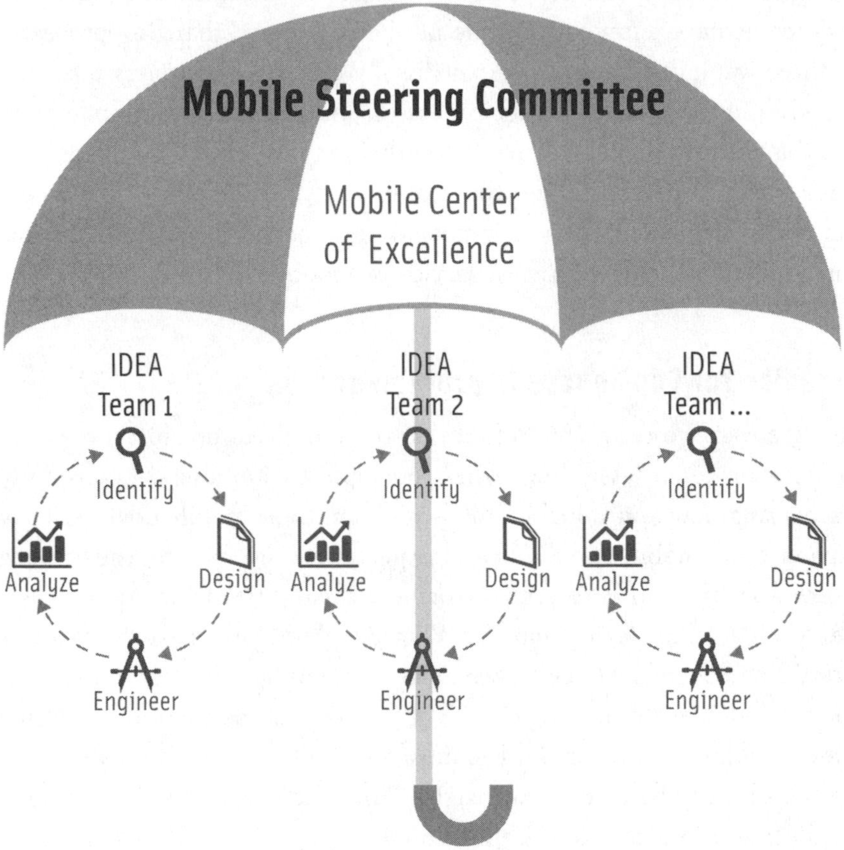

The basic development unit is the *IDEA team* comprised of people from technology, design, business, and, sometimes, from partners helping with technology or with business elements. The core of the team is typically dedicated to a single mobile application for a year or more, though some people may be part time or come in for a quick contribution. Some IDEA teams have only five people, while some have 20; it depends on the scope of the effort. Team members report to their functional managers but have dotted-line responsibility to the product owner. Many companies start with a single agile team focused on a mobile app and then find the organizational model so successful that they expand to other initiatives. ING Bank, for example, has 170 agile teams working across the company on different technology projects.

This team uses an *agile development process* to release new software every few weeks. Every successful mobile app we've encountered is built by a multidisciplinary team using agile development and delivery techniques. This process allows the team to develop, test, assess, and extend features continuously. (Developers call this continuous delivery.)[2] It also helps a company avoid a big mistake, which is to spend too much time and money on a feature that nobody uses but that some manager has staked his career on.

Because agile development is so important, we include it explicitly in our description of the IDEA cycle. To deliver great mobile moments that get better over time, you will use the agile technique to develop software and engineer your business operations, just as ING does.

The management decisions come from a *mobile steering committee* and its execution body, a *mobile center of excellence*. Because mobile touches so many lines of business, departments, and technology systems, you will need an executive leadership team to prioritize and coordinate the work across every business function and operation. And if your mobile strategy extends beyond an app or two, you will also need a mobile center of excellence to coordinate the skills, investments, and partnerships your company is developing.

While this may all sound daunting, we'll make it easier: In this chapter, we'll describe the new team, explain how it works, and define the leadership charter for your new mobile center of excellence.

Put an IDEA Team in Charge of the Mobile App

Historically, when businesspeople or marketers created software, they jotted down ideas and pitched them over to their technology department or to technology partners like Accenture, Deloitte Digital, Infosys, SapientNitro, or Razorfish. Or perhaps they slaved away for months working with their technology staff or vendors, meticulously guessing which features will matter and writing them all down. Either way, they then built and launched the application, often to find out they guessed wrong about what was important.

For mobile apps, these approaches simply don't work—they are too slow and inflexible.

What pioneers like ING, Nordstrom, and Starbucks have learned (and what every mobile entrepreneur has built into his corporate culture) is that great mobile moments don't happen unless the business employees responsible for the success of the application—product owners—work side-by-side and continuously with both designers and developers. This small group—business people, designers, developers—is the IDEA team.

There are two organizational insights that apply here.

First, designers and developers must work closely together. Dave Wolf, the head of research and development for mobile engagement provider Cynergy (now part of KPMG), describes it this way: "We used to separate designers and developers because they really didn't like each other anyway. But it meant they designed things that we couldn't build or that ran really slowly. One day we made them sit together. It was hard at first, but once they got to know each other and how their brains worked, they started to create beautiful things that work really well."

Designers and developers are two halves of a genius—great mobile moments happen only when you mash a designer's right brain and developer's left brain together. Keeping designers and developers on separate teams leads to apps with a pretty face but no value. You must put designers and developers onto a single team united by the common aspiration and a motivation to build an app that people use again and again in their mobile moments.

And it's not just designers and developers on the team. The second organizational insight is that *product owners* from the business must work closely with designers and developers. To deliver a great mobile experience, you must treat the app or site not as a *project* to be built and left alone, but as a *product* to be designed, built, operated, monitored, enhanced, and built again. This means the team needs a full-time product owner with a business frame of reference, someone who's on the hook for the business outcome. Product owners are the bridge between your customer and the mobile moments you are tackling.[3]

Beyond the business people, designers, and developers, the composition of the team may vary somewhat based on your specific situation. At Starbucks, for example, the cross-functional team includes store operations so that baristas and store managers are prepared for any change to the customer mobile app, plus a liaison from the legal department to make sure the app adheres to the company's customer data protection policies. At Dish Network, the team includes field operation managers responsible for everything from the dispatch process to the uniforms designed to hold the mobile device. At American Airlines, the team includes representatives of the back-end transaction systems, ensuring that a feature like seat selection won't overwhelm the mainframe computer running those systems. But the core of the IDEA team remains the business people, the designers, and the developers.

Because this organizational principle of multidisciplinary teams and agile process is so important, let's hear from another company that's learned how to work collaboratively across functional boundaries: the hospitality company IHG.

CASE STUDY: How IHG's Mobile Team Succeeds with Agile Development

At IHG, the parent company of InterContinental Hotels, Bill Keen's mobile app product team and James Prolizo's design and development team build the hotel's booking app together. They work in the same building. They are motivated and united by a single metric: room nights booked. With this shared goal, the teams collaborate to build a great mobile experience that keeps hotel guests coming back.

Because Bill's and James's groups use an agile development process, they are always learning and adapting to find ways to improve the experience. They work together to generate business ideas and technology ideas for improving the guest experience. Here's how they do it.

Bill Keen, director of mobile solutions, manages a team of eight product managers that focus on the business problem and product. These product managers ultimately decide which features to put on the road map and which to focus on in any given release. Because they work side-by-side with the developers, they understand the challenges and complexities of app development and mobile marketing across multiple platforms. They tailor their expectations and contributions accordingly.

James Prolizo, director of mobile and installed applications delivery, manages a development group of 12 people. His people have particular expertise in mobile app design and development as well as in building APIs that access the key transaction systems, the content system, and public services such as maps or the weather.

These two groups operate together as a single unit, sharing and trading off responsibilities. They meet daily to plan, develop, and test new features. Each accepts responsibility for all aspects of the process, from ideation to deployment. The product managers focus more on the first three steps—ideation, conceptualization, and requirements—but remain involved in design and testing as well. Similarly, designers and developers focus on the last three steps—design, build, and deploy—but are very aware of the goals and mechanisms to improve customer engagement.

The team operates in two-week sprints using agile development techniques. As development director James describes it, "The product managers pick the next features to focus on. We let them know what can be done in the next two-week sprint, and they make the final decision on which ones to do." What makes this system work is that product managers participate in the daily standup meetings in which developers review their progress and discuss solutions. Each group knows the capabilities and limitations of the other. That makes it easier for them to solve problems and improve the mobile app.

Why Agile Development Processes Work Best

What works for ING Bank and IHG will also work for your IDEA teams. By adopting an agile development and business process, you will accomplish four goals.

First, your business and technology teams are united to engage customers in their mobile moments. There is no artificial separation, only unification around a single goal: serve customers. We've seen how IHG does this. At ING Bank, the metrics of success include customer satisfaction, transaction volume, and repeat contacts. At Delta Air Lines, a unifying metric is the number of mobile check-ins.

Second, you will move quickly to find and develop new mobile moments. In the agile process, you build, test, and learn in rapid cycles. That means you can quickly see what's working and what to do next to take advantage of the mobile moment. Charles Teague, the CEO of the company that developed LoseIt!, says, "Let's not pretend we know the endgame; let's do the least amount of features to know if it will work. Then improve it if people use it." Just as with the connected products like the Nest Learning Thermostat we described in chapter 7, you should build a minimum viable mobile product, then improve it over time.

Third, you will mitigate the financial risk of building the wrong thing. Some early mobile apps failed because they focused on the wrong thing: marketing instead of service transactions, for example. The agile process helps avoid this by chunking your investments into short cycles with immediate market feedback so you won't throw good money after bad. Nordstrom's vice president of IT, John Mayfield, says, "We now speak of investment themes and six-month positive returns, not capital investments over two years."

Fourth, you will learn how to apply agile development to business processes, not just technology development. At Alex and Ani, the team learned how to adapt its store operations process for package wrapping, for example, to match the speed of the mobile checkout process. This is a collateral benefit to having business and technology people on the same IDEA team: Business people learn the power of rapid cycles of building, testing, and learning to shape customer processes. One of the biggest lessons for business people is that it's okay to fail if you quickly correct the problem and move on. This requires a leap of belief that customers will forgive mistakes if they don't happen twice. But it's a necessary part of staying focused on the mobile moment.

If you need help getting started, you'll probably find that you have an agile team already up and running in your technology management organization or development group. If not, you can find detailed tutorials and how-to guides for agile development, including Forrester's published research on development methods and the works of Dean Leffingwell and Donald Reinertsen.[4]

So much for the team structure. But how do you organize mobile development in a large company, where many different parts of the organization work on mobile applications? You create an executive team to drive it. That's what American Airlines did.

CASE STUDY: American Airlines Organizes Mobile with a Steering Committee

We met Maya Leibman and Phil Easter of American Airlines in chapter 3. Phil manages the IDEA team building the traveler app. Maya is the CIO of the company. She's very busy these days integrating American Airlines and US Airways technologies but she still finds time to spearhead American Airline's mobile steering committee.

Once it was clear that the traveler app was a success, every business group—sales, marketing, loyalty, flight operations, catering, baggage handling, customer service—wanted its features presented to travelers in a mobile moment. Phil and his team couldn't do it all and certainly not all at once. So they needed a mobile steering committee to set the investment priorities.

American Airlines' mobile steering committee includes executives from every facet of the business, both from operational groups, such as sales and marketing, and from groups that would be affected by apps, such as technology and flight operations. Only in this way can the company engage resources from across the company to deliver a great mobile experience.

Phil Easter takes this charter from the mobile steering committee and executes it. His technical organization, which we would call a mobile center of excellence, has doubled in size every year over the past three years to 80 technical staff in 2014. Most of his staff are on agile IDEA teams. He uses some outside resources for things like interface design, but mobile development has become a core competency of the airline. Mobile moments are too important to American Airlines to do it any other way.

Charter a Mobile Steering Committee to Oversee the Strategy

Some companies' early mobile efforts have been burned with poor app store ratings, attracting concerned attention from CEOs and boards of directors. That's often when senior management sets up an executive mobile steering committee. But don't wait for that disaster. Even if you start small with a single IDEA team, get a charter from an executive committee. That will set the stage for continuous improvement and mobile moment success.

If you're a retailer and your retail customers bring smartphones into your store to beat you down on price or quality, this steering committee gives you the organizational commitment to make changes in everything from store operations all the way through to investments in mobile technology platforms. The challenges may be different by industry, but the authority of the steering committee is crucial to retaining a consistent commitment to winning in the mobile moment.

A mobile steering committee is responsible for overseeing a company's mobile initiatives. Here's how it works.

The committee of between four and 10 executives from every part of the organization meets monthly. As American Airlines learned, because mobile touches so many parts of your company, you need a representative from each domain. For example, at Starbucks this team is led by chief digital officer Adam Brotman, and includes executives from store operations in every region, digital strategy, marketing, legal, and technology.

The committee typically focuses on four things. First, what are the mobile priorities? For example, is it more important to focus on mobile marketing or, as ING did, on transactions? Second, what is the status and level of business success for each of the initiatives? IHG reports app metrics and business outcomes. Third, is the right staff in place internally or does the company need to pay a partner? Fourth, what are the investment themes and where will the money come from?

The committee is also responsible for seeing problems and finding solutions. For example, if an organizational barrier prevents business and technology people from working together on IDEA teams, the steering committee could recommend starting with a single agile team to see how it goes. If the technology systems are not ready for mobile moments, the steering committee might support the CIO by making a board-level decision to invest in technology, as Home Depot did.

The Role of the Mobile Center of Excellence

The mobile steering committee is an executive decision body. It needs an execution arm to implement the decisions. This has led to the rise of the mobile center of excellence (sometimes called digital center of excellence or digital transformation group) that operates by authority of the mobile steering committee. There is no single organizational model for a mobile center of excellence. To create the one that works best for your company, you'll need to figure out three things.

First, decide if the mobile center of excellence will also include the people who build applications—will it encompass the resources on the IDEA teams? At GE, the mobile center of excellence based in Detroit has more than 900 people dedicated to improve the mobile and customer experience across the firm. At American Airlines, the center of excellence has 80 full-time employees. But not all mobile centers of excellence build things. For example, at Northwestern Mutual, ten people appointed by the steering committee meet weekly to keep mobile initiative on track, but they don't actually build them—they work with the teams or agencies and integrators that do.

Second, figure out which department hosts the multidisciplinary center of excellence. A mobile center of excellence may be part of the eBusiness organization, as at IHG; the digital strategy organization, as at Starbucks; or the technology department, as at American Airlines.

Third, determine how you will staff your mobile center of excellence. The positions might be full time as at GE or part time as they are at some other companies. Some centers of excellence have implemented programs where people cycle through to master the skills. At IBM, developers and product managers take crash courses in the Austin design center. At GE, employees from different product teams come to Detroit in three-month assignments to master the process. But other employees in GE's center are permanently assigned and full-time members of an IDEA team.

Once you have made those decisions, you must next decide what parts the IDEA team, center of excellence, and steering committee play in making and implementing decisions ranging from the brand experience to the development technology (see Table 12-1). For the mobile center of excellence and its sponsoring steering committee, decide where to educate people, where to coordinate activities, and where to control outcomes.

Educate people to create and share best practices. Some mobile practices are best handled with guidelines and assistance rather than restrictions and oversight. For activities like a mobile moment audit or experience design, the mobile center of excellence plays an education role. At GE, for example, the mobile center of excellence offers strategy workshops to bring business and technology teams together. This kind of education unites staff around common goals and interests to launch them in the best direction to complete a mobile product.

Coordinate activities that need clear leadership but where many people are working on execution. Most organizations won't and shouldn't centralize mobile initiatives or even mobile app development.[5] The breadth of mobile products makes it impossible to control output. But simply educating people on the topic is often not enough to keep an app moving forward at the right pace. Sometimes, the mobile center of excellence needs to implement a decision and coordinate activity around that decision. For example, at one global bank, the center of excellence designated the software development tool to bring consistency to the application.

Table 12-1: One Example of How a Mobile Organization Could Function

Responsibility	Mobile steering committee	Mobile center of excellence	IDEA teams
Setting investment priorities	Set and audit the investment themes.	Make recommendations based on collective needs.	Create the case for mobile apps and associated systems.
Defining the brand experience	Work with marketing to define.	Audit brand experience.	Implement the brand experience.
Designing apps	Establish design as an investment priority.	Set up design choices, training, and services.	Incorporate design into the agile development process.
Building mobile apps and sites	Ensure commitment of supporting groups and systems.	Broker changes in processes, systems, and organizations.	Build and continuously improve the mobile experience.
Handling security, privacy, and compliance	Authorize, support, and audit the policies.	Build policies with the help of legal, security, and compliance teams.	Adhere to the security, privacy, and compliance policies.
Determining a skills plan	Assess skills mix needs, determine whether to train or acquire.	Create job descriptions, including salary levels.	Hire or train team members with the right skills mix.
Building technology platforms	Prioritize platform requirements.	Aggregate requests across IDEA teams.	Define the platform requirements for mobile apps.
Managing technology choices	Enforce technology decisions.	Recommend technology choices.	Adhere to technology guidelines.
Managing agency or development partnerships	Ensure compliance with strategic partners.	Own agency or integrator relationships.	Manage agency or integrator relationships.

Control outcomes that give you scale or put you at high risk. The technology group typically owns the security policy, while marketing is usually the watchdog of the brand. For these elements, the mobile center of excellence must insist on compliance to a standard. At Cisco, for example, all apps for the Apple App Store go through a single senior manager. But the center should be careful to govern only the things that carry the most risk, like security, brand, and access to back-end transactions systems such as the customer database. Too much control will turn what should be an enabling organization into a major barrier to deployment and success.

What to Worry About When Organizing for Mobile

Few companies have mastered the mobile organization that we outline in this chapter. We have drawn on the best practices of different companies to paint a picture of best practices. So don't fret if it takes you time to put the right organization in place. Start with the basic building block: the multidiscipline IDEA team using an agile development process. And keep an eye out for some common mistakes.

Look out for the conflict that comes from overcoming channel barriers. If there's one certainty, it's that your customers will expect more from you on their mobile devices next year than they do today. Keep an eye out for an eCommerce team that gets squirrely about supporting the mobile app or a store operations group that avoids looking at the impact of mobile on retail customers. You must overcome the channel conflict, but because of potential turf issues, this may need high-level attention even from the CEO.

Make sure that even if you use partners to accelerate your progress, you also acquire the skills you need to make mobile moments a core competency. At ING Direct in Australia (another ING Group company), the head of digital and emerging channels, Janelle McGuinness, learned this the hard way. The company started with a hybrid app (app plus mobile website) that it launched and then didn't update. As Janelle said, "The market moved on. Customer expectations surpassed us." On the second go-round, her team used outside expertise to design and code the app but then hired a full-time user experience specialist to continue the company's commitment to a better mobile experience. Today it has a four-star app and also the skills in-house to design and develop mobile apps along with the necessary back-end APIs.[6]

One last thing: Have the courage to occasionally scrap the whole app and start from scratch. As you continuously add features, the app inevitably starts to become bloated and tired looking. When you can no longer see where to cram in new features or stretch your existing design paradigm to fit the new capabilities, throw it away. American Airlines did this brilliantly when it launched a completely redesigned application on the same day that Apple upgraded its operating system to iOS 7. By doing so, American got the jump on other airlines and created a beautiful and elegantly functional application with room to grow further in the relentless cycle of improvement. This is a great reason to charter a mobile center of excellence that sits outside the IDEA teams—it helps break the lock the IDEA team has on its app.

How to Know When You Are Doing It Right

In the first part of this book, we described what the mobile mind shift is and how to approach it. In the second part, we showed how the mobile mind shift affects customer-facing groups. The third part described how to engineer your company and technology to deliver on the promise of mobile moments.

The key is the mobile moment, not the app. Companies must unite the elements we describe—the IDEA cycle, continuous improvement, and re-engineered platforms and processes—to win in a mobile moment.

Here are three signals that a company is poised for success in the mobile mind shift:

1. Any officer of the company can explain why he is investing in his customers' and employees' mobile moments. This is what makes Starbucks and Nestlé successful.

2. Employees are able to move across functional siloes and business boundaries to work together on the platforms and processes to support a great mobile moment. This is why ING Bank and USAA are able to innovate at scale.

3. Business budget holders are queued up to fund new applications and features that make customers and employees successful in their mobile moments. This is why American Airlines' mobile apps improve dramatically every year.

. . . .

In the next chapter we will peer over the horizon to describe what the mobile mind shift looks like 10 years from now.

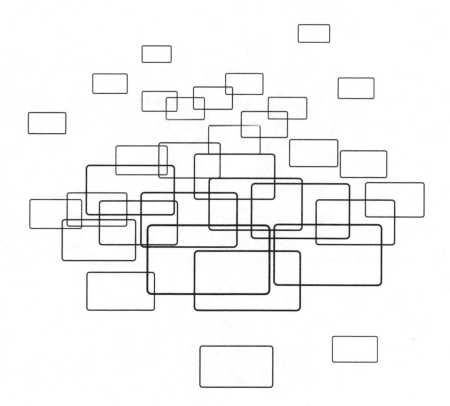

PART IV
The Future Shift

13

· · · · · · · · ·

The Future Shift
Mobile Moments Will Blanket the World

"**K**ids are amazing everywhere in the world. There's so much hope and potential and ambition in a child. Then, slowly, the hope and potential gets killed." That's Shannon May, the co-founder of Bridge International Academies, talking about the challenge of teaching in Kenya. "The real problem is that children aren't learning. If children aren't learning, they can't support themselves, their family, their community, their country. It leaves the children vulnerable. How can you totally change the trajectory?"

Shannon realized that it was possible to change trajectory in Kenya, and it didn't need to be expensive, either.

Shannon understood that children need educators with the best curriculum available to break a cycle of poverty and enter the modern world. She and her co-founders Jay Kimmelman and Phil Frei launched an educational solution using mobile technology that has now reached more than 250 academies and 80,000 Kenyan school children.

The idea is simple: Enable parents to place their children in schools with professionally developed curriculum, even in villages with no electricity or running water. Put the cost of that education within reach of people living on $2 per day. Keep the children in school long enough to give them a fighting chance to pass an exam to enter secondary education and break out of a cycle of subsistence. And use mobile technology to do it.

Here's how it works. Bridge International Academies hires professional educators to develop curriculum and lesson plans in both Nairobi and Cambridge, Massachusetts. It hires local teachers and administrators for the academies. And then the company uses mobile to distribute the lesson plans.

The environment in rural Kenya is challenging for technology. There's basic mobile phone network coverage but sometimes no electricity. Bridge International Academies found a way around that. Each school's administrator gets an inexpensive mobile phone with administrative, testing, and billing apps to run the school. Bridge updates the phones over the cellular network with seven days' worth of teaching materials. The phone also operates as a Wi-Fi hotspot so teachers can download the teaching materials and day's lesson plans to an eReader. These eReaders can run for days without needing to be recharged.

The teaching materials appear on the eReaders. Teachers also use them to enter the test scores, which are then communicated back to the phone and subsequently back to Bridge headquarters. The content expertise is central, the teaching is local, and the learning is mobile.

One master teacher can now empower hundreds of classroom teachers with secondary educations to teach thousands of schoolchildren the educational necessities of the modern era. To you, this may sounds simplistic. But to a Kenyan child who has little alternative, it's enlightenment.

The cost is just over $6 per student per month. For this price, Bridge makes a whole day full of education moments possible for tens of thousands of children. They're planning on tripling the number of students every year for the next four years. We're betting they'll succeed.

Mobile Moments Multiply to Define the Future

Here's what you need to understand about the wave of change that is the mobile mind shift: It is on a vastly bigger scale than any digital technology that's come before.

When PCs became commonplace in the 80s, they changed things. Over the next 15 years, hundreds of millions of people sat in front of a screen and started to create their own content, rather than just consuming it. Workers became masters of their own information instead of slaves to their central information services department.

When the Internet and laptops became ubiquitous in the 90s, people connected. Over the next 15 years, social media exploded to reach a billion people. Companies put up websites so people could serve themselves on a single screen. Workers demanded and received instant access to information and each other. Both consumers and workers began to see information as a resource, and everything accelerated.

But the changes created by PCs and by the Internet are dwarfed by what's coming. Why? Because the mobile mind shift affects more people in more parts of their lives. And it's happening much more quickly.

As we see in Kenya, mobile technology will reach billions more people than PCs and the Web did. The mobile mind shift means that *most people on the planet* will see mobile as the answer, no matter what the question. That expectation for instantaneous assistance will transform every aspect of our world—*and* your business.

Here at Forrester Research, our clients ask us to look into the future. The mobile mind shift is such a profound transformation that, frankly, we can't definitively tell you how things will look in 10 years. But we can see some interesting things coming. Let's shift our view from what's already happening to what will happen next.

Mobile Moments Will Fill Your Day As Everything Connects

As we write this, in 2014, 21% of online American adults are Shifted, reliant on their mobile devices to get most things done. That could easily be 50% or more by 2020. Younger consumers raised on touchscreens and voice control will find mouse-and-keyboard interactions clunky and slow. Toddlers already tap on TVs, tablets, and tabletops expecting to make the images dance.

And it's not just screens. Communications chips and sensors are so cheap now that any real-world object can be instrumented. This will give us wearables to track our every step, eyeglasses that shine a universe of media onto an eyeball, wristwatches with a kitbag of buzz tones to uniquely identify a texter, garments endowed with body sensors to monitor our health, and ingestible medications that broadcast their dosage to a caregiver.

What does this all mean? It means that any moment in which someone touches a product or object or structure can also be a mobile moment.

You will ask your dress whether you wore it last week. Your shoes will nag you to take the stairs instead of the elevator. Your car—well, your car is a moving computer already, with access to media, directions, maintenance information, and, in the case of Mercedes-Benz Mbrace system, even recommendations on where to get a nice dinner. How long will it be until the door to your house knows you're coming and warms up the house in anticipation or the peaches in the bowl tell you this is the exact right moment to eat them?

Phones were first. Tablets came next. But in the next few years, these devices will be joined by dozens more that will address your needs in a mobile moment. By 2020, your customers could have 30 connected products delivering mobile moments, not just the handful they have today. Here's what this means for your business.

If you have a product, connect it. Consider the ecosystem of other objects it interacts with (beverages with refrigerators, tires with cars, conference rooms with video walls) and keep a close watch on how those other objects are connecting—look for partnerships you can build on.

If you have information, shrink it or atomize it. The real estate available to you to communicate with your customers has already shrunk from a 19-inch monitor to a 4-inch mobile device. Next it will shrink to a 2-inch screen on a wrist or cornea.

If you have apps, consider a future in which they've gone underground. The next inconvenient step people will bypass is clicking on each and every app. Our phones or wearables will know where we need to be when, whether or not we have an applicable coupon while we stand in line at Target, or if we have enough money to make a payment. The app will notify us to take action without the hassle of opening it. Google Now already gives us a glimpse of this future by waking us up earlier if there is traffic on our route to work.

So, stop thinking only about phones and apps. Think instead about the moments in your customers' and employees' lives, and what service you can provide in those moments. Because phones will become just another device, but mobile moments will proliferate endlessly.

Privacy Will Be Your Differentiator or Your Peril

Protesters gathering on January 21, 2014, in Kiev, Ukraine, received this text message on their mobile phones: "Dear subscriber, you are registered as a participant in a mass disturbance."[1] Oy! This kind of surveillance is entirely within the (brand new) law of the land, spotting protestors from location data spun off their mobile phones. But it reminds us just how visible our every move is in the mobile mind shift. Governments, corporations, and employees will be seduced by the power of information. In an age filled with paranoia generated from NSA spying and shocking corporate privacy violations, how companies use or abuse the data they gather will determine how people think about them. A customer's trust is a cornerstone of a twenty-first-century brand.[2] Lose trust, lose a customer.

It's even more of an issue because these mobile devices are so intimately part of our lives. Nest CEO Tony Fadell had to reassure customers that once the company was part of Google, their data would still be protected from prying eyes, and that all policy changes would be "opt in;" customers will have to choose to share information rather than have to explicitly restrict its use.[3]

Connected cars are a nexus for concern here. Each time you start a Nissan Leaf, it pops up a message warning you that "Your vehicle wirelessly transmits recorded vehicle data to Nissan" and requires you to accept or decline. Ford executives recently revealed how much data the GPS in its cars is collecting, and while insisting that privacy comes first, acknowledged that it would be possible to know when and where someone is speeding.[4]

As Forrester's expert on big data, analyst Brian Hopkins said, "You are entering new business-ethics territory that will test your resolve to put your customers' interests first." Beginning right now, you must make customer privacy your personal responsibility.

If you run a company, let the dinner table guide your decisions. If over dinner you described what you were doing to your children or your parents, how would they feel about it? If they would wrinkle their brow, sour their smile, or blank their face, then don't do it. Start with trust. Seek to serve rather than sell in a mobile moment.

If you create public policy, anticipate the backlash of surprise. If a citizen finds she is running around naked to scrutiny and exploitation because of the information her mobile device or thermostat gathers, she will lash out. Don't let the public be surprised. Find and head off the dangers even if people don't yet see them.

If you work with young people, teach them about disclosure and sharing. Collecting birthdates may appeal to a marketer, but it's probably more information than a 12-year-old should share with a brand. Teach children about privacy settings and data disclosure.

As with any mobile functionality, the key to appropriate privacy policy is *context*.[5] Collecting and using personal data should be consensual and for a mutually agreed upon purpose. If Nissan wants to upload your data, it should ask you once then remember your preference. People are quite willing to let companies collect and use data—and its context—to help serve them, but only if you prove that you will always get the appropriate permission. Smart companies will collect only the information they need to serve people and keep it only as long as it can help deliver that service. Companies that behave like that will earn the trust that's essential in the age of the customer.

Mobile Moments Will Transform the Physical World

People hate waiting in line. Mobile moments help them skip it.

Companies hate paying for space that doesn't generate sales. Mobile moments help them avoid wasted space. Mobile moments also let them avoid building traditional retail points of presence in the first place, as we saw in Kenya with M-Pesa's mobile payments.

Nobody with a mobile airline app needs to wait in line at a kiosk or check-in counter. Airlines are leaving desks dark and starting to take them away altogether as passengers go directly to security, mobile boarding pass in hand.

Checkout counters are disappearing in retail stores. Apple Stores don't have them. We explained how Alex and Ani uses mobile devices to reduce the need for checkout counters in chapter 2. Hointer, a Seattle clothing store, has taken this idea to a new level. In its stores, shoppers encounter a thinly populated rack of clothes. They scan a barcode and enter a few fitting details, then head to the dressing room where the garment shows up ready to be tried on. The shopping experience is reduced to its essentials with less staff and less rack space clutter.

eBay is one company that is pursuing a new vision for retail that thinks very differently about location. Steve Yankovich used to be eBay's vice president for mobile. As we described in chapter 4, mobile is huge for eBay; people have posted more than half a billion listings using its app. But Steve is leaving all that mobile commerce behind in his new position as VP of innovation and new ventures, with a focus on eBay Now, a commerce business that facilitates traditional (non-auction) sales from local merchants and delivers to a person in real time, wherever they happen to be.

"We are building on two core principles," Steve says. "First, mobile has made consumers more impatient—they want instant gratification. Second, they want control—especially over delivery. We give them both with eBay Now. We deliver what they want, when they want it and to where they want it—even if it's a park bench in Union Square." Steve has recognized that mobile moments can happen anywhere. He understands that the important location is not where the store is, it's where *you* are.

In financial services, banks are closing branches, not only in response to economic pressures, but also because more customers are using online and mobile banking services. First Niagara Financial Group, a regional bank with branches concentrated in western New York, Pennsylvania, and Connecticut, is cutting branches and retraining staff to handle more complex services as more customers conduct business away from the branch. In January 2014, Mark Rendulic, the bank's executive vice president, said that more than 40% of its customers are registered to bank online and 140,000 had downloaded the mobile app in the first year.[6] Bank of America, SunTrust Bank, PNC Financial Services Group, Lloyds Bank, BNP Paribas, and Bankia are other examples of banks cutting branches, partially in response to lower demand for branch services.

In the mobile mind shift, real estate plays a different role: to bring people together to share product and service experiences. Transactions and service delivery happens on a mobile device, not a kiosk or counter. Think of the car rental return person greeting you as they walk around the car and check you in. China Eastern Airlines girds staff with vests complete with a boarding pass printer to greet and serve travelers where they stand.

Every retail branch experience will be reconstituted in the mobile mind shift. It may be your real estate, but to your customers, it's just another place where mobile moments can make or break the experience.

Mobile Payments Will Upend the Economics of Loyalty

A battle is coming for mobile payments. Incumbents like Visa and Master-Card and disruptors like Apple and PayPal are bringing payment services in the form of digital wallets that make payment just part of a deeper relationship. Subway, for example, is using a mobile payment system from Paydiant in its loyalty application to establish a platform for new services and promotions similar to what we described for Starbucks in chapter 6.[7]

After years of planning and with the help of Worldline, McDonald's has taken mobile payments to 1,200 restaurants across France in 2013. The killer app? Order on the phone and pick up in the restaurant with no waiting. But the spinoff value is that McDonald's has a platform to extend new services, perhaps even some outside the restaurant, to loyal customers.

Jean-Noël Penichon, head of digital strategy and transformation at McDonald's, told us, "The question is how can we be more than just an ordering tool? How can we transform the customer experience, to bring value before, during, and after the purchase?"

We are moving out of the experimentation stage into a world where more and more transactions will flow through mobile devices. By 2018, US retailers will take $26 billion in payments directly off of mobile devices.[8] And that's just the start. It will take time to develop, but the payment industry will look entirely different in a world populated by mobile payment and loyalty moments.

Mobile Data Will Create More Competitive—and More Volatile—Pricing

We've already seen how mobile devices expose the prices and price variability in your store versus online or at a competitor. Mobile shopping moments guarantee that your customers will be too smart to fool with channel-based pricing.

Mobile devices also enable performance-based pricing.

For example, a mobile device now makes it possible for Progressive Insurance to reward good driving behavior through performance-based pricing. A driver agrees to put a gadget called Snapshot in her car to track speed, acceleration, and time of day for 30 days. Good drivers get up to 30% off their car insurance bill.[9]

Similarly, self-insured company health plans are experimenting with performance-based pricing. In one company, employees and family members use "life miles," a point system that tracks exercise with a fitness wearable and encourages members to report their health, get regular checkups, and work with a clinician on sticky issues. The payoff for people with healthy habits? As much as $400 in cash.

These are examples where mobile sensors enable companies to create more accurate prices, customized to individuals. But can companies adjust prices by the moment, like a stock price, based on current conditions?

That's exactly what Uber did in San Francisco on New Year's Eve, just before and after the calendar ticked over to 2014. Uber used "surge pricing" to charge passengers more than three times as much after midnight as in the hours leading up to it, because there was much higher demand during that time period. Because it wanted to be transparent, it warned people ahead of time with an email that included a chart of how prices would change (see Figure 13-1).

Figure 13-1: Uber Notifies and Practices Variable Pricing to Match Supply and Demand

Before 8pm:	8-10pm:	10:30-12:15am:	12:15-2:30am:	3:00am-dawn
Fast, easy rides at normal prices.	May be moderate surge as people hit the town	Ultra-pro-tip: open Ubers are everywhere right before the ball drops.	Most EXPENSIVE time of the evening; everyone is on the move at exactly the same time	Prices will quickly drop and return to normal rates

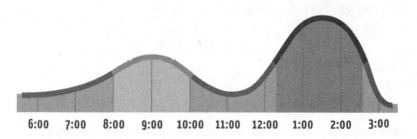

Source: Uber New Year's Eve 2014 blog and email notification

The question "what is the right price" depends on information. Much more information—and more context—is available in a mobile world. Companies will be able to charge more when demand is high (like Uber) and charge less for customers who prove they deserve it (like Progressive). Here's what this means for you. If you have an ongoing relationship, you must instrument your apps and products to provide you with the information you need to optimize prices. To minimize a backlash, you must follow Uber's example and be transparent in the way that you do this. And if you don't set prices this way, be ready for your competitors to do so. If your internal systems don't allow you to change prices quickly and in a flexible way, you may find yourself flatfooted when the competition changes its pricing mechanisms.

All three pricing forces put power into the hands of individuals and reward companies willing to bring pricing to the forefront of business strategy.

Medicine, Too, Will Gain Mobile Moments

In chapter 7, we learned how Withings is tying weight and fitness together through a connected bathroom scale. Connected devices and mobile health can deliver more effective and cost-effective care: telemedicine, connected medical devices, even medications that signal when they've been swallowed.

A few years ago, the Serono division of Merck, the pharmaceutical giant, was winning only 1 in 12 new patients in the UK who needed human growth hormone (HGH), an important therapy for undersize children and people recovering from a debilitating disease. Don Cowling, then vice president and managing director of Merck Serono UK, knew he needed to find a way to differentiate his product.

The answer lay in the mobile moment of injection. If Merck could show that the new drug was more effective when it was used properly, it could win more prescriptions.

Don's team turned to a connected medical device that injects medicine through the skin with a hidden needle.[10] Sensors on the bottom of the injector detect contact with skin as well as monitoring the depth, angle, and speed of the injection—important adjustments in an effective treatment. But because the device is connected, it can also track the time and place of the injection, which shows a clinician and insurer that a patient is keeping up with the treatments.

This attracted insurance payers. Because it could monitor compliance with the treatment and tweak the injection parameters to maximize efficacy, Merck's HGH treatment solution outperformed the competition. In just one year, Merck shifted its acquisition rate from 8% to 55% of new

HGH treatment patients. It took market share even from rivals who were cutting their prices. Don went on to become senior vice president, commercial programs of Proteus Digital Health, a company building medical technology based on the idea that medications, including pills, should be able to report on whether they're being used effectively.

The HGH treatment that Merck succeeded with was demonstrably better because it was connected. What about your product? As we described in chapter 7, many products are becoming commodities. Mobile apps to control them and mobile sensors that indicate how they're doing will create differentiation in all products. If you make products, this is your new competitive dynamic.

Data Will Become the New Currency of Competition

More sensors. Privacy concerns. Competitive pressures creating mobile-connected products. Pricing based on real-world information. There's a pattern in all of these trends: data. Lots and lots of data.

Data drives the advertising businesses of Google, Facebook, and Flipboard. It also extends the value of the Nest Learning Thermostat, Withings bathroom scale, and Nissan Leaf. Data is also the prime way in which brands like Starbucks and retailers like Sephora derive insight from loyalty programs. Data is rapidly becoming a competitive weapon.

Mobile moments generate more data than any technology before, data from photos, location metadata, and contextual searches and posts, for example.

When thousands or millions of people share their immediate experiences in a mobile moment, the accumulated data can be a powerful, competitive weapon and a force for good. When citizens report potholes and burned out streetlights from a mobile app, the city of Boston can repair roads ravaged by the polar vortex. When MyFitnessPal collects data from its community of more than 40 million customers, it's a piece of cake to create a database with nutritional information on three million food items.

Data from the crowd remakes maps. You can tell Google Maps on your iPhone that a store or a street is closed. Waze (now owned by Google) automatically collects data on how fast the traffic is moving on side streets and thoroughfares and on breakdowns, accidents, and construction. It uses this information to reroute drivers around traffic jams (and turns once-quiet streets into rush hour byways in the process).

In Lahore, Pakistan, a cheap mobile device lets city workers track insecticide use and report the data to the public. City health officials correlate that data with infected cases of dengue fever, a mosquito-borne illness, to see how effectively the health strategy is working. In one year, the number of confirmed cases plummeted from 21,292 to just 255 (with no fatalities) as mobile data flowed in to drive the insecticide program.[11]

Companies can tap into customer data in new ways, too. Intu Properties, United Kingdom's biggest shopping center owner with 350 million visits every year, has made being "digitally connected" a core strategy. It provides free Wi-Fi and is working on a mall navigation app. It then uses Cisco wireless technology to aggregate data about where people walk ("internal footfall tracking") and where they spend time ("dwell-time analytics"). Gian Fulgoni, Intu's chief information officer, explains that Intu will use this data to work with its retail partners to direct traffic, offer promotions, and be smarter about helping people get where they want to go.

Lastly, every mobile startup has made customer intelligence based on the behavioral data they collect off mobile phones a foundation of the business. Nest Labs guides people to conserve energy by tracking how they use the thermostat and the room it's in. Nike+ FuelBand tells consumers how they are doing relative to people like them. Grocery iQ taps the data to offer coupons to shoppers.

Data scientists and analysts who can turn this torrent of bits into useful intelligence are the key here. Data is useless unless you can synthesize it into insight. As mobile matures, the Analyze stage in the IDEA cycle is where companies will invest to gain an edge.

How to Think Differently for the Mobile Future

You've now seen how mobile moments change the expectations of people waiting in the rain for the next pope to arrive and how mobile moments transform taxi companies ferrying passengers through that rain. You've witnessed disruptive changes in retail, travel, media, banking, and healthcare. You've experienced augmented business models in consumer products, manufacturing, and apparel.

That's just a prelude.

Ten years from now, any business not built on mobile moments will seem as outdated as a cassette player.

You need to think further ahead.

Think like Brad Smith, the CEO of Intuit, who counsels his company to think five years out, not quarter-to-quarter. He has created a CEO Fund to invest in ideas that may not bear fruit for years, but must be developed in a world so rapidly changing. You need to do the same.

Imagine that you have $15 million to invest in mobile moments that could transform your company and completely disrupt your industry. Think of it as a team of 10 people, three partners, and a lot of technology for the next three years. What will you do with that money?

Think big. And think disruptively—that's how the entrepreneurs targeting your business are thinking. (If you want to know more about thinking like a disruptor, see James McQuivey's definitive book on the topic, *Digital Disruption*.[12]) Here are four principles for how to apply your thinking:

1. **Start with your customers and your assets.** Don't start by thinking about your current business. Think about your customers— what do they need? What's their biggest problem? When Johnson & Johnson thinks about its customers—parents of new babies—it realizes that they need help with getting the baby to bed. That's why the company created an app called Bedtime, not one called Mobile Baby Powder. Alternatively, think about your assets—partnerships, manufacturing plants, institutional competencies. In what new ways could you apply those assets in a world of mobile moments?

2. **Design for mobile moments.** That's where your customers will be. Even if they're in your store, they are mobile. Even if they are on your website, they are mobile. Even if they are waiting for your call center agent, they are mobile. That means you must "follow them home" in the words of Intuit CEO Brad Smith. Know their habits and context because you care to serve them. Know what tasks they care about, what actions they want to take, what information they need to feel confident in taking that next step.

3. **Rent what you need, own what you must.** Don't expect to have all the equipment and skills you need at first. Rent servers and software. Hire expertise. A horde of technology and service providers is out there to help. But don't abdicate responsibility for the essential

components of the application and platform. Transfer skills from partners to your staff. Establish long-term relationships. Pay for success, not just completion.

4. **Be ready to launch, learn, and adjust.** Nobody gets it right the first time. It's why we've continually reinforced the importance of agile, multidisciplinary teams throughout this book. No successful person we've interviewed has done it alone. The teams include business and marketing and design and technology people that use two- or three-week development sprints and a continuous improvement cycle. There's a lot buried in that idea: testing on every device and network, setting up the right feedback loops, listening carefully, analyzing the data you've collected, rapidly fixing broken things, and explaining why. So start by thinking of a small engagement, but prepare for how you will grow and improve it.

Get your executives or your team together and mull this over. Brainstorm your best ideas to win in mobile moments. And after that, don't just go home. Make a plan, and do it.

The mobile mind shift will rock your world. It's inevitable. The only question is whether you or someone else will do it first.

WHAT'S NEXT

· · · · · · · · ·

Wondering how to act on what you've just read? Here are some things you can do next:

- **Get help.** We'd be happy to work with you and your company on strategy and execution for the mobile mind shift. We can help you understand the mobile mind shift of your customers, identify the mobile moments of your customers and employees, and develop or improve your mobile strategy. Learn more and contact us at http://mobilemindshift.com.

- **Get resources.** We have complimentary reports, interactive tools, and self-assessments on the mobile mind shift at http://mobilemindshift.com.

- **Get a speech.** We can speak at your corporate and public events to inspire and educate people on how to embrace the mobile mind shift. To line up a speech, contact us at speakersbureau@forrester.com.

- **Get connected.** Follow us here:

	Twitter	Blog
Forrester Research	@forrester	blogs.forrester.com
Ted Schadler	@TedSchadler	blogs.forrester.com/ted_schadler
Josh Bernoff	@jbernoff	blogs.forrester.com/josh_bernoff
Julie Ask	@JulieAsk	blogs.forrester.com/julie_ask

ACKNOWLEDGMENTS

· · · · · · · · ·

This was a hard book to create. There were a lot of people involved. Every single contribution was essential, and we are grateful for them all.

First, you should know that the "fourth Beatle" in this collaboration is Lizzie Ryckewaert. As the research associate for the book project, she set up many of the interviews, tracked them, and generally kept this whole loony project humming along while the analyst/authors were traveling off to who knows where for who knows what—and all in her first six months on the job. Without her help and the help of Naxin (Nancy) Wang, Griffin McGrath, and Jin Di, this book would never have happened.

Forrester has an awful lot of knowledge on mobile, and we tapped into all of it. We leaned especially hard on Thomas Husson for international perspective and John C. McCarthy, who with Ted originally conceived of our analysis of systems of engagement. Much of Julie's foundational research on mobile and context has been tightly entangled with insights from Jeffrey Hammond, our mobile development guru. We also tapped the collected wisdom of Dane Anderson, Kurt Bittner, Victoria Bough, John Brand, Eric Brown, Matt Brown, David Cooperstein, John Dalton, Michael Facemire, Nigel Fenwick, Charles S. Golvin, JP Gownder, Katyayan Gupta, Brad Holmes, Carrie Johnson, Patti Freeman-Evans, Christian Kane, Khalid Kark, TJ Keitt, Craig Le Clair, Deanna Laufer, Sharyn Leaver, Mark Lindwall, Diego Lo Guidice, James McQuivey, Sucharita Mulpuru, Melissa Parrish, Michelle Pelino, Doug Roberge, Sarah Rotman Epps, Ron Rogowski, Clay Richardson, Tim Sheedy, James Staten, Bryan Wang, Kelland Willis, and Jenny Wise. Thanks also to Mary Beach and Natan Abraham, and in Asia, to Tomoko Aihara, Chris Perrine, and Maynard Zhang.

We're grateful for the full-throated support—emotional and budgetary—of Forrester's senior leaders, Cliff Condon, Dennis van Lingen, Tom Pohlmann, Ellen Daley, and, of course, George F. Colony.

Insight depends on data. In this case, the data came into being when Roxie Strohmenger brought her creative insights to bear on this topic and offered to conduct a survey on mobile attitudes and expectations, a survey that became the basis for the Mobile Mind Shift Index. Colin Campbell was tireless in his efforts to make our data correct and useful, with assists from Vikram Sehgal, and Jeff Wray. Anjali Lai chimed in with insights from our online community, Community Speaks.

The data graphics are more beautiful because of help from the estimable Ryan Morrill. Jens Kueter saved us more than once in the creation of the rest of the graphics. Paddy McCobb, Sarah Lukachko, and the whole Forrester design team created the book jacket and directed the rest of the design. Merlina McGovern expertly copyedited the whole manuscript.

The book's success depends in part on our excellent marketers. Erica Sahin was highly effective in herding our many marketing cats, which include Cassandra Calawa, Jenny Castaneda, Jeff Ernst, Annarose Kitzelman, Amy Lewis, and Lisa Walker. Our peerless team of publicists includes Lara Cole, Phil LeClare, Simone Levien, Laura Moran, Deborah Ng, Belinda Simmelink, and Jon Symons.

Gail Mann was our counselor, in all the meanings of that word.

We'd also like to recognize the essential contributions of our publishing team at Greenleaf Book Group, including Hobbs Allison, Bryan Carroll, and Kami Smith.

Finally, we'd like to thank our families for putting up with and supporting us during this all-consuming endeavor—Deirdre, Sophie, and Rory; Kimberley, Ray, and Isaac; and James.

And thanks to all the entrepreneurs, technologists, mobile developers, device makers, and cloud engineers who made the mobile mind shift possible. We're ready to embrace the new world you have created for us!

—Ted Schadler, Josh Bernoff, and Julie Ask
Cambridge, Massachusetts, and San Francisco, California

ABOUT THE AUTHORS

. . . .

Ted Schadler

Ted is the co-author of *Empowered: Unleash Your Employees, Energize Your Customers, and Transform Your Business* (Harvard Business Review Press, September 2010). *Empowered* shows how companies must empower their employees to directly engage with and solve the problems of empowered customers. *Empowered* has been featured several times on the 800-CEO-READ bestseller list, which lists the most popular books among corporate book buyers.

As a VP and principal analyst, Ted leads Forrester's analysis of the impact of mobile on corporate processes and systems. His report "Mobile Is The New Face Of Engagement" was the most popular report among Forrester clients in 2012.

Ted has 26 years of experience in the technology industry, focusing on the effects of disruptive technologies on companies and the technology industry. His research history includes breakthrough analyses of the impact of web, open source, cloud, and mobile technologies on businesses and consumers.

Ted's research and analysis have been widely cited in publications including *The Wall Street Journal*, *The New York Times*, *Forbes*, *ZDNet*, and *CIO* magazine, as well as on NPR and PBS.

Ted has a master's degree in management from the MIT Sloan School of Management and an M.S. in computer science from the University of Maryland as well as a B.A. in Physics from Swarthmore College. Ted's first career was as a singer and bass player for Crash Davenport, a popular Baltimore-based rock-and-roll band.

Josh Bernoff

Josh is a bestselling author and senior vice president, idea development, at Forrester Research.

He is the co-author of the *Businessweek* bestselling book *Groundswell: Winning in a World Transformed by Social Technologies* (Harvard Business Review Press, 2008), a comprehensive analysis of corporate strategy for dealing with social technologies. Abbey Klaassen, editor of *Advertising Age*, picked *Groundswell* as "the best book ever written on marketing and media." Josh was also the co-author of *Empowered: Unleash Your Employees, Energize Your Customers, and Transform Your Business* (Harvard Business Review Press, 2010).

Josh is also the editor of two other books: *Outside In: The Power of Putting Customers at the Center of Your Business* (New Harvest/HMH, 2012) by Harley Manning and Kerry Bodine, and *Digital Disruption: Unleashing the Next Wave of Innovation* (Amazon Publishing, 2013) by James McQuivey.

Josh's job at Forrester is to identify, develop, and promote the company's most influential and forward-looking ideas. He joined Forrester in 1995 and created the company's Technographics segmentation, a classification of consumers according to how they approach technology, which is still in use more than 15 years later.

Josh is frequently quoted in publications like *The New York Times* and *The Wall Street Journal*. Josh has keynoted major conferences on television, music, marketing, and technology in Barcelona, Beijing, Brussels, Cannes, London, New York, Rome, Tokyo, São Paulo, and Seoul.

Prior to joining Forrester, Josh spent 14 years working for startups in the technology industry and studying mathematics in the Ph.D. program at MIT. His hobbies include recreational biking, the futile pursuit of wellness, and standup comedy.

Julie Ask

Julie has authored more than 120 reports on mobile in her 14 years as an analyst, and she has helped establish Forester as a mobile research leader since 2009. Her research includes "The Future Of Mobile Is Context," one of Forrester's most downloaded reports, and the foundation for many of the ideas in *The Mobile Mind Shift*. She currently coordinates Forrester's research on the impact of mobile technologies and has helped hundreds of clients with mobile strategy.

Julie's 25 years of work experience are balanced between the engineering and management consulting work she did in the first half of her career and her work as an analyst for the past 14 years. She began her career in telecom as a microwave circuit engineer at Comsat Laboratories in 1988. As a management consultant, she worked in the US, Germany, Poland, the Czech Republic, Hungary, Romania, and Slovenia solving business problems.

Julie's research and analysis have been widely cited in publications including *The Wall Street Journal*, *The New York Times*, *USA Today*, *Businessweek*, and *The Onion* and on CBS, NBC, and PBS. She was cited as one of the 25 "Mobile Women to Watch" by *Mobile Marketer* in 2013. She has given speeches on mobile in Australia, Austria, Brazil, China, Germany, Israel, Korea, Spain, the UK, and across the US.

Julie holds a B.S.E.E. and a Master of Science in electrical engineering and computer science from the Massachusetts Institute of Technology (MIT). She also holds an M.B.A. from the University of Michigan. Julie has played ice hockey in the Budesliga in Germany and climbed Mt. Kilimanjaro.

ABOUT FORRESTER RESEARCH

. . . .

Forrester Research (Nasdaq: FORR) is one of the most influential research and advisory firms in the world. Our focus: help our clients win, serve, and retain customers by successfully navigating the disruption unleashed by digitally empowered customers and technology's relentless progression forward. We do so by providing proprietary research, consumer and business data, custom consulting, events, and peer-to-peer executive programs—all based on independent, fact-based insight. For more information, visit forrester.com.

CASE INDEX

· · · · · · · · ·

by Industry

Numbers indicate chapters in which these cases and examples appear. (Italic type indicates full case studies.)

CASE INDEX

· · · · · · · · ·

by Geography

Numbers indicate chapters in which these cases and examples appear. (Italic type indicates full case studies.)

METHODOLOGY

. . . .

Most of the data in this book comes from the Forrester's US Mobile Mind Shift Online Survey, Q3, 2013, which was fielded in September 2013 to 8,249 US individuals ages 18 to 88. For results based on a randomly chosen sample of this size (N=8,249), there is 95% confidence that the results have a statistical precision of plus or minus 1.08% of what they would be if the entire population of US online individuals ages 18 and older had been surveyed. Forrester weighted the data by age, gender, income, broadband adoption, and region to demographically represent the adult US online population (defined as those who go online weekly or more often). The survey sample size, when weighted, was 8,224. (Note: Weighted sample sizes can be different from the actual number of respondents to account for individuals generally underrepresented in online panels.) The sample was drawn from members of an online panel managed by MarketTools, and respondents were motivated by receiving points that could be redeemed for a reward. The sample provided by MarketTools is not a random sample. While individuals have been randomly sampled from MarketTools' panel for this particular survey, they have previously chosen to take part in the MarketTools online panel.

The international data came from four other surveys, described below.

For its North American Technographics® Online Benchmark Survey, 2013, Forrester conducted an online survey fielded in April 2013 of 61,167 US individuals and 5,800 Canadian individuals ages 18 to 88. For results based on a randomly chosen sample of this size (N=61,167 in the US and N=5,800 in Canada), there is 95% confidence that the results have a statistical precision of plus or minus 0.4% of what they would be if the entire population of US online individuals ages 18 and older had been surveyed and plus or minus 1.3% of what they would be if the entire population of Canadian online individuals ages 18 and older had been surveyed. Forrester weighted the data by age, gender, income, broadband adoption, and region to demographically represent the adult US and Canadian online populations (defined as those who go online weekly or more often). The survey sample size, when weighted, was 61,104 in the US and 5,778 in Canada. (Note: Weighted sample sizes can be different from the actual number of respondents to account for individuals generally underrepresented in online panels.) Please note that respondents who participate in online surveys generally have more experience with the Internet and feel more comfortable transacting online.

For its Asia Pacific Technographics Online Benchmark Survey, 2013, Forrester conducted an online survey fielded in May 2013 of 9,007 individuals in Australia, Indonesia, Japan, South Korea, metropolitan China (including Beijing, Chengdu, Dalian, Guangzhou, Nanjing, Ningbo, Shanghai, Shenyang, Suzhou, Wuhan, Wuxi, and Xian), Hong Kong, and metropolitan India (including Ahmedabad, Bangalore, Chennai, Hyderabad, Jaipur, Kolkata, Mumbai,

New Delhi, and Pune). This survey is based on an online population of people ages 18 and older who are members of the Ipsos-MORI online panel. Ipsos weighted the data in all countries by age, gender, and geographical distribution to be representative of the adult online population in each country surveyed. In metropolitan China, the data was also weighted by income level for each city surveyed. In metropolitan India, the data was also weighted by the SEC AB groups. For results based on a randomly chosen sample of this size (N=9,007), there is 95% confidence that the results fall within a range of statistical precision of plus or minus 2.0% to 4.3% of what results would be if each country's entire population of online individuals (defined as those online weekly or more often) ages 18 and older had been surveyed. The survey sample size, when weighted, was 9,007. (Note: Weighted sample sizes can be different from the actual number of respondents to account for individuals generally underrepresented in online panels.) Please note that this was an online survey. Respondents who participate in online surveys have more experience with the Internet in general and feel more comfortable transacting online. The data is weighted to be representative for the total online population on the weighting targets mentioned, but this sample bias may produce results that differ from data collected offline. The sample used by Ipsos is not a random sample; while individuals have been randomly sampled from the Ipsos panel for this survey, they have previously chosen to take part in the Ipsos online panel.

For its European Technographics Online Benchmark Survey, 2013, Forrester conducted an online survey fielded in May 2013 of 22,027 European individuals in the UK, France, Germany, Italy, the Netherlands, Poland, Spain, Sweden, and Turkey. This survey is based on an online population ages 16 and older who are members of the Ipsos-MORI online panel. Ipsos weighted the data by age, gender, and online frequency to demographically represent the online adult population in each country. In Turkey, the data was weighted by age and gender only. For results based on a randomly chosen sample of this size (N=22,027), there is 95% confidence that the results have a statistical precision of plus or minus 0.7% of what they would be if the entire population of Western European online (defined as those online weekly or more often) individuals age 16 and older had been surveyed. This confidence interval can widen to 3.1% when the data is analyzed at a country level. The survey sample size, when weighted, was 22,027. (Note: Weighted sample sizes can be different from the actual number of respondents to account for individuals generally underrepresented in online panels.) Please note that respondents who participate in online surveys have more experience with the Internet in general and feel more comfortable transacting online. The data is weighted to be representative of the total online population on the weighting targets mentioned, but this sample bias may produce results that differ from data collected offline. The sample used by Ipsos is not a random sample; while individuals have been randomly sampled from the Ipsos panel for this survey, they have previously chosen to take part in the Ipsos online panel.

For its Latin American Technographics Online Benchmark Survey, 2013, Forrester conducted an online survey fielded in May 2013 of 5,994 individuals ages 16 to 75 in top metropolitan areas/provinces of Argentina and top metropolitan areas/states of Brazil and Mexico.* For results based on a randomly chosen sample of this size (N=1,995 for Argentina; N=2,001 for Brazil; N=1,998 for Mexico), there is 95% confidence that the results have a statistical precision of plus or minus 2.2% of what they would be if the entire metropolitan population of individuals ages 16 and older had been surveyed in each country. Forrester weighted the data by age, gender, socioeconomic level (representing ABC1, C2, and C3 levels in Argentina; AB1, B2, and C1C2 levels in Brazil; and ABC+, C, and D+ levels in Mexico), and city. The survey sample size, when weighted, was 5,994. (Note: Weighted sample sizes can be different from the actual number of respondents to account for individuals generally underrepresented in survey data.) Please note that this was an online survey. Respondents who participate in online surveys have in general more experience with the Internet and feel more comfortable transacting online. The data is weighted to be representative of the total online population of each country on the weighting targets mentioned, but this sample bias may produce results different from data collected offline. The sample provided by Ipsos Livra is not a random sample. While individuals have been randomly sampled from Ipsos Livra's panel for this particular survey, they have previously chosen to take part in the Ipsos Livra online panel.

For its Russian Technographics Online Benchmark Survey, 2013, Forrester conducted an online survey fielded in May 2013 of 2,000 Russian online individuals ages 16 and older who are members of the Ipsos-MORI online panel. Ipsos weighted the data by age and gender to demographically represent the online adult population of metropolitan Russia. For results based on a randomly chosen sample of this size (N−2,000), there is 95% confidence that the results have a statistical precision of plus or minus 2.2% of what they would be if the entire population of metropolitan Russian online (defined as those online weekly or more often) individuals ages 16 and older had been surveyed. Please note that respondents who participate in online surveys have more experience with the Internet in general and feel more comfortable transacting online. The data is weighted to be representative of the total online population on the weighting targets mentioned, but this sample bias may produce results that differ from data collected offline. The sample used by Ipsos is not a random sample; while individuals have been randomly sampled from the Ipsos panel for this survey, they have previously chosen to take part in the Ipsos online panel.

ENDNOTES

· · · · · · · · ·

Much of the information in this book comes from direct in-person, telephone, and email interviews by the authors with the people and representatives of the companies described in the book. Facts and quotes that do not have a note are either from public sources or from these personal interviews.

In these notes, when citing a long Web address, we typically use an equivalent address of the form http://forr.com/mmsX-Y. We created these site references for the convenience of the reader. Enter the web address into your browser and you will be redirected to the appropriate site online.

Please note that, as in all cases with Web addresses, people sometimes change or remove content that we have cited. Web content cited was visible at the time the book was written.

Many of these citations are Forrester reports. If you are a Forrester client with appropriate access, the cited address will take you to the report page online where you can read or download the full report. If you are not a client or your relationship with Forrester does not include access to the report, you'll see a short excerpt of the report. If you're still interested in the full report, you can sign up to become a client or purchase the report.

Chapter 1

1. Nathan Ingraham, "Apple announces 1 million apps in the App Store, more than 1 billion songs played on iTunes radio," *The Verge*, October 22, 2013, http://forr.com/mms1-1 .

2. Song Jung-a, "South Korean mobile messenger app expands reach into Asia," *The Financial Times*, November 5, 2013, http://forr.com/mms1-2 .

3. Forrester Research World Smartphone Adoption Forecast, 2012 to 2017 (Global), Forrester Research World Tablet Adoption Forecast, 2013 to 2018 (Global).

4.　"February 2014 Web Server Survey," Netcraft, http://forr.com/mms1-4.

5.　Results from 158 community members in Forrester Research's ConsumerVoices, a market research online community that synthesizes qualitative insights on consumer technologies and behaviors. This is a community of 600 individuals in the US and 600 individuals in the UK, http://forr.com/mms1-5.

6.　David M. Cooperstein, "Competitive Strategy In The Age Of The Customer," Forrester report, October 10, 2013, http://forr.com/mms1-6.

7.　James McQuivey, *Digital Disruption: Unleashing the Next Wave of Innovation* (Amazon Press, 2013) http://forr.com/mms1-7.

8.　Andrew S. Grove, *Only the Paranoid Survive: How to Exploit the Crisis Points That Challenge Every Company* (Crown Business, 1999), http://forr.com/mms1-8 .

9.　To avoid the awkward "his or her" formulation, we balance pronouns in this book, referring to generic customers, workers, or executives with female pronouns in odd-numbered chapters and male pronouns in even-numbered chapters.

Chapter 2

1.　Julie A. Ask, "The Future Of Mobile eBusiness Is Context," Forrester report, May 1, 2012, http://forr.com/mms2-1.

2.　"The Home Depot's CEO Hosts 2013 Investor and Analyst Conference (Transcript)," Seeking Alpha, December 11, 2013, http://forr.com/mms2-2. Frank Blake is the chairman and CEO of The Home Depot. Matt Carey is the head of technology responsible for applications like these. Because the effort has Frank's commitment, the company is ready to cut across organizational boundaries to achieve the goal.

3.　Shelly Banjo, "Home Depot To Offer Same Day Delivery," *The Wall Street Journal*, December 11, 2013, http://forr.com/mms2-3.

4.　Geoffrey Moore, "A Sea Change in Enterprise IT," *AIIM*, January 17, 2011, http://forr.com/mms2-4. We interviewed Geoffrey Moore to get his thoughts on our definition of systems of engagement, http://www.geoffreyamoore.com.

5.　Forrester Research interview with Zappos in 2011. The company has since rectified the problem and now offers a 4.5 star app in Apple's App Store that offers the same inventory and pricing as the online site. It uses a hybrid mobile app design to do it.

Chapter 3

1.　Austin Carr, "Facebook Mobile Ad Revenue Rockets 478% Year-Over-Year," *Fast Company*, October 13, 2013, http://forr.com/mms3-1.

Chapter 4

1.　Josh Bernoff and Ted Schadler, *Empowered: Unleash Your Employees, Energize Your Customers, and Transform Your Business*, (HBR Press, 2010). We describe how E-Trade first embraced mobile trading on page 75.

2.　Rating information retrieved from Apple App store on January 15, 2014. Refers to all versions of the iPhone app, http://forr.com/mms4-2.

3. In this chapter, differences that we describe as statistically significant are significant at the 5% level. However, many of these differences are also significant at the 1% level.

4. The Mobile Expectation Scores for all the Mobile Intensity segments show statistically significant differences from each other.

5. When reading comparisons between countries on the Mobile Mind Shift Index, keep three caveats in mind: First, we only survey online consumers. Second, we weren't able to conduct these surveys simultaneously—while all the data is from 2013, the US data is a few months more recent than the Asian data, for example. And finally, for practical reasons, we survey only metropolitan consumers in the countries labeled "Metro" in this chart—Argentina, Brazil, China, India, Mexico, and Russia—so it's not strictly accurate to compare scores in those countries to the others.

Chapter 5

1. Susan Huynh, "Forrester Research Mobile Commerce Forecast, 2012 to 2017 (US)," Forrester report, August 8, 2012, http://forr.com/mms5-1.

2. "Smartphones will Influence $689 Billion in Retail Store Sales by 2016: Deloitte Study," Deloitte, June 27, 2012, http://forr.com/mms5-2.

Chapter 6

1. Mike Dano, "Starbucks counts 10M active mobile customers, 4M mobile payments per week," *FierceMobileIT*, April 29, 2013, http://forr.com/mms6-1.

2. Sean Corcoran, "No Media Should Stand Alone," Forrester report, December 16, 2009, http://forr.com/mms6-2. If you're familiar with the well-known concept of owned, earned, and paid moment, you may see a parallel here. The owned/earned/paid media concept was embraced by thinkers including Pete Blackshaw (now at Nestlé) and former Forrester Research analyst Sean Corcoran.

3. Jay Baer, *Youtility: Why Smart Marketing is About Help, Not Hype,*" (Portfolio Hardcover, 2013) http://forr.com/mms6-3.

4. Harley Manning and Kerry Bodine, *Outside In: The Power of Putting Customers at the Center of Your Business*, (New Harvest, 2012) http://forr.com/mms6-4.

5. The 100 minutes per week statistics for Line users applies to traffic in September 2013.

Chapter 7

1. Steven Levy, "Brave New Thermostat: How the iPod's Creator Is Making Home Heating Sexy," *Wired*, October 25, 2011, http://forr.com/mms7-1.

2. Christopher Mines and Michele Pelino, "Mapping The Connected World," Forrester report, October 31, 2013, http://forr.com/mms7-2.

3. Jeff St. John, "Whirlpool Launches the Wi-Fi Smart Appliance," Greentech Media, April 25, 2013, http://forr.com/mms7-3.

4. Sarah Perez, "Apple's App Store Hits 50 Billion Downloads, 900K Apps, $10 Billion Paid To Developers; iTunes Now With 575M Accounts," *TechCrunch*, June 10, 2013, http://forr.com /mms7-4.

5.   Of course dads use Philips products, too, but the company knows that its primary market is mothers and concentrated on learning more about what mothers need.

6.   Eric Ries, *The Lean Startup: How Today's Entrepreneurs Use Continuous Innovation to Create Radically Successful Businesses* (Crown Publishing Group, 2011) http://forr.com/mms7-6. Eric Ries has written about the principle of minimum viable products.

7.   Ajaz Ahmed and Stefan Olander, *Velocity: The Seven New Laws for a World Gone Digital* (Random House UK, 2012) http://forr.com/mms7-7.

8.   Tony Long, "Jan. 28, 1807: Flickering Gaslight Illuminates Pall Mall," *Wired*, January 28, 2008, http://forr.com/mms7-8.

9.   "iPads to make street lights smarter," *West London Today*, http://forr.com/mms7-9.

10. "LeafNut controls Westminster's Christmas lights," *LEDs Magazine*, November 30, 2012, http://forr.com/mms7-10.

Chapter 8

1.   "Nike Redefines 'Just Do It' With New Campaign," Nike, August 21, 2013, http://forr.com/mms8-1.

2.   Brian Dolan, "Why Aetna acquired iTriage app maker Healthagen," *MobiHealthNews*, December 16, 2011, http://forr.com/mms8-2.

3.   Dara Kerr, "Google reveals it spent $966 million in Waze acquisition," Cnet, July 25, 2013, http://forr.com/mms8-3.

4.   Matt McFarland, "How iBeacons could change the world forever," *Innovations* (blog), *The Washington Post*, January 7, 2014, http://forr.com/mms8-4.

5.   Megan Rose Dickey, "Insanely Popular Game Candy Crush Saga Is Bringing In An Estimated $633,000 A Day," *Bloomberg Business Insider*, July 8, 2013, http://forr.com/mms8-5.

6.   Bradley Johnson, "10 Things You Should Know About the Global Ad Market," *Ad Age*, December 8, 2013, http://forr.com/mms8-6.

7.   Michael O'Grady, "Forrester Research Mobile Advertising Forecast: 2013 To 2018 (US)," Forrester report, May 2, 2013, http://forr.com/mms8-7.

8.   Susan Huynh, "World Smartphone Adoption Forecast, 2012 To 2017 (Global)," Forrester report, March 25, 2013, http://forr.com/mms8-8a; tablet forecast: Michael O'Grady and Vikram Sehgal, "The Worldwide Tablet Forecast," Forrester report, June 13, 2013, http://forr.com/mms8-8b. People, particularly in developing economies, choose tablets and smartphones over computers as their first device. Wireless access, subsidized purchase models, and lower cost are three reasons why.

9.   "Kenya Uses Text Messages To Track Elephant," CBS News, October 11, 2008, http://forr.com/mms8-9.

10. Craig Le Clair, "Business Agility Drives Higher Performance," Forrester report, November 12, 2013, http://forr.com/mms8-10.

Chapter 9

1.   Frank E. Gillett, "Info Workers Will Erase The Boundary Between Enterprise And Consumer Technologies," Forrester report, February 21, 2013, http://forr.com/mms9-1. Two forces cause this massive adoption. First, mobile devices and wireless networks flow directly from home to work as employees find creative ways to use personal devices to get work done in markets as diverse as farming in Kenya, fishing in Sri Lanka, and manufacturing in the Philippines. Second, more companies deploy cloud-hosted applications to new kinds of employees that previously had no computer at all. We've looked at many of these examples in this book already.

2. Kathleen Masterson, "Reducing fertilizer waste with GPS," *Harvest Public Media*, January 2, 2012, http://forr.com/mms9-2.

3. Paul E. Waggoner, "James Gordon Horsfall: Nonconformist and Founding Father," *Annual Review of Phytopathology* 41 (September 2003): 27–39, http://forr.com/mms9-3.

4. Forrsights Global Workforce Benchmark Survey, Q4 2013.

5. "Josh Constine, "Dropbox Hits 200M Users, Unveils New 'For Business' Client Combining Work And Personal Files," TechCrunch, November 13, 2013, http://forr.com/mms9-5

6. Your company controls your business Dropbox for your work files, complete with security and sharing privileges. When you leave the company, your business Dropbox and its files disappear from your devices, but you keep your personal Dropbox with your personal files.

7. "BBVA banks on the Google cloud," BBVA press release, January 11, 2012, http://forr.com/mms9-7.

8. This information comes from APAN.org and Forrester interviews. The All Partners Access Network (APAN) is an unclassified, non-dot-mil network providing interoperability and connectivity among partners over a common platform. APAN fosters information exchange and collaboration between the United States Department of Defense (DoD) and any external country, organization, agency, or individual that does not have ready access to traditional DoD systems and networks.

9. "Disaster Response: APAN Aids in Haiti Relief Efforts," APAN, http://forr.com/mms9-9.

Chapter 10

1. "Nordstrom Reports March Sales," Nordstrom press release, April 5, 2012, http://forr.com/mms10-1.

2. Brad Strothkamp, "Case Study: USAA Makes Mobile Remote Deposit A Core Mobile Offering," Forrester report, November 11, 2011, http://forr.com/mms10-2. USAA found demand for its mobile services to be *six times higher* than it originally forecast.

3. Mark Walsh, "ESPN's Mobile Traffic Edges Desktop Again," *Online Media Daily*, November 26, 2013, http://forr.com/mms10-3.

4. Michael Facemire, "Mobile Needs A Four-Tier Engagement Platform," Forrester report, October 18, 2013, http://forr.com/mms10-4.

5. Drew Fitzgerald, "Avon to Halt Rollout of New Order Management System," *The Wall Street Journal*, December 11, 2013, http://forr.com/mms10-5.

6. George Colony and Peter Burris, "Technology Management In The Age Of The Customer," Forrester report, October 10, 2013, http://forr.com/mms10-6.

Chapter 11

1. Ted Schadler and John C. McCarthy, "Wanted: Mobile Engagement Providers," Forrester report, August 6, 2013, http://forr.com/mms11-1. Companies will spend roughly three times as much on internal systems and process changes as they do with development partners. As the market for mobile engagement services grows to $32.4 billion by 2018, that means they will spend $130 billion in total. The text cites and updated projection of $189 billion that was not yet published at the time this book went to press.

2. Megan Burns, "The Customer Experience Index, 2014," Forrester report, January 21, 2014, http://forr.com/mms11-2.

3. Ted Schadler and John C. McCarthy, "Mobile Is The New Face Of Engagement," Forrester report, February 23, 2012, http://forr.com/mms11-3. Atomizing the process means breaking it down into its discrete components so they are readily accessible on a tiny screen in a few moments of time.

The challenge is what to do with your complex SAP and legacy transaction systems. You will need to expose only enough functionality to take the next step.

4. Jeffrey S. Hammond, "Building Five-Star Apps," Forrester report, November 7, 2012, http://forr .com/mms11-4. There are hundreds of thousands of mobile apps out there, and they're all competing for the same mobile users. If you want to reach your customers with a custom mobile app, then you want to make sure you create one that will get high ratings. We spoke with more than a dozen leading mobile app developers about how they build, test, and release their top-rated mobile apps. We've identified the common development best practices that these shops use to help you build your own five-star app.

5. "TV Viewers Rate AT&T U-verse Highest in Customer Satisfaction in J.D. Power Study," AT&T press release, September 26, 2013, http://forr.com/mms11-5. According to the release, "AT&T U-verse received the highest numerical score among television service providers in the North Central region in the proprietary J.D. Power 2013 US Residential Television Service Provider Satisfaction Study. The study was based on 22,593 total responses measuring eight providers in the North Central region (IL, IN, MI, OH, WI) and measures consumer satisfaction with television service. Proprietary study results are based on experiences and perceptions of consumers surveyed in November 2012 and January, April, and July 2013. Your experiences may vary."

6. Craig Le Clair, "Smart Process Apps—One Year Later," Forrester report, December 10, 2013, http://forr.com/mms11-6. A new software category—which we call smart process apps—helps employees tackle the untamed processes that most firms struggle with. These apps put people first, are lighter, easier to change, assume mobile, and use big data and analytics to predict events and drive actions. This report provides a snapshot of current trends in the emergence of smart process apps.

7. "Mondelēz International Celebrates Its First Anniversary," Mondelēz International press release, October 1, 2013, http://forr.com/mms11-7.

8. Tcho reports that its Peruvian farmers took the top five spots in the "VI Concurso Nacional de Calidad" contest in 2012.

9. Clay Richardson, "Design For Disruption: Take An Outside In Approach To BPM," Forrester report, June 14, 2013, http://forr.com/mms11-9. To redesign processes for mobile moments, business architects and business process professionals will need to shift from "systems thinking" paradigms that emphasize process modeling to "design thinking" paradigms that emphasize creativity and customer experience. This will require teams to adopt emerging strategies and practices for integrating design-thinking principles into their business process management initiatives.

10. Michael Hammer, "Reengineering Work: Don't Automate, Obliterate," *Harvard Business Review* (July/August 1990), 104–112.

11. Ted Schadler and John C. McCarthy, "Mobile Is The New Face Of Engagement," Forrester report, February 23, 2012, http://forr.com/mms11-11. Here we define mobile as: Devices that are mobile; applications designed specifically to run on mobile devices; communications equipment to support mobile devices; consulting services to provide guidance to companies on how to use mobile and how to integrate from mobile devices to core systems; wireless telecom services; and managed wireless network outsourcing. Using data from Forrester's global technology industry market sizing for business and government in 2011 versus 2015, we calculate that the mobile spend will increase from 23% of the total in 2011 to 35% in 2015, or doubling from $675 billion to $1.301 trillion.

Chapter 12

1. Agile development is a software development practice that delivers new functionality every two to four weeks. Customers get new features on a regular cadence, and the company gets to rapidly launch, learn, and extend without taking huge risks. Agile development is more like iterative evolution with change built in the process: Features that work are extended; features that don't work are changed or retired ("deprecated" is the word your software teams will use).

2. Kurt Bittner, "Continuous Delivery Is Reshaping The Future Of ALM," Forrester report, July 22, 2013, http://forr.com/mms12-2.

3. In customer experience organizations, this person is often called a business analyst, but if so it's one with veto power and responsibility for outcomes.

4. Diego Lo Guidice, "Embrace Holistic Change To Achieve Agile Results," Forrester report, April 27, 2012, http://forr.com/mms12-4. Agile is popular for development teams, but in order to get the benefits across the organization, something more fundamental is required: holistic change—a change or transformation to processes, organizational models, development practices, tools, and architecture. Forrester recommends a holistic change approach based on Lean principles that includes building the right change team and aligning delivery and business teams.

5. This information is from a Forrester report by Jeffrey A. Hammond that was not yet published at the time this book went to press.

6. Ted Schadler and John C. McCarthy, "Wanted: Mobile Engagement Providers," Forrester report, August 6, 2013, http://forr.com/mms12-6. The challenge of making a simple, intuitive app that fronts a complex system of engagement stretches the abilities and swamps the resources of most firms. For help, firms increasingly turn to vendors that possess a connected portfolio of engagement competencies and management skills. The result will be a new market for mobile engagement providers that will grow to $32.4 billion by 2018. No vendor can do all of this today, but suppliers from six categories—digital agencies, management consultancies, mobile specialists, product development specialists, systems integrators, and telecommunications companies—are chasing the prize. The payoff for vendors that make this investment will be to earn a seat at your table as a long-term partner in your engagement success.

Chapter 13

1. Andrew E. Kramer, "Ukraine's Opposition Says Government Stirs Violence," *The New York Times*, January 21, 2014, http://forr.com/mms13-1.

2. David M. Cooperstein, "Brands Must Adapt To Customers' Higher Standards," Forrester report, August 20, 2012, http://forr.com/mms13-2.

3. Nick Summers, "Nest CEO Tony Fadell vows to make any privacy policy changes transparent and opt-in," *The Next Web*, January 20, 2014, http://forr.com/mms13-3.

4. "Ford VP: 'We have GPS in your car, so we know what you're doing'," RT, January 10, 2014, http://forr.com/mms13-4.

5. Fatemeh Khatibloo, "The New Privacy: It's All About Context," Forrester report, December 19, 2013, http://forr.com/mms13-5.

6. Matt Glynn, "First Niagara cutting 170 jobs, closing 10 branches," *The Buffalo News,* January 8, 2014, http://forr.com/mms13-6.

7. "Subway Restaurant Chain Selects Paydiant to Power Mobile Wallet," Paydiant press release, October 2, 2013, http://forr.com/mms13-7.

8. This information is from a Forrester report by Denee Carrington which was not yet published at the time this book went to press.

9. Meghan Walsh, "Pay-As-You-Drive Insurance Gets a Push From Progressive," *Bloomberg Businessweek*, July 9, 2012, http://forr.com/mms13-9.

10. You can find more information on Merck's human growth hormone injector at the Saizen website, http://www.saizenus.com/.

11. "Zapping mosquitos, and corruption," *The Economist,* June 1, 2013, http://forr.com/mms13-11.

12. James McQuivey, *Digital Disruption* (Amazon Press, 2013) http://forr.com/mms13-12 .

INDEX

business to business, 79
  Cisco, 91
  mobile moments in, 33
  salespeople with tablets, 79
BYOD (bring your own device),
  131–33

C

Candy Crush Saga, 121
Carlson, Erik, 167–73
Carrefour, 87
Caterpillar, 147
Celltick, 61
Chambers, Dwayne, 91
channels
  channel conflict, 198
  mobile eliminates, 86
  mobile is not a channel, 72
Charles Schwab, 51–52
Chawla, Sona, 70–72
China, 61–62, 160–61
  2G networks in, 94
  Carrefour, 87
  China Eastern Airlines, 146–47
  Cmune, 121
  Coca-Cola marketing in, 92–94
  mobile behaviors in, 61–62
  Mobile Mind Shift Index of, 95
  Renren, 93
  WeChat, 93
  Weibo, 93
China Eastern Airlines, 146–47,
  209
Cinquin, Isabelle, 85
CIO, 162–63
Cisco
  Binary Game app, 91

employee applications at, 143
governance at, 198
mobile facilities applications,
  180–81
mobile workforce at, 131–33
ClearSlide Outside, 79
Cleveland Clinic, 105
click to call, 95
Clorox, 89–90
cloud
  as mobile delivery platform, 157
  cloud platform vendors, 141
  Concur Travel and Expense
    Cloud, 153
  for mobile employee apps, 143
  platforms for process apps, 174
Cmune, 119–21
Coca-Cola, 92–94
collaboration, 145–46
Columbia Sportswear, 90–91
Comcast, vii
commerce, role of mobile in, 67–80
Commonwealth Bank of Australia,
  63
Concur, 153–54
Constellation Brands, 139–40
consumerization of IT, 138
consumers. *See* customers
content management, 156
context, 21, 35–36
  as a technology requirement, 151
  determines privacy policy, 208
  emotional, 35–36
  in employee applications, 141
  location, 35
  physical, 35
  profile and history, 36